EXTRA- AND NON-DOCUMENTARY WRITING IN THE CANON OF FORMATIVE JUDAISM

VOLUME TWO

PALTRY PARALLELS

EXTRA- AND NON-DOCUMENTARY WRITING IN THE CANON OF FORMATIVE JUDAISM

VOLUME TWO

PALTRY PARALLELS

THE NEGLIGIBLE PROPORTION AND PERIPHERAL ROLE OF FREE-STANDING COMPOSITIONS IN RABBINIC DOCUMENTS

Jacob Neusner

Academic Studies in the History of Judaism
Global Publications, Binghamton University
2001

Copyright © 2001 by Jacob Neusner

All rights reserved. No portion of this publication may be duplicated in any way without the expressed written consent of the publisher, except in the form of brief excerpts or quotations for review purposes.

Library of Congress Cataloging-in-Publication Data

Neusner, Jacob, 1932-
  Extra- and non-documentary writing in the canon of formative Judaism / Jacob Neusner.
      p. cm. -- (Academic studies in the history of Judaism)
  Includes bibliographical references.
  ISBN 1-58684-106-8 (pbk : alk. paper) -- ISBN 1-58684-107-6 -- ISBN 1-58684-113-0
  1. Midrash--History and criticism--Theory, etc. 2. Talmud--Criticism, Form. 3. Rabbinical literature--History and criticism--Theory, etc. 4. Becker, Hans-Jürgen, 1956- Die großen rabbinischen Sammelwerke Palästinas. I. Title. II. Series.
  BM514 .N466 2001
  296.1'206--dc21

2001003604

Published and Distributed by:
Academic Studies in the History of Judaism
Global Publications, Binghamton University
LNG 99, Binghamton University
State University of New York at Binghamton
Binghamton, New York, USA 13902-6000
Phone: (607) 777-4495 or 777-6104; Fax: (607) 777-6132
E-mail: pmorewed@binghamton.edu
http://ssips.binghamton.edu

THE SERIES

Extra- and Non-Documentary Writing in the Canon of Formative Judaism. I. The Pointless Parallel: Hans-Jürgen Becker and the Myth of the Autonomous Tradition in Rabbinic Documents

Extra- and Non-Documentary Writing in the Canon of Formative Judaism. II. Paltry Parallels. The Negligible Proportion and Peripheral Role of Free-Standing Compositions in Rabbinic Documents

Extra- and Non-Documentary Writing in the Canon of Formative Judaism. III. Peripatetic Parallels

ACADEMIC STUDIES IN THE HISTORY OF JUDAISM

Editor-in-Chief

Jacob Neusner
Bard College

Editorial Committee

Alan J. Avery-Peck, *College of the Holy Cross*

Bruce D. Chilton, *Bard College*

William Scott Green, *University of Rocheste*

James Strange, *University of Southern Florida*

TABLE OF CONTENTS

PREFACE

PART ONE

EXTRA- AND NON-DOCUMENTARY WRITING

1. THE BAVLI'S MASSIVE MISCELLANIES

    i. Extra- and Non-Documentary Writing and the Bavli
    ii. Differentiating the Types of Writing in the Bavli
    iii. The Bavli's Paramount Mode of Discourse: The Propositional, Analytical Composite
    iv. The Composition and the Composite
    v. The Rationality of a Major Massive Miscellany: Bavli Abodah Zarah Chapter One
    vi. The Problem of Agglutinative Discourse
    vii. Traits of Agglutinative Discourse in the Bavli

PART TWO

EXTRA- AND NON-DOCUMENTARY WRITING IN PROPORTION AND POSITION

QUANTITATIVE:

SHOWING THAT A MINISCULE PROPORTION OF RABBINIC DOCUMENTS IS COMPRISED BY FREE-STANDING STORIES

AND
QUALITATIVE:
SHOWING THAT THESE FEW FREE-STANDING STORIES
ARE TANGENTIAL IN THE COMPOSITIONS WHERE
THEY DO OCCUR

2. **PROPORTION AND POSITION: EVIDENCE OF SHARED, AUTONOMOUS TRADITIONS IN A SAMPLE OF THE MISHNAH AND THE TOSEFTA**

   i. When a Later Document Cites an Earlier One
   ii. The Special Situation of the Mishnah
   iii. The Free-Standing Composition in the Tosefta. Tosefta Hullin 2:21-24
   iv. The Negligible Proportion and Peripheral Role of Free-Standing Stories: Tosefta Moed Qatan Chapter Two
   v. The Reception by the Yerushalmi and the Bavli of the Non-Documentary Composite of Tosefta Moed Qatan Chapter Two
   vi. The Autonomous, Documentary Standing of the Mishnah and the Tosefta

3. **PROPORTION AND POSITION: EVIDENCE OF SHARED, AUTONOMOUS TRADITIONS IN A SAMPLE OF SIFRA**

   i. The Documentary Traits of Sifra
   ii. The Sample: Sifra Parashat Tazri'a 122-124
   iii. The Negligible Proportion of Free-standing Stories
   iv. The Peripheral Role of Free-Standing Stories

4. **PROPORTION AND POSITION: EVIDENCE OF SHARED, AUTONOMOUS TRADITIONS IN A SAMPLE OF GENESIS RABBAH**

    i   The Documentary Traits of Genesis Rabbah
    ii.   The Sample: Genesis Rabbah Parashah One
    iii.   The Considerable Proportion of Free-standing Stories
    iv.   The Peripheral Role of Free-Standing Stories
    v.   Documentary, Non-Documentary, and Extra-Documentary Writing: The Case of Genesis Rabbah
        1.   Documentary Writing
        2.   Non-Documentary Writing
        3.   Extra-Documentary Writing
    vi.   The Documentary Complex

CONCLUSION

    i.   Summary
    ii.   Pointless Parallels, Paltry Parallels
    iii.   Imagining the Rabbinic Canon: Toward a General Theory
    iv.   The Two Theories of the Rabbinic Canon: Documents *versus* Scrapbooks — And Why They Matter

BIBLIOGRAPHY

EXTRA- AND NON-DOCUMENTARY WRITING IN THE CANON OF FORMATIVE JUDAISM

VOLUME ONE

THE POINTLESS PARALLEL

Hans-Jürgen Becker and the Myth of the Autonomous Tradition in Rabbinic Documents

Table of Contents

Preface

PART ONE

SHOWING THAT, IN INDICATIVE TRAITS, ONE DOCUMENT IS DIFFERENT FROM ANOTHER DOCUMENT

1. Differentiating Kindred Documents: Genesis Rabbah and Leviticus Rabbah

    i. The Documentary Reading of the Rabbinic Canon in the Formative Age
    ii. The Program of Genesis Rabbah
    iii. The Program of Leviticus Rabbah
    iv. Comparing the Programs of Genesis Rabbah and Leviticus Rabbah
    v. The Centrality of Redaction in the Formulation and Selection of Exegeses of Scripture

PART TWO

SHOWING THAT A SHARED PERICOPE IS PRIMARY TO ONE DOCUMENT, SECONDARY TO ANOTHER

2. The Shared Pericope and the Prior Claim of Leviticus Rabbah: the Relationship between Leviticus Rabbah and Pesiqta deRab Kahana. The Form-Analytical Perspective

   i. Literary Structures of Pesiqta deRab Kahana Pisqa' 6
   ii. Literary Structures of Pesiqta deRab Kahana Pisqa'ot 14 and 22
   iii. Pesiqta deRab Kahana 27 = Leviticus Rabbah 30
   iv. The Shared Pisqa'/Parashah: Where Does It Belong?

3. THE SHARED PISQA' IN PESIQTA DERAB KAHANA AND PESIQTA RABBATI

   i. Introduction
   ii. The literary Structures of Pesiqta Rabbati
   iii. Pesiqta Rabbati Pisqa One
   iv. The Forms of Pesiqta Rabbati Pisqa One
   v. The Thematic Program and Proposition of Pesiqta Rabbati Pisqa One: Syllogism, Collage, or Scrapbook?
   vi. The Order of the Forms of Pisqa' One
   vii. Recurrent Literary Structures: Types of Units of Discourse, their Order, and their Cogency
   viii. The Rhetorical Plan of Pesiqta deRab Kahana
   ix. Comparative Midrash [1]: The Rhetorical, Logical, and Topical Aspect. The Plan and

        Program of Pesiqta deRab Kahana and Pesiqta Rabbati
x.   Comparative Midrash [2]: The Two Pesiqtas side by Side
xi.   Leviticus Rabbah, Pesiqta deRab Kahana, and Pesiqta Rabbati: The Three Kindred Compilations and the Documentary Reading of the Rabbinic Canon

PART THREE

SHOWING THAT SHARED TRADITIONS, PRIOR TO AND AUTONOMOUS OF THE TWO TALMUDS DO NOT LINK THE BAVLI TO THE YERUSHALMI

4.   Do the Yerushalmi and the Bavli Point toward an Autonomous Tradition?

       I.   A NULL-HYPOTHESIS: THE YERUSHALMI AND THE BAVLI DRAW ON COMMON SOURCES OTHER THAN THE MISHNAH, THE TOSEFTA, AND COUNTERPART CANONICAL DOCUMENTS
      ii.   A Common Source Utilized by both Talmuds
      III. DO THE BAVLI AND YERUSHALMI DRAW ON (A) "Q"? AND DOES A TOPICAL PROTOCOL DEFINE THE TALMUDS' MISHNAH-EXEGESIS?
      iv. Does a Topical Protocol Define the Talmuds' Mishnah-Exegesis?
      v.   Does a Shared Program of Questions Dictate the Shape of the Talmuds' Mishnah-exegesis?

vi. Does a Common Exegetical Program Dictate the Talmuds' Reading of the Same Tosefta-Pericope
vii. Do the Yerushalmi and the Bavli Form Distinct Expressions of a Single Tradition? The Null-Hypothesis Revisited

PART FOUR

TOWARD A GENERAL THEORY OF THE FORMATION OF THE RABBINIC TRADITION

5. The Prior Rabbinic Tradition and the Autonomous Tradition: The Three Stages in the Formation of Canonical Documents

   i. A Theory of the Formation of the Rabbinic Documents: Accounting for Different Kinds of Writing
   ii. The Three Stages in the Literary History of the Rabbinic Canonical Documents and How We Discern Them
      1. The Latest Stage in the Literary History of the Rabbinic Documents: Writings That Conform to the Particular Document's Indicative Traits
      2. An Intermediate Earlier Stage in the Literary History of the Rabbinic Documents: Writings That Can Have Served Redactors of Documents But That Did Not Serve the Redactors of The Particular Documents That We Now Have

3. A Still Earlier Stage in the Literary History of the Rabbinic Documents: Writings Autonomous of a Particular Document's Indicative Traits. The Peripatetic Composition
4. Classes of Writing, Stages of Formation
iii. The Correct Starting Point
iv. Redaction and Writing. The Extreme Case of The Mishnah
v. When The Document Does Not Define The Literary Protocol: Stories Told But Not Compiled And The Autonomous Tradition
vi. Pericopes Framed for the Purposes of the Particular Document in Which They Occur
vii. Pericopes Framed for the Purposes of a Particular Document But Not of a Type We Now Possess
viii. Pericopes Framed For A Purpose Not Particular To, or Realized in, a Type of Document Now in Our Hands
ix. The Three Stages of Literary Formation

Appendices

A. POINTLESS PARALLELS AND SUPERFICIAL FRAMING OF ISSUES: HANS-JUERGEN BECKER, *DIE GROSSEN RABBINISCHEN SAMMELWERKE PALAESTINAS. ZUR LITERARISCHEN GENESE VON TALMUD YERUSHALMI UND MIDRASH BERESHIT RABBA*

B. BUT WHAT IF WE HAVE NO DOCUMENTS? THE PROBLEM OF ESTABLISHING THE TEXT AND THE

Preface xvii

> SOLUTION OF FORM-ANALYSIS. THE DEBATE WITH
> ARNOLD GOLDBERG AND PETER SCHAEFER

BIBLIOGRAPHY

PREFACE

A free-standing composition or composite in a document of the Rabbinic canon is one that ignores the indicative conventions of rhetoric, topic, and logic of cogent discourse that otherwise characterize that document. Moreover, such a composition may occur in two or more documents and ignore the differentiating traits of all of them — and even of all the extant documents all together. That is a still more striking indicator that that composition ignores documentary conventions. Such a composition is called "extra-documentary,"

The canon of Rabbinic Judaism in its formative age, from the Mishnah through the Bavli, encompasses not only documentary, but also free-standing compositions and composites. Some of these occur in two or more compilations and are called *"extra-documentary."* That is because they entirely ignore documentary boundaries. Others of these free-standing compositions and composites occur in only one document but do not replicate the indicative traits in rhetoric and topic of their home-document. These are called *"non-documentary."*

I.

For reasons to be spelled out, this study samples the other-than-documentary components of the Bavli, Mishnah, Tosefta, Sifra, and Genesis Rabbah. It shows that, for the analyzed samples of Bavli, Mishnah, Tosefta, and Sifra, the extra- and non-documentary writing forms a paltry proportion of the whole. Free-standing compositions (I found no composites to speak of) furthermore undertake no critical documentary task within the document(s) in which they occur. For Genesis Rabbah the proportion of free-standing compositions is not paltry. But the autonomous writing is of a single classification and yields a workable hypothesis on one type of non- and pre-documentary writing. That in all five compilations the role of free-standing compositions proves entirely peripheral is set forth not as a subjective opinion. It is a fact that is founded on the basis of objective criteria of analysis. The results of the sample can be replicated by others interested in the problem treated here.

Why do these facts produced by the sample at hand make a difference, and to whom? The answer lies in an ongoing debate about the fundamental characterization of the canonical documents of Rabbinic Judaism in its formative age. Two theories of the formation of the Rabbinic canon presently contend. One, broadly held, regards documentary bounds as null. The other deems them consequential and determinate. At stake is the possibility of the characterization of Rabbinic Judaism as a cogent structure and system, a contextual description based on coherent canonical documents. These are matters that require considerable amplification.

The former theory sees the Rabbinic tradition as a vast corpus of disorganized bits and pieces — a mass of contradictory opinions about we know not what, yielding no category-formations, let alone temporal aggregates of focused opinion. The compilations of Rabbinic writing begin with the smallest whole units of discourse, and these are random and unformed. The free-standing stories and other composites form a body of evidence that points to an extra-documentary origin of the compositions and composites of the Rabbinic compilations of late antiquity. First came the bits and pieces, and only later on the agglutination of these bits and pieces into the compilations we now have. Everything floated free in its day. Then, for reasons we know not, in some arbitrary manner, people collected and arranged this ready-made writing in the posterior collections now in our hands. On that theory of agglutination, we cannot hope to discern cogent category-formations of coherent opinion, building blocks of a religious structure, components of a religious system: Judaism. By definition, the formal building blocks and components are null, mere accidents and random composites, not purposive statements of a propositional character.

The contrary theory maintains the opposite. The canonical compilations are purposive. Rabbinic writing begins in the whole units formed by documents with their definition of distinctive rhetoric, topic, and logic of coherent discourse. The consequent documents register convictions, prove propositions, speak to a particular time and place and in behalf of a determinate corporate body. This characterization of the canonical writings adopts for itself a historical-temporal model of a determinate character. First came the program of forming a document with determinate qualities of rhetoric (form), topic (proposition), and logic of coherent discourse (how matters form coherent statements). Then came the preparation of compositions and composites exhibiting the determinate traits of the document.

This contrary theory, however, contains an important qualification. It also recognizes that a variable proportion of the Rabbinic documents is comprised by non- and extra-documentary writing. By no means do all of the units of coherent thought and expression ("paragraphs") in the several canonical writings adhere to the indicative traits of the documents in which they appear. The documentary reading of the canonical compilations accommodates that fact without difficulty. In accord with its theory of the formation of the Rabbinic tradition, along the way, perhaps before writing *for* documents, *within the rules of* particular documents, began — so this theory maintains — writings of a non- and extra-documentary character were undertaken. Then these too found their way into the nascent documents.[1] The non- and extra-documentary compositions generally supplement the expositions to which they are tacked. They do not take a primary part in the documentary exposition of propositions.

One way or another, the parties to the debate take up the same data. But they evaluate it differently. Specifically, advocates of the documentary reading of the canonical writings must address the free-standing components of the documents — the other-than-documentary-writings, whether external to all documents or to a particular compilation. The advocates of an atomistic reading of the same compilations must deal with the distinctive traits of rhetoric and topic and logic of coherent discourse that, all together, define a given document and no other. Since they build upon the free-standing compositions, they have to account for the disciplined, rhetorically-formal and propositionally-purposive compositions and composites. Those who follow matters do not need to be told my position on this debate. And the contrary position has been set forth, most often casually and dismissively, but in some instances in a serious and weighty manner. The former may be passed over in silence. They have not yet done their homework. Evidence for their views consists of pronouncements of their own opinions, and little more than that. Off-hand footnotes, casual dismissal in a sentence or so of massive bodies of data — these in the end cannot prevail. The latter, however, are best represented by the Goldberg-Schaefer-Becker school, which has the dignity of a fully expounded and worked out position.

---

[1] In Chapter Five of *Pointless Parallel*, the companion of the present work, entitled "The Prior Rabbinic Tradition and the Autonomous Tradition: The Three Stages in the Formation of Canonical Documents," I have elaborated on this general theory of the formation of the Rabbinic tradition in writing. This brief summary suffices for the present purpose.

Preface

As the source and author of the documentary, form-analytical reading of the Rabbinic canon of late antiquity,[2] from the Mishnah through the Bavli, from Sifra and the two Sifrés through Song of Songs Rabbah and the Fathers According to Rabbi Nathan, I have maintained that the canonical writings sustain distinctive definitions, each for itself. Each may be characterized with indicative, definitive traits of rhetoric (form), topic (proposition) and logic of coherent discourse. What of the acknowledged presence of the extra- and — more consequential still! — the non-documentary writing contained by every document except the Mishnah?[3] I face the challenge, to that characterization of matters, presented by those compositions and composites, now situated within the canonical compilations, that do not conform to a given document's distinctive traits. Because these demonstrably find a place in any document or in none, they call into question whether documentary boundaries govern — or even make a difference — in the formation of the Rabbinic canon. They call into question the identification, as the generative category-formation, of the several Rabbinic documents, from the Mishnah through the Bavli. That renders null any account of the religious structure and system, Rabbinic Judaism in the formative age, which identifies large-scale, coherent propositions represented by documentary statements. So the issues are not negligible.

---

[2] The main items that pertain are listed at the end of this book in the bibliography of my monographs and research reports and form-analytical translations and commentaries of the Rabbinic canon of the formative age.

[3] The effort to identify in the Mishnah "sources" characterized by distinctive formal patterns yields some special cases, e.g., Eduyyot or Kelim Chapter Twenty-Four or Tamid-Middot. But documentary rules govern here too. No Rabbinic document is more successfully formatted than is the Mishnah, bearing in its wake the Tosefta and Sifra, as we see in these pages.

II.

Let me now expand on these matters and fully expose the issues as I see them. The principal documents are subject to characterization by the criteria of the congeries of traits, distinctive to each document, indicated by rhetoric (form-analysis), topic (propositional program) and logic of coherent discourse. Each document exhibits its own particular qualities in combination, and no document is identical to any other in rhetoric, topic, and logic. But there are groups of kindred documents, e.g., the Mishnah and the Tosefta, Leviticus Rabbah and Pesiqta deRab Kahana, and the like. These are established facts.

As to my documentary reading of the Rabbinic canonical compilations, the constructive enterprise is now in print. In the works listed in the bibliography, I have shown how documents distinguish themselves. I have described each of the principal parts of the Rabbinic canon and compared and contrasted the major components thereof. The present project advances the argument. Now concomitantly, I take up the extra- or non-documentary compositions and composites in those same documents. My position on extra- and non-documentary compositions, briefly stated, is very simple.

[1] The proportion of extra- or non-documentary writing in the canonical compilations in most of the sampled documents is negligible.

And [2] the role of that writing in all of them is peripheral. So while the documentary hypothesis of the Rabbinic canon makes provision for other-than-documentary writing, it assigns to that classification of compositions and composites a subordinate role in the process of documentary-formation.

The model that I invoke is simple. Whatever the state of Rabbinic writing of compositions and composites, the ca-

Preface

nonical documents for their part begin whole. They commence in a definitive plan and program that form-analysis discerns. The several documents, respectively, originate in that initial decision

[1] to write a book on a given topic,

[2] to impose upon the writing particular traits of formalization, and

[3] to join the bits and pieces of composed writing into composites by appeal to one theory of logical coherence rather than some other.

The greater part by far of each of the several documents is comprised by precisely that sort of documentary writing. But, as I said, circulating probably before but certainly at the time of the compilation of the canonical documents was a body of non- and extra-documentary writing. Materials of that corpus were chosen for, or found their way into, the canonical documents — I repeat, ordinarily in modest proportion, always in a peripheral role. That is what this book proves for a sample of the several, principal documents.

In the first part of this trilogy, *Pointless Parallels*, I reviewed the affirmative evidence for the hypothesis that the canonical compilations, respectively, exhibit determinate traits of rhetoric, topic, and logic — thus the "pointless" of the title. Here I amass the negative evidence that other-than-documentary writing plays no material part in the canonical documents — thus the "paltry" of the title.

I do the work in two stages, marked as Parts One and Two of the present work. The former consists of a single, long chapter; the latter of three sizable ones.

First, in Chapter One,[4] I take up the most noteworthy challenge to the documentary reading of the Rabbinic canon,

---

[4] That chapter forms a reprise of my *The Bavli's Massive Miscellanies*, further drawing on *The Talmud of Babylonia. A Complete Outline*.

which is the miscellaneous character of the Talmud of Babylonia, the Bavli. Here I address the crux of the matter: the sizable corpus of free-standing composites in the Bavli — the canon's largest single body of writing that on the surface ignores all documentary traits and preferences. The miscellanies that fill the pages of the Bavli violate the program of the Bavli, which is systematic and orderly exegesis of the Mishnah and of the Halakhic principles invoked thereby. They therefore call into question the documentary hypothesis. That is because, on the surface, these protracted, topical conglomerates, ignoring the context of discussion that precedes and follows, mark the Bavli as a disorganized mess. They account for the characterization of the Bavli in that way, even by experienced scholars of that Talmud, e.g., Adin Steinsaltz.[5] They disrupt the flow of argument. They form appendices inserted squarely in the middle of a systematic exposition. They compile topical information utterly unconnected to any argument, let alone to the Bavli's analytical argument that they disrupt. So they further make the disciple of the Bavli wonder about the order and program that animate the document. That is if there is such an order or program, if the Bavli can be called a document at all. I devote considerable attention to this problem.

Why do these massive miscellanies matter to the documentary reading of the Rabbinic writings? The Bavli is the crown jewel of the Judaic canon. It is also the theological culmination of Rabbinic Judaism in its formative age.[6] If we

---

[5] I refer here to *How Adin Steinsaltz Misrepresents the Talmud. Four False Propositions from his "Reference Guide."* Atlanta, 1998: Scholars Press for South Florida Studies in the History of Judaism. But Steinsaltz is not the only one to represent the Bavli as disorganized within Western philosophical categories of logic and order.

[6] I refer to *The Theology of Rabbinic Judaism. A Prolegomenon.* Atlanta, 1997: Scholars Press for South Florida Studies on the History of Judaism.

cannot establish its programmatic qualities, then any characterization of the entire canon along documentary lines is thwarted by a huge exception to the alleged rule. But I maintain, and through a systematic outline of the Bavli have proved, that even in the inclusion (though not necessarily original compilation) of the massive miscellanies, the Bavli follows a documentary convention as rigidly and successfully as the greatest realization of form-analytical rules, the Mishnah itself. *But* it is a different convention, framed by the Bavli's own distinctive task and program. Only when we understand their function and position in the Bavli's plan can we comprehend the elegant conception of matters that defines the Bavli whole and complete. So much for Chapter One, which stands by itself but forms the foundation of all that follows.

Second, in Part Two I turn to most of the canonical compilations of a more coherent quality than the Bavli. Thus, in Chapters Two and Three, I proceed to survey the free-standing stories and compositions of the Mishnah and the Tosefta and Sifra, the two Sifrés. In Chapter Four I turn to a representative of compilations of Aggadic exegesis, a sample of Genesis Rabbah. Here for both the Halakhic and the Aggadic compilations (Mishnah-Tosefta-Sifra and Genesis Rabbah, respectively) I sample the documents in search of answers to two questions, one quantitative, and the other qualitative. I set forth the affirmative defense of the documentary hypothesis by conceding that the documents encompass non- and extra-documentary writing, but maintain that in proportion and documentary function, free-standing writing is ordinarily paltry and always trivial. To show that that is the fact, I select a sample of each document for analysis. Then I ask, for the sample at hand, two questions:

[1] exactly how large a proportion of a given sample is comprised by free-standing stories or compositions; and

[2] how significant a task in the sample such stories are assigned, meaning, are they primary or tangential in context?

To define that context, I give very ample citations of the documents in which the same story or saying occurs, not only, e.g., Genesis Rabbah, but the intersecting documents, whether Sifra or Yerushalmi or Bavli. That sizable representation of the intersecting documents allows us to assess the importance of the shared saying or story or exegetical construction as it makes its way from our base-document (here: Genesis Rabbah) to the parallel appearances in other documents, as indicated. So when I claim that extra-documentary writing does not undertake an important assignment in the documentary plan of our base-document, I advance the further claim that extra-documentary writing also does not play a weighty part in any document in which it occurs. It is ordinarily extra-documentary everywhere, critical and central nowhere. Ample evidence sustains that point.

How do I read that evidence? I determine the "role" of the non-documentary components of the sample by reproducing my outline of the document.[7] That presents visual signals of the task, primary or subordinate or utterly tangential, assigned to a given composition (unit of discourse) of a given composite. What we see, time and again, is that the non-documentary composition(s) bear no important role in the exposition of the sample's proposition, that is, in the accomplishment of its task as assigned by the plan of the document as a whole.

From periperality, we turn to the matter of proportion. I establish proportion by word- or line-count, the entire

---

[7] That is set forth, for the Midrash-compilations, in the form-analytical translation with semiotic markings and the outline of each of the documents in my *The Components of the Rabbinic Documents: From the Whole to the Parts*.

Preface

number of words (in English translation) as against the number of words[8] (also in English translation) used in the non- or extra-documentary component of the sample (or, in some instances, the entire number of lines in the standard printed edition as against the lines utilized for extra-documentary compositions). In this way I deal with quite proper questions that any theory of the nature of the canonical documents must address.

III

Since the issues are clearly drawn, I owe an explanation of how, exactly, do these exercises address the position of those who dismiss as null the claim to discern documentary plan and program of the several canonical compilations? Since critics of the documentary reading of the Rabbinic canon use the language of "parallels," I introduce the same word-choice. They mean by "parallels" exactly what I mean by the language, "free-standing stories" or "…compositions." My "extra-" and "non-documentary writing" makes a distinction important to my larger theory but not critical to the debate at hand, hence the variety of word-choices for the same phenomenon in the canonical corpus.

That is to say, proponents of both positions in common refer by "parallels" to writing that serves in more than a single documentary setting and so, on the surface, violates the boundaries of a single document. As I have already made clear, that is precisely what I mean by "extra-" and "non-

---

[8] I count the words of the American translation, since at issue is proportion, not absolute number, the result will be roughly the same for American as for Rabbinic Hebrew. But I welcome any effort at counting the total number of Hebrew words in a sample as against the number of words of the free-standing composition(s) of the same sample. Where I have spot-checked matters, I produced the same proportions for Hebrew as for American.

documentary" writing. With reference to the challenge of "parallels," accordingly, I offer this sample of evidence of two propositions.

[1] "Parallels" — stories occurring in two or more compilations — from the perspective of the documentary hypothesis are pointless; in the context of a given document's propositional program, they play no part. And their presence proves nothing about the documents that accommodate them.

[2] And, as I said, in a variety of documents, particularly the Halakhic ones, they are paltry, adding up to very little in those documents.

That is argued on two bases, as the divisions of Chapters Two, Three and Four indicate, (1) the negligible proportion formed of the sample in hand by free-standing compositions, (2) the peripheral role played by them.

[1] The canonical documents are subject to differentiation, one from another, by appeal to indicative traits of an objective character. These indicative traits form unique congeries of combinations that distinguish one document from another. Parallels/free-standing/non-documentary stories ignore these indicative traits and tell us nothing about the integrity of the documents that utilize them.

[2] While the documents also encompass compositions that ignore the indicative traits characteristic of one or another of the canonical compilations, these are negligible in proportion and null in impact.

So I address the question, do the free-standing compositions form a grave challenge to the very conception of documents, not merely formless scrapbooks, for the Rabbinic canon? What I mean to demonstrate then is simple. These free-standing stories or compositions or composites in quantity and in quality, modest proportion and subordinate position, do not destroy the integrity of the documents that con-

Preface

tain them. That is because, my sample will suggest, they form a paltry proportion of the documents where they occur, and they also are subordinate and tangential and not primary and central in the context framed by their host-documents.

Accordingly, this monograph carries forward the argument begun in *The Pointless Parallel: Hans-Jürgen Becker and the Myth of the Autonomous Tradition in Rabbinic Documents*.[9] There I laid out form-analytical evidence and argument for the documentary reading of the Rabbinic canonical writings. I showed that each document finds a distinctive definition for itself in the indicative traits of rhetoric, topic, and logic of coherent discourse that characterize that document and no other. I further offered a theory of the literary history of the Rabbinic tradition in antiquity: kinds of writing and when and how they took place. By defining "document" phenomenologically and inductively, allowing the distinctive traits to designate one document and distinguish it from all others, I dealt with the problem of variant readings and diverse versions of particular documents. In that way I dealt with one component of the critique of the documentary reading of the Rabbinic canon, parallels and what they show or do not show about documents.

But if variant readings and "parallels" do not affect the documentary reading of the canonical writings, the latter do require attention in their own right. Here I turn to the challenge to the documentary reading that derives from a simple fact. Some sayings and stories not only do not exhibit the distinctive traits of any one document but neatly fit in two or more compilations equally well. What does that fact tell us about the character and definition of those documents? So the documentary hypothesis must address the compositions

---

[9] Binghamton 2001: Global Publications. ACADEMIC STUDIES IN THE HISTORY OF JUDAISM SERIES.

and composites that move from one document to another and so are autonomous of any one compilation.

What about the diverse wording of "parallels" as they move from document to document? I originally addressed that matter in *The Peripatetic Saying*.[10] Now I revise that monograph and impose upon its data the focus that the present debate defines. The result is the third and final part of this study, *Extra- and Non-Documentary Writing in the Canon of Formative Judaism*. III. *Peripatetic Parallels*.

IV.

Let me now dwell for a moment on the principal exercise worked out in this research report, the matter of proportion and position of the free-standing compositions. For Part Two forms the shank of the monograph and its proposition, data, and argument therefore should be spelled out in some detail. My purpose now is to show two simple facts, one concerning quantity and proportion, the other, quality and consequence.

Negligible Proportion of Free-Standing Stories in Rabbinic Documents

First, the peripatetic saying or free-standing story forms a negligible proportion of the crafted and purposive documents, where they do occur. Documents defined by characteristic traits of rhetoric, topic, and logic of coherent discourse do not depend for more than a tiny fraction of their compositions and composites upon writing shared with other

---

[10] *The Peripatetic Saying: The Problem of the Thrice-Told Tale in Talmudic Literature*. Chico, 1985: Scholars Press for Brown Judaic Studies. Reprise and reworking of materials in *Development of a Legend; Rabbinic Traditions about the Pharisees before 70* I-III.

compilations.[11] When we ask, just how significant a proportion of a document is comprised by stories autonomous of a particular document and common to two or more, the answer is, quantitatively a minor proportion.

The Tangential Position, in Documentary Context, that is Assigned to the Free-Standing Composition

Second, when we ask about the importance of free-standing stories in the canonical documents, we find that they play a tangential role. They provide useful information, they illustrate, they amplify, they constitute a topical appendix or a footnote. But they do not bear the principal burden. They do not carry the documentary message where they do occur. How do we know that fact? It is by identifying the main lines of exposition and argument of a given composite. If we outline a composite, we see that the free-standing story always takes a subordinate position and never defines a principal part in the composite in which it figures.

So I mean to show through specific cases that the free-standing story or saying in no way forms an obstacle to the documentary reading of the canonical compilations. The rule is, the constituent components of the document conform to the distinctive rhetorical, topical, and logical program of a given document; the exception is the free-standing story. But that exception reinforces the rule, because the free-standing story or staying serves as filler, in one way or another serving the purpose of the compiler of the document. It is a footnote in the documentary text, not a principal part of the text itself.

---

[11] I summarize the matter systematically in *Introduction to Rabbinic Literature*. N.Y., 1994: Doubleday. THE DOUBLEDAY ANCHOR REFERENCE LIBRARY. This is based on systematic studies of each of the principal writings of the canon, from the Mishnah through the Bavli, and from the earliest to the latest compilations of Midrash-exegeses.

Part Two forms a simple exercise. I choose as a sample a standard unit of the given document, a chapter (a *pisqa* or *parashah*), and through variations in type-faces — specifically, in lower case caps — I mark out those components of the *pisqa* or *parashah* that are shared with another document besides the one under discussion. So I proceed systematically through principal parts of the canon, from the Mishnah-Tosefta through the Bavli, and from the earlier (Sifra) to the later (Genesis Rabbah) Midrash-compilations. Of each sample of the representative document in succession, I ask, does this document as represented by the sample in prospect systematically or significantly utilize writing ("traditions") that serves other documents as well? Or does this document make a statement that is, sum and substance, unique to itself, calling only seldom if at all upon writings shared with other documents? On the basis of the result, I allege, the parallels establish no point. The claim that there is an influential autonomous tradition on which the various documents draw but which is prior to and separate from them all is a myth: not true.

Then, in each chapter, the presentation doubles back over the composites reviewed at the outset. I reproduce an outline of the context in which the cited non- or extra-documentary passage occurs, and that clearly shows the position, in the exposition of matters, that is accorded to the free-standing saying. Visually once more we are able to discern the tangential and subordinate role in the documentary exposition that is assigned to the free-standing saying. So my argument is that the free-standing saying is quantitatively negligible and qualitatively tangential in the canonical compilations of Rabbinic Judaism in the formative age. That disposes of an argument against the documentary reading of those compilations that the free-standing or autonomous stories present.

V.

Perspective will illuminate matters. How did the debate, running on now for twenty years or more, get underway? The debate began before I had even enunciated the documentary reading of the Rabbinic canon. The documentary hypothesis of the Rabbinic canon came to merely implicit expression in my work on the Mishnah (together with the Tosefta), *Judaism: The Evidence of the Mishnah*.[12] Willy-nilly, I precipitated a considerable row. I did so by writing on a single document in the context of the systemic description, analysis, and interpretation of a religious system. Reading a Rabbinic writing in such a way, which struck me as self-evidently required, represented an innovation, bearing implications of both a methodological and a theological sort.

But I did not at that time think through and articulate the implications of a work that read the Mishnah in its own terms and framework, in dialogue with the Tosefta. That is because it struck me as a self-evidently necessary first step: this text by itself, then that text by itself, then both, each in its consequent context established in a canon of documents continuous with one another.[13] Why not read the Mishnah in its

---

[12] *Judaism. The Evidence of the Mishnah.* Chicago, 1981: University of Chicago Press. *Choice*, "Outstanding academic book list" 1982-3. Paperback edition: 1984. Second printing, 1985. Third printing, 1986. Second edition, augmented: Atlanta, 1987: Scholars Press for Brown Judaic Studies. The work appeared also in Italian and in Hebrew.

[13] I backed into the entire matter. I turned to the Mishnah because I realized historical work of a critical character could not be done as it was being done, ignoring the venue of the sayings and stories that at that time sustained historical study. After *Development of a Legend, Rabbinic Traditions about the Pharisees before 70,* and *Eliezer ben Hyrcanus, The Tradition and the Man,* I had come to the end of the line of form-criticism (as I then understood it), and the models of Tanakh and New Testament studies for historical research ceased to instruct me. I determined to start back at the beginning, taking as my problem the historical use of the Rabbinic documents, from the Mishnah, the first of them, onward. I quickly became ab-

own terms, since it was, after all, the first document of Rabbinic Judaism beyond Scripture? Beyond Scripture, the Mishnah had no past. It marked the starting point. It therefore seemed to me self-evidently the right way to commence work on the documentary history of the ideas of Rabbinic Judaism. And that is what I contemplated, starting with the first writing. So I read the Mishnah (with the Tosefta) as an autonomous document. I understood that canonical documents also are connected one to another, and, further, that being formed into the canon of Judaism, they form a continuity from each to all.[14]

But reviewers, most of them benign and intellectual but some few of them memorably brutal and political, imme-

---

sorbed by the Halakhic structure and system in its own terms — thus "Judaism: the evidence of the Mishnah" as a history and analysis of the Halakhic data. I was simply oblivious to the fact that one does not isolate a single document out of the corpus of the oral Torah. All the documents — so people held — serve as mere utensils for the preservation of free-standing "traditions" about this and that, and the work of learning was to collect and arrange these "traditions" in new patterns. My documentary history of Rabbinic Judaism presented an unwanted alternative. But it took many years to reread the canonical writings one by one, describing, analyzing, and interpreting each in its own framework and context. And with the results now in hand, I am inclined to think a recapitulation of the work a productive project for the future. At the end point, new beginnings present themselves always.

[14] Not only so, but I had as my model the greatest exegete the Mishnah has ever had, that is, Maimonides, who not only re-founded the tradition of Mishnah-exegesis, but defined it for all time. His commentary to the Mishnah centers upon the Mishnah in its own terms, absorbing other Halakhic data within his representation of Mishnah-matters. His precursors in Mishnah-commentary hardly compare, and those that came later simply aped his model and paraphrased his results. With him in mind, I never imagined that I was doing other than an established procedure in Mishnah-exegesis, to be sure with my own program and generative problematic, which differed radically from Maimonides' but drew heavily upon his results to accomplish a new purpose.

Preface

diately perceived and challenged the unacknowledged premise of my work. That was, a given Rabbinic document could be defined as autonomous of all other documents, with distinctive traits of topic, rhetoric, and logic of coherent discourse. I took for granted that one could speak of "the Judaism of the Mishnah," that is, the religious structure and system that the Mishnah (and the Tosefta, which I treated as integral to Mishnah-commentary, the Mishnah's first talmud) set forth. I thought it self-evident that the Mishnah and the Tosefta provide their own first, best commentary: the very signals embodied in the rhetoric, topic, and logic of coherent discourse that characterize those compilations. That is what I expounded in *Judaism: The Evidence of the Mishnah*.

That work dictated its own succession: Could the other documents sustain the descriptive, analytical, and interpretative enterprise, one by one? Indeed so, for in subsequent studies, in a systematic way, I examined further documents, the Yerushalmi and Bavli in the line of the Mishnah, and Sifra, the two Sifrés and Mekhilta, and the Rabbah-Midrash-compilations of antiquity, in the line of Scripture, as well as Abot deRabbi Natan in the line of tractate Abot. So I did not neglect the other components of the ancient canon. So much for the autonomy of the canonical documents, each read on its own.

I further pursued the other two of the three dimensions of canonical context, connection and continuity. That is, I saw each document in succession as autonomous of all others, connected with some others, and continuous, by reason of canonical standing, with every other Rabbinic writing (inclusive of the liturgical documents, so far as these originate in late antiquity). I compared and contrasted two or more documents, e.g., two kindred Midrash-compilations, the two Talmuds, and the like.

Nonetheless, the possibility of describing a document as a systematic statement of a cogent system, not only as a component of a larger construction, was challenged. The challenge to what was implicit, in a variety of studies precipitated by my *Judaism: The Evidence of the Mishnah*, then, imposed on me the task of proceeding from the Mishnah to all the other documents of the Rabbinic canon, meaning, the Yerushalmi and Bavli, the several Midrash-compilations, and the like. That work of documentary description, analysis, and interpretation for the main part of the Rabbinic canon of late antiquity has required twenty years and is now complete, so far as I can accomplish it. Another generation will improve upon and refine the results. But I know of no assuredly-pre-Islamic, clearly-Rabbinic documents of any integrity, weight and consequence that await documentary description.

Now, as a matter of fact, the direction of criticism I scarcely anticipated proved the most engaging. I have already spelled it out, so a brief reprise suffices. That criticism held that the very conception of a document with a set of determinate traits, a document that is to be described, analyzed, and interpreted, in the Rabbinic canon cannot stand. Rabbinic writings are random, scrapbooks not documents of purpose.

That is for three reasons, which certainly require systematic attention.

[1] the indeterminacy of the readings of documents by reason of textual variants;

[2] the porous character of documentary boundaries by reason of the presence of a given composition or composite in two or more documents, thus the composition or composite autonomous of any single document; and

[3] the matter of intertextuality, the flow of thought from document to document, even when a particular passage is not explicitly cited by one document from another.

Now let us take up each of these foci of criticism of the documentary hypothesis of the Rabbinic canon.

VI.

What about variant readings? Much excellent computer-work — self-evidently — goes forward, both in Germany and in the State of Israel, in collecting and collating variant manuscript-readings of the principal documents of the Rabbinic canon — and has for a hundred years and more. That excellent work carries forward the traditions of the classical Yeshivot, both in times past and in our own day, of identifying and interpreting the meaning of variant wordings of Halakhic and Aggadic writings alike. While computer-science has made easy the collection and collation of manuscript-variants, it has not innovated in material ways in the work of producing "critical editions," whatever people mean by that language.

Collecting and collating variant readings of the several canonical documents represent a shibboleth in the contemporary scene of the study of ancient Judaism. For my part, I have relied on the best editions and commentaries available to me at the time I have done my work,, e.g., of translation and form-analysis. But I have never made my task the provision of "critical" texts, meaning, texts that reproduce the variety of manuscript evidence of a given document. I have left that work to others and have used their results. I have always taken account of the possibilities of manuscript variation of a given text and never constructed an account of matters based on a single reading rather than some other reading. I have analyzed large aggregates of data and proposed characterizations that accommodate diversity of readings of those data. That is the very heart of form-analysis: recurrent patterns, exhibited by vast proportions of the document under analysis.

From my initial presentation of the Mishnah-Tosefta in my *History of the Mishnaic Law*, however, I failed to articulate the way in which I took account of variation in manuscript representation of documents. As a result, critics focused upon what I did not undertake to do — the collation of manuscript variations — and ignored how I framed matters in full cognizance of the state of the evidence at hand. Put simply, as I said, where text-scholars have produced superior editions and commentaries, I was among the first to build upon their work, and where I was left to depend upon the standard printed editions, I controlled for the range of uncertainty defined by the state of learning at that time.

Now, as a matter of fact, critics, represented in *Pointless Parallels* by H.-J. Becker[15] and his teacher Schaefer and *his* teacher Goldberg, have maintained that the variations in manuscript testimony are so vast as to deny cogency and coherence to any compilation. That may be so for the Qabbalah-documents that Schaefer studied, but it is not so for the Rabbinic ones on which I work. There the variations, however sizable, do not call into question the integrity of the documents that we know through diverse manuscript representations. Unfairly, I was accused of ignoring the matter of variant readings, even though my Mishnah- and Tosefta-work systematically attended to them. That systematic work for the Mishnah and the Tosefta, the former by me and my students in the manuscript-representations of the Mishnah, the latter by Lieberman for most of the Tosefta and by overseas counterparts for the rest of it, yielded no grounds for denying the integrity of the Mishnah and the Tosefta, even in full recognition of variations among the manuscript representations of

---

[15] I refer to *Die grossen rabbinischen Sammelwerke Palaestinas. Zur literarischen Genese von Talmud Yerushalmi und Midrash Bereshit Rabba* Tuebingen, 1999: J. C. B. Mohr (Paul Siebeck). 218 pp. My review of that dissertation is in Volume One of this project.

those documents. Where critical texts, collating variant readings, existed for the documents when I worked on those documents, I used those texts, Bernard Mandelbaum's for Pesiqta deRab Kahana, M. Margoliot's for Leviticus Rabbah, for example. My translations of both of those documents were the first to use the critical texts. My Yerushalmi translation was complete before Schaefer's collations of manuscript-variants began to appear, so I could not use them. I take note of these matters only to deal with the criticism that I ignore manuscript variants. I address them as required.

But still, I plead guilty. For, it is true that, in the framework of form-analysis, I am not paralyzed by the availability of two or more readings of a given passage or even representations of a given document. Variant readings do not pose a problem that, within the documentary hypothesis, requires intense engagement, because of what is claimed, and not claimed, by that hypothesis. Stated simply but with heavy emphasis: *at no point is the characterization of a document within the documentary reading of the canonical writings made to depend upon one reading rather than another, or on one MS version rather than another.* That is for a fundamental reason, which I do not think has been grasped by the critics of the documentary reading who base their criticism on the variations in manuscript-wording. It is this: the formal traits produced by documentary description repeat themselves throughout — that is the very point of form-analysis.

The form-analysis, the systematic description of the topical program, the characterization of the logic of coherent discourse — all three elements of documentary definition address large aggregates of data, not variant readings. We can define the documentary qualities of, e.g., Genesis Rabbah or the Mishnah, even though the wording of the documents — and even entire compositions — may vary from one manuscript to the next. Becker, for one, is so impressed by variant readings that he posits more than one Genesis Rabbah, each "version" defined by its own singular manuscript. The fact is, confronted by an unassigned variant, if the unassigned variant exhibits the indicative traits of a document, we are ordinarily quite able to identify the document to which it belongs, when we address the differentiating formal, topical, or logical traits of said variant.

That manuscript evidence provides us with diverse accounts of a given documents brings no news to me or anyone I know. Variant readings captured my interest early on. My initial encounter with textual variants came with the Mishnah and the Tosefta, and while cognizant of the findings of Y. N. Epstein in his *Mevo lenussah hammishnah* (1954) and lesser works, I saw no variation so fundamental as to deny to the Mishnah all formal and intellectual cogency. It is one thing to recognize variations in wording of particular passages. It is another to deny that the Mishnah has distinctive and definitive traits that characterize the whole: no rhetorical patterns, no topical program, no logic of coherent discourse everywhere took charge of matters. But the variant readings rarely if ever call into question the indicative traits identified by form-analysis; forms are forms because they recur and define and dominate. In Saul Lieberman's Tosefta edition and the German counterparts, which I used for the first four and the sixth divisions, respectively, where the variants are carefully collated, variations in detail likewise left ample space for the recognition of something we may regard as a stable and coherent whole: *the* Tosefta, not merely this manuscript's version of the Tosefta and that manuscript's version of the same. Nothing in Lieberman's discussion suggested otherwise. And that is so, even though there are significant MSS variations, as everyone knows. Lieberman's apparatus articulates these variations; but he offers us a text, *the* Tosefta, and variants, not three or ten or fifty different Toseftas, as, by extension from what he says, Becker would maintain: each manuscript a document.

True, the relatively stable text-tradition of the Mishnah represents a particularly felicitous situation. Some of the Rabbinic compilations, as well as Judaic but not necessarily Rabbinic compilations, e.g., the Hekhalot texts, are represented in text-traditions of considerable diversity. Among them, indeed, are compilations with simply chaotic text-traditions. These are problems to be taken into account. Much depends on whether the definition of a given document — its rhetorical, topical, and logical program — can accommodate diverse textual representations of said document. When we invoke the three criteria of documentary definition, we define the document as a writings that conform to those indicative criteria and no others. That serves nicely for nearly the entire Rabbinic canon of late antiquity.

VII.

What of compositions autonomous of documents? The matter of "parallels" — the "pointless parallels" of the title of the companion-study, Volume One of this project — comes to the fore. Critics have argued that the occurrence of the same story or saying in two or more documents calls into question the conception that the compilers of documents exercised taste and judgment in selecting for their distinctive purpose the materials they present to us. The ubiquity of parallels shared by two or more documents bears a compelling implication, some have held. It is that compilers in no way carried out a systematic labor of composition, collection, and arrangement, a labor aimed at making a cogent statement of a systemic order. People made up compositions and even composites, and editors used these ready-made writings when they compiled their collections.

What is the upshot of the matter of variant readings, free-standing compositions, and the documentary hypothesis? It suffices to say, I concur entirely that variant readings are to be noted, especially where they represent a distinction that makes a difference; and that stories and sayings autonomous of particular documents require study in their own terms. Both approaches are necessary. But they are not sufficient. The full characterization of the canon requires the recognition of the simple fact that the Mishnah is different from Genesis Rabbah, which is different from the Yerushalmi, which is different from the Siddur and Mahzor; and that all the canonical documents participate in a single system in common.

VIII.

To summarize the two main points of debate: The critics thus have pursued two lines of attack on the documentary reading of the Rabbinic canon:

[1] textual variants vitiate the conception of a determinate document to begin with, and

[2] peripatetic sayings and stories demonstrate the irrelevance of documentary boundaries.

Both emphasize the diversity of documentary representations, both in the manuscript traditions and in the inclusion of the same story in more than one document. Each body of evidence is seen to invalidate the claim that the various compilations respond to distinctive programs and purposes, respectively. One approach is to compare and contrast versions of the same story as these occur in two or more Rabbinic documents. The other is to focus upon manuscript variations, some of them of a considerable order, that pertain to a single document. One manuscript represents the document in one way, another in quite a different way, the one including, the other omitting, sizable stretches of writing.

Preface xlv

These two matters present no surprises to anybody who studies the canonical writings. They are commonplaces of learning. Differences arise only from diverse assessments of the matters' importance. From the early 1970s forward, I have addressed both matters, textual variations and multiple citations of a single story or saying.

As to the diverse manuscript testimonies to a given document, I addressed the question — important to me as much as to those who regard the canon as essentially chaotic — in two ways.

First, in my commentary to the Mishnah (*A History of the Mishnaic Law* [Leiden, 1974-1986: E. J. Brill, in forty three volumes]) I collated a fair portion of the variant readings of the Mishnah-text for some of the divisions; I found they yielded distinctions that rarely made much of a difference except as to Halakhic ruling, which did not concern me. And from the perspective of the description, analysis, and interpretation of free-standing documents, the variant readings made no difference at all. That is because, more important, I defined the documentary reading of the canonical documents in such a way as to take account of variations in manuscript representation of documents. The definition of a document — its description, analysis, and interpretation — never rests on one reading as against another, but on the indicative traits that everywhere characterize the whole and establish the paradigm that governs the parts. Within that definition, the inclusion or exclusion of one detail or another makes little difference.

Second, as to variant readings of a given document, I furthermore dealt with the matter explicitly in my debate with Schaefer. Since to my knowledge he has not replied in print, in systematic book, to my systematic response to his critique of 1986, I cannot guess at what he may be thinking. But there is evidence that suggests he lays heavy stress on variant MSS evidence of a given document. The evidence takes the form of a series of "books" comprised by computer printouts of collated variants. Alas, what difference the distinctions in readings make is difficult to assess. Schaefer's printouts do not encompass systematic reading and interpretation of what is collated. Specifically, Schaefer and his co-workers mechanically collate variant readings of the various Yerushalmi-tractates. But to my knowledge they have yet to interpret these variants. I have not seen their Yerushalmi-commentaries, based on their collation of variant readings, and I do not know how they interpret these variants in the context of the Halakhic issues to which, in general, they pertain.

There is another aspect of matters, the nihilism of the =Goldberg-Schaefer-Becker school. That is shown by how they treats variant reading. It is as though they contained no implications for the exegesis of the document and for its contents. Anyone at home in the Rabbinic study of Rabbinic literature knows that a variant reading, e.g., of a Halakhic texts, commonly embodies a Halakhic theory of what is at stake in the text at hand. It is not a mere formality, it is a clue to the logical possibilities of the Halakhic issue before us. Everybody in the classical Yeshiva-world understands that fact. I do not think the Goldberg-Schaefer-Becker school does. Implicitly, then, their presentation of manuscript variants — a mere collation, without comment or interpretation, of the variants — treats the variations as formalities, lacking all meaning. That school explicitly does little to establish their cultural (e.g., logical or intellectual) consequence. I cannot overstress, in this context, that the Rabbinic tradition in the classical contexts of learning knows full well the meaning of diverse wordings and readings of Halakhic rulings. The received approach to Talmudic exegesis is able to discern the Halakhic theory that has generated one reading in preference

Preface xlvii

to another. The freshest beginner in the authentic study of these texts is introduced to the problem of implications of variant wordings and readings, e.g., by Rashi and the Tosafists, among many. Schaefer and his co-workers have thus far declined to pursue the implications of their computer-collations. Accordingly, to date they have given us distinctions that make no difference to learning. But they have made much of that little.

Still, they owe themselves to make the effort. For the documentary reading of the Rabbinic canon concerns itself with precisely the matter of Rabbinic culture. Not only so, but the classical exegetical tradition of the Halakhic documents takes full account of not only the presence, but also the meaning, of variant readings of Halakhic rulings — the legal theory behind this version as against that — and of this fact, Schaefer and his co-workers exhibit remarkably slight appreciation. So the entire enterprise stands for little more than a formality of arid academicism: collecting and arranging information of no consequence to speak of. On that basis I characterize that school as nihilistic.

What, second, about the free-standing story or the peripatetic saying? As to the circulation of a given story or saying, complete with variations, over two or more compilations, I dealt with that phenomenon systematically between 1969 and 1974. Specifically, I undertook such systematic studies in the comparison and contrast of the same saying or story in circulation in a number of compilations, e.g., *Development of a Legend. Studies on the Traditions about Yohanan ben Zakkai; Rabbinic Traditions about the Pharisees before 70;* and *Eliezer ben Hyrcanus: The Tradition and the Man.*[16] In a long sequence of charts of

---

[16] *Development of a Legend. Studies on the Traditions Concerning Yohanan ben Zakkai.* Leiden, 1970: Brill; *The Rabbinic Traditions about the Pharisees before 70.* Leiden, 1971: Brill. I-III; I. *The Rabbinic Traditions about the Pharisees before 70. The Masters;* II. *The Rabbinic Traditions about the Pharisees before 70. The*

comparisons of stories common to two or more documents, I laid out the differences in detailed charts and proposed theories to explain them. Struck by the heavy emphasis on these stories autonomous of particular documents, I restated the main results of those studies as well as others in *The Peripatetic Saying: The Problem of the Thrice-Told Tale in Talmudic Literature*.[17] But I have never addressed the implications of the peripatetic saying or story for the documentary reading of Rabbinic literature. And that brings us, in the setting of three decades of critical work on the Rabbinic culture, to the present exercise. Specifically, just how important, proportionately, are these peripatetic sayings and stories in the setting of the documents that preserve them?

IX.

My answer now is perfectly clear. I find the parallels pointless in function, paltry in proportion. By "the pointless parallel," then, in the companion-volume I mean, the existence of parallels in two or more documents, stories that occur here and there but make a documentary difference no where. By "the paltry parallel," in the present part of the study, I mean, such parallels as we do have play no substantial role in the documents in which they occur. A documentary difference would impose variables upon the definitive traits of the document. Stated simply: traditions autonomous of particular documents are parachuted down into particular documents, ordinarily for purposes we can readily discern. Their presence never requires the redefinition of the documentary traits of rhetoric, topic, and logic of coherent dis-

---

Houses' III. *The Rabbinic Traditions about the Pharisees before 70. Conclusions' Eliezer ben Hyrcanus. The Tradition and the Man.* Leiden, 1973: Brill. I. *Eliezer ben Hyrcanus. The Tradition and the Man. The Tradition;* II. *Eliezer ben Hyrcanus. The Tradition and the Man. The Man.*

[17] Chico, 1985: Scholars Press for Brown Judaic Studies.

course that prevail throughout the document. Their presence signifies the intent to draw upon extra-documentary data to amplify or illustrate a documentary point.

What comes next? What I have left is the claim that the Rabbinic tradition circulated in autonomous traditions, unaffected by documentary considerations. Those autonomous traditions in stories and sayings that occur in two or more documents, it is held, vitiate the documentary reading of the Rabbinic canonical books. Rabbinic Judaism circulated in free-circulating "traditions" or "texts," and localizing these "traditions" here rather than there forms a happenstance. If texts can fit anywhere, they belong. no where in particular. It is argued that the presence of peripatetic sayings renders null the claim that data in a given compilation has been selected and arranged purposefully. I have maintained that the compilers of a given document impart to their compilation distinctive traits of rhetoric, topic, and logic of coherent discourse.

Others take the view that utilization of a saying or story in a variety of documents calls into question the allegation that documentary lines signal the imposition of a distinctive program, whether of law or theology, upon what lies within those boundaries. The Rabbinic literature, others maintain, is comprised by a formless mass of free-standing traditions, unaffected by the intent and purpose of documentary authorships let alone the authors of the compositions and composites collected by those authorships.

X.

To Professor William S. Green, University of Rochester, I owe the formation of the title, therefore the clarification of the plan of the work. That is no negligible debt!

I consulted upwards of twenty-five colleagues on this project as I routinely do on kindred ones. I appreciate their on-going interest in my research and the suggestions that they make in improving it.

Well-settled now at Bard College, I express my pleasure at this ideal situation for my research. My colleagues, particularly Professor Bruce D. Chilton, create a pleasant environment in every way, and, in his case, a stimulating one as well.

JACOB NEUSNER
RESEARCH PROFESSOR OF RELIGION AND THEOLOGY
SENIOR FELLOW, INSTITUTE OF ADVANCED THEOLOGY
BARD COLLEGE
ANNANDALE-ON-HUDSON, NEW YORK 12504 USA
neusner@webjogger.net

PART ONE

EXTRA- AND NON-DOCUMENTARY WRITING

1.

THE BAVLI'S MASSIVE MISCELLANIES

The Talmud of Babylonia contains a sizable component of enormous miscellaneous composites. These by definition constitute non-documentary writing, and important parts of some of them may be classified as extra-documentary. The documentary reading of the Rabbinic canon must take up the Bavli's massive miscellanies.

First, let me once again review the definitions that are in play in this project. By "extra-" and "non-documentary writing," as I explained in the Preface, I mean, compositions or composites that ignore the indicative rhetorical, logical, and topical traits of the document in which they are now located. "Extra-documentary" writing occurs in two or more documents and belongs to none of them in particular. "Non-documentary" writing occurs in only one document but ignores the definitive traits of that document.

Indeed, both types of such writing ordinarily neglect the indicative traits of any of the Rabbinic documents of the formative canon. Compositions and composites that ignore the conventions of their documentary venues constitute a considerable challenge to the hypothesis that Rabbinic writing in the formative age takes shape in purposive compilations, not random aggregates of free-standing "traditions." The Mishnah with the Tosefta contains a negligible proportion of non- or extra-documentary writing; it is formally more uniform than any document of Rabbinic Judaism in the formative age. At the other end of the canonical age, the Bavli contains a massive proportion of such writing, a huge component of what appears on the surface miscellaneous. Accordingly we begin with the largest, and most intractable, problem, then proceed through the more uniform compilations.[1]

Let me spell out what is at issue here. The Bavli is comprised in part by proportionately-huge composites of a formally- and programmatically-miscellaneous character. In a few tractates, by my estimate, they form 40% of the whole. These massive miscellanies cannot be dismissed as paltry or exceptional. Though they do not necessarily circulate from document to document, they certainly appear from the perspective of the tractate in which they occur to be simply pointless, calling into question as they do the documentary integrity of the Bavli. And the document assigns to them a role of sufficient consequence that we cannot dismiss them as tangential. So the first task is to show that the superficially-non-documentary composites of the Bavli in fact adhere to documentary norms in the Bavli, if not in form then in function. They adhere to rules that pertain to their venue and exhibit traits of editorial rationality. The issue is, how do these formally-miscellaneous composites exhibit traits of documentary purpose? May we treat these composites as integral to a documentary program that nearly everywhere guides the compilers of the Bavli? I have argued that we may, and here present a reprise of the matter.[2]

---

[1] As we shall see in Chapter Two, the problem of non-documentary writing scarcely makes an appearance in the Mishnah (ca. 200 C.E.), and, concomitantly, the Tosefta (ca. 300 C.E.) too is comprised in large measure by compositions that adhere to determinate conventions of rhetoric, topic (here: problematic), and logic of coherent discourse. These, all together, characterize the Tosefta and no other compilation. So in the Mishnah-Tosefta we address a fine instance of the paltry proportion of non-documentary writing in principal Rabbinic compilations.

[2] I summarize in this chapter the main points of my *The Bavli's Massive Miscellanies. The Problem of Agglutinative Discourse in the Talmud of Babylonia*. At-

I. Extra- and Non-Documentary Writing and the Bavli

Once we define the documentary program of the Bavli, which is [1] Mishnah analysis, then [2] Halakhic inquiry and amplification, we realize that by its own definition of its task, that Talmud contains a fair proportion of non-documentary writing. That is writing that not only has no bearing on the exegesis of the Mishnah but also — and more to the point — exhibits no obvious links to the context in which it appears. It represents a formidable obstacle to the proposition that (among the canonical compilations of Rabbinic Judaism) the Bavli is characterized by purposive qualities of form and program. Only when we understand how in its large aggregates, if not in every small detail, such non- and extra-documentary writing fits into the Bavli shall we be able to set into place the capstone of the construction represented by the documentary reading of the Rabbinic canon.

The pages of the Bavli contain long stretches of apparently disorganized and disconnected writing, on one subject after another, In these miscellaneous entries we have the equivalent of paragraphs but none of those larger compositions of paragraphs setting forth sustained and connected arguments — chapters of thought — that in general characterize the Bavli. Partly because of these massive miscellanies, the Bavli appears to many to be disorganized or to adhere to no principle of arrangement that we can discern. If that were so, then the Bavli would radically diverge from the character of the other compilations that make up the Rabbinic canon. For the

---

lanta, 1992: Scholars Press for South Florida Studies in the History of Judaism.

prior writings[3] commonly exhibit traits of order and coherence, and, while some contain non-documentary writing, none is comprised in so significant a proportion by vast conglomerations of free-standing thoughts. None but the Bavli contains sizable sequences that exhibit the appearance of a mere scrapbook — this and that, haphazardly thrown together, in no apparent order, for no visible purpose.

In this chapter I demonstrate that these miscellaneous composites adhere to rules of discourse that we can discern. We identify regularities, rules that show miscellanies to be anything but haphazard. In the end, we shall find, on the contrary, the miscellanies, adhering to rules of agglutinative, not propositional and syllogistic, discourse, serve as Mishnah-commentaries, as do the cogent composites that predominate in the Bavli. But what they contribute to the elucidation of the Mishnah is information, not analytical argument. And how they connect to the topical program of Mishnah-commentary requires patient inquiry. It is not always obvious.

Seeing the documentary task undertaken by massive miscellanies in the Bavli seems to me to lay to rest the last shreds of the argument, so far as it is based on data, that the Bavli lacks indicative traits of a documentary character. People maintain that it is disorganized or unorganized; that the document adheres to no clear principles of order and that it is really just this, that, and the other thing, all thrown together. Based

---

[3]I am not sure that this statement would accurately characterize the Yerushalmi, not having done for that Talmud studies equivalent to those on the basis of which I characterize, e.g., the Mishnah, Tosefta, and all Midrash-compilations without exception. My impression, based on the work done for *The Talmud of the Land of Israel. A Preliminary Translation and Explanation.* Chicago: The University of Chicago Press: 1983. XXXV. *Introduction. Taxonomy*, and also *Judaism: The Classical Statement. The Evidence of the Bavli.* Chicago, 1986: University of Chicago Press, is that the Yerushalmi contains much less miscellaneous material than the Bavli. But that is only an impression.

on a profound misunderstanding of the document's agglutinative properties and revealing deep ignorance of all principles of cogency but the coherence of words and phrases into sentences and paragraphs, that opinion is broadly held. It shows that, until now, the Bavli has really not been properly understood at all. That proper understanding derives from a broad perspective on the whole, a grasp of the large-scale principles of organization, extension, and secondary amplification. Lest my claim prove implausible, I point to prior writings of mine, where I have extensively cited both received and contemporary statements of the theory that the Bavli is not a well-crafted and carefully edited document. In fact the Bavli is a commentary to the Mishnah, and in this work of literary analysis, I take up the most intractable type of material — vast stretches of the Bavli that appear to be little more than miscellanies — and I now show that that too is little more than Mishnah-commentary, of a rather special kind to be sure.

II. DIFFERENTIATING THE TYPES OF WRITING IN THE BAVLI

Now we turn to the heart of the matter. Two conflicting characteristics mark the Bavli. It is, first, a disciplined and well-organized, carefully crafted piece of writing. Most of the document is formulated in accord with a few simple rules, so that it is well-organized and easily followed. The Bavli, viewed whole, is carefully set forth as a commentary to the Mishnah, and the vast majority of its composites are put together so as to elucidate the statements of the Mishnah.

But in the pages of the Bavli we observe, second, very large composites, not formed into Mishnah-commentaries at all. These composites do not follow the rules that govern the formation of the composites that serve as commentaries to the Mishnah. Mishnah-commentaries proceed along orderly lines, treating a subject in a way that conforms to our logic, beginning with first things, moving onward, within the limits and logic of the subject, to more complex ones, ending then in subsidiary questions. But the miscellanies go from this to that to the other thing, and it is not easy to explain why one thing is joined to some other, or why one passage is presented before, or after, some other.

Not only so, but the large-scale aggregates to which I refer both have, and also give to the Bavli, when it is viewed by an undiscerning reader, a miscellaneous quality: this, that, the other thing, with no clear pattern or purpose much in evidence. These massive miscellanies — composites that on first glance seem to follow no clear rules of composition at all — are made up of a substantial number of free-standing compositions. They in no way serve the paramount purpose of the Bavli, which demonstrably is to explain the Mishnah. Whoever put the miscellanies together had a different program in mind. And if the framers of the miscellanies had in mind that they ultimately would be collected in a piece of writing of some dimensions, then that writing that they imagined bears no resemblance to the writing in which their miscellanies did end up, that is, the Bavli. To substantiate these allegations I shall set forth the rules of conglomeration and agglutination that govern the formation of these massive miscellanies and define the program that, in my view, governed the formation of the Bavli's miscellanies.

III. THE BAVLI'S PARAMOUNT MODE OF DISCOURSE: THE PROPOSITIONAL, ANALYTICAL COMPOSITE

Most of the Bavli is made up of extended exercises of Mishnah-exegesis and amplification, with, first, exegesis of the

Mishnah's language, rules, sources, and authority; and, second, secondary discussions of laws and principles of laws pertinent to a given Mishnah-paragraph. These sustained passages, running on for many pages at a time, are remarkably cogent. Even though made up of diverse materials, ready made and rarely recast or rewritten for the occasion, nearly everything in a given composite will relate in some way or another to the purpose of the composite as a whole; will contribute facts; will provide examples; will address secondary or subsidiary issues; or will otherwise carry forward the analytical, and even propositional, program of Mishnah-exegesis that is realized in the entire composite.

    Let us begin with one fine example, among countless candidates, of first rate Mishnah-commentary in the Bavli's sustainedly excellent manner. Indeed, the Bavli is so elegant, so magnificent a piece of disciplined writing that it is difficult to select one instance over some other. But it must be done. In what follows, we begin with a Mishnah-paragraph and proceed to a systematic commentary on its components. The passage marked **I.1** then cites a clause of the Mishnah; it further raises an analytical question, in this instance, the implications of the statement of the Mishnah. What serves our purpose — the identification of an already-completed, quite cogent piece of writing — follows at C: a clear citation of a prior document. The presentation differentiates in three type faces. Citations of the Mishnah and the Tosefta are in bold face type. The voice of the Talmud when in Hebrew is in plain type. The voice of the Talmud when in Aramaic is in italics. What we see is that the analytical discourse takes place in Aramaic, and that is a fixed trait of the Bavli.[4]

---

[4] See my *Language as Taxonomy. The Rules for Using Hebrew and Aramaic in the Babylonian Talmud.* Atlanta, 1990: Scholars Press for South Florida Studies in the History of Judaism.

MISHNAH-TRACTATE BABA QAMMA 1:1

A. [There are] four generative causes of damages: (1) ox [Ex. 21:35-36], (2) pit [Ex. 21:33], (3) crop-destroying beast [Ex. 22:4], and (4) conflagration [Ex. 22:5].

B. [The definitive characteristic] of the ox is not equivalent to that of the crop-destroying beast;

C. nor is that of the crop-destroying beast equivalent to that of the ox;

D. nor are this one and that one, which are animate, equivalent to fire, which is not animate;

E. nor are this one and that one, which usually [get up and] go and do damage, equivalent to a pit, which does not usually [get up and] go and do damage.

F. What they have in common is that they customarily do damage and taking care of them is your responsibility.

G. And when one [of them] has caused damage, the [owner] of that which causes the damage is liable to pay compensation for damage out of the best of his land [Ex. 22:4].

I.1 A. **four generative causes of damages:**

B. *Since the framer of the passages makes reference to* **generative causes,** *it is to be inferred that there are derivative ones as well.* Are the derivative causes equivalent [in effect] to the generative causes or are they not equivalent to them in effect?

C. *We have learned with reference to the Sabbath:* **The generative categories of acts of labor [prohibited on the Sabbath] are forty less one [M. Shab. 7:2A].** *Since the framer of the passages makes reference to* **generative categories,** *it is to be inferred that there are derivative ones as well.* Are the derivative categories equivalent to the generative categories or are they not equivalent to them?

D. *Well, there is no difference between one's inadvertently carrying out an act of labor that falls into a generative category, in which case he is liable to present a sin-offering, and one's inadvertently carrying out an act of labor that falls into a derivative category of labor, in which case he is also liable to present a sin-offering. There is no difference between one's deliberately carrying* out an act of labor that falls into a generative category, in which case he is liable to the death penalty through stoning, and one's deliberately carrying out an act of labor that falls into a derivative category of labor, in which case he is also liable to the death penalty through stoning.

E. *So then what's the difference between an act that falls into the generative category and one that falls into the derivative category?*

F. *The upshot is that if one simultaneous carried out two actions that fall into the class of generative acts of labor, or two actions that fall into the classification of a derivative category, he is liable for each such action, while, if he had performed simultaneously both a generative act of labor and also a derivative of that same generative action, he is liable on only one count.*

G. *And from the perspective of R. Eliezer, who imposes liability for a derivative action even when one is simultaneously liable on account of carrying out an act in the generative category, on what basis does one classify one action as generative and another as derivative [if it makes no practical difference]?*

H. *Those actions that are carried out [even on the Sabbath] in the building of the tabernacle are reckoned as generative actions, and those that were not carried out on the Sabbath in the building of the tabernacle are classified as derivative.*

2. A. *With reference to uncleanness we have learned in the Mishnah:* **The generative causes of uncleanness [are] (1) the creeping thing, and (2) semen [of an adult Israelite], [2B] and (3) one who has contracted corpse uncleanness, [and (4) the leper in the days of his counting, and (5) sin offering water of insufficient quantity to be sprinkled. Lo, these render man and vessels unclean by contact, and earthenware vessels by [presence within the vessels' contained] airspace. But they do not render unclean by carrying] [M. Kel. 1:1].** And their derivatives are not equivalent to them, for while a generative cause of uncleanness imparts uncleanness to a human being and utensils, a derivative source of uncleanness imparts uncleanness to food and drink but not to a human being or utensils.

3. A. *Here what is the upshot of the distinction at hand?*

B. Said R. Pappa, "There are some derivatives that are equivalent in effect to the generative cause, and there are some that are not equivalent in effect to the generative cause."

4. A. *Our rabbis have taught on Tannaite authority:*

   B. Three [of the four] generative causes of damage are stated with respect to the ox: horn, tooth, and foot.

5. A. How on the basis of Scripture do we know the case of the horn?

   B. *It is in line with that which our rabbis have taught on Tannaite authority:*

   C. "If it will gore..." (Ex. 21:28) — and goring is done only with the horn, as it is said, "And Zedekiah, son of Chenaanah, made him horns of iron and said, Thus saith the Lord, with these shall you gore the Aramaeans" (1 Kgs. 22:11);

   D. and it is further said, "His glory is like the firstling of his bullock, and his horns are like the horns of a unicorn; with them he shall gore the people together" (Dt. 33:17).

   E. *What's the point of "and it is further said"?*

   F. *Should you say that teachings on the strength of the Torah are not to be derived from teachings that derive from prophetic tradition, then come and take note:* "His glory is like the firstling of his bullock, and his horns are like the horns of a unicorn; with them he shall gore the people together" (Dt. 33:17).

   G. *Yeah, well, is this really a deduction out of a scriptural proof text? To me it looks more like a mere elucidation, showing that "goring" is something that is done by a horn.*

   H. *What might you otherwise have supposed? That where Scripture makes an important distinction between an ox that was not known to gore and one that is a certified danger, that concerns a horn that is cut off [as in the case of the first of the two examples, that of 1 Kgs. 22:11], but as to one that is actually attached to the beast, all goring is classified as done by an ox that is an attested danger. Then come and take note:* "His glory is like the firstling of his bullock, and his horns are like the horns of a unicorn; with them he shall gore the people together" (Dt. 33:17).

6. A. *What are the derivatives of the horn?*

   B. Butting, biting, falling, and kicking.

C. *How come goring is called a generative cause of damages? Because it is stated explicitly,* "If it will gore..." (Ex. 21:28). *But then in reference to butting, it also is written,* "If it butts" (Ex. 21:35).

D. *That reference to butting refers in fact to goring, as has been taught on Tannaite authority:* Scripture opens with a reference to butting [Ex. 21:35] and concludes with a reference to goring [Ex. 21:16] to tell you that in this context "butting" means "goring."

7. A. *What, when the Scripture refers to injury to a human being, does it say,* "If it will gore" (Ex. 21:28), *while when Scripture refers to an ox's injuring an animal, it uses the language,* "if it will butt" (Ex. 21:35)?

B. *In connection with a human being, who is subject to a star [planetary influence], will be injured only by* [Kirzner: willful] *goring, but an animal, who is not subject to a star, is injured by mere accidental butting.*

C. *And by the way, Scripture tangentially informs us of another matter, namely, an animal that is an attested danger for a human being is an attested danger for other beasts, but an animal that is an attested danger for beasts is not necessarily an attested danger for injuring a human being.*

8. A. Biting: *does this not fall into the classification of a derivative of Tooth?*

B. *Not at all, for what characterizes injury under the classification of "tooth" is that there is pleasure that comes from doing the damage, but biting is not characterized by giving pleasure in the doing of the damage.*

9. A. falling, and kicking: *do these not fall into the classification of derivatives of Foot?*

B. *Not at all, for what characterizes injury under the classification of "foot" is that it is quite common, while damage done by these is not so common.*

10. A. *Now, then, as to those derivatives that are not equivalent to the generative causes [from which the derives come], to which R. Pappa made reference, what might they be? Should we say that he makes reference to these? Then how are they different from the generative cause? Just as Horn is a classification that involves damage done with intent, one's own property, and one's responsibility for adequate guardianship, so these too form classifications that involve damage done with intent, one's own property, and one's responsibility for adequate guardianship. So it*

one's responsibility for adequate guardianship. *So it must follow that the derivatives of Horn are equivalent to the principal, the Horn, and R. Pappa must then refer to tooth and foot.*

11. A. *Where in Scripture is reference made to tooth and foot? It is taught on Tannaite authority:* "And he shall send forth" (Ex. 22:4) — this refers to the foot, and so Scripture says, "That send forth the feet of the ox and the ass" (Is. 32:20). "And it shall consume" (Ex. 22:4) — this refers to the tooth, in line with this usage: "As the tooth consumes **[3A]** to entirety" (1 Kgs. 14:10).

12. A. The master has said: "'And he shall send forth' (Ex. 22:4) — this refers to the foot, and so Scripture says, 'That send forth the feet of the ox and the ass' (Is. 32:20)."

B. *So the operative consideration is that Scripture has said,* "That send forth the feet of the ox and the ass." *Lo, if Scripture had not so stated, how else would you have interpreted the phrase,* "And he shall send forth" (Ex. 22:4)? *It could hardly refer to horn, which is written elsewhere, nor could it mean tooth, since this too is referred to elsewhere.*

C. *No, the proof nonetheless was required, for it might have entered your mind to suppose that "send forth" and "consume" refers to tooth, in the one case where there is destruction of the principal, in the other where there is no destruction of the principal, so we are informed that that is not so.*

D. *Now that you have established that the cited verse refers to foot in particular, then how on the basis of Scripture do we know that there is liable for damage done by the tooth in a case in which the principal has not been destroyed?*

E. *It would follow by analogy from the case of damage done by the foot. Just as in the case of damage done by the foot, there is no distinction to be drawn between a case in which the principal has been destroyed and one in which the principal has not been destroyed, so in the case of damage done by the tooth, there is no distinction to be drawn between a case in which the principal has been destroyed and one in which the principal has not been destroyed.*

13. A. The master has said, "'And it shall consume' (Ex. 22:4) — this refers to the tooth, in line with this usage: 'As the tooth consumes to entirety' (1 Kgs. 14:10)."

B. *So the operative consideration is that Scripture has said,* "As the tooth consumes to entirety." *Lo, were it not for that statement, how might we have interpreted the phrase anyhow? It could hardly have been a reference to horn, for that is stated explicitly in Scripture, and it also could not have been a reference to foot for the same reason.*

C. *No, it was necessary to make that point in any event. For it might otherwise have entered your mind to suppose that both phrases speak of foot, the one referred to a case in which the beast was going along on its own, the other when the owner sent it to do damage, and so we are informed that that is not the case. [So we are informed that that is not the case.]*

D. *If then we have identified the matter with tooth, then how could we know that one is liable under the category of Foot when the cattle went and did damage on its own?*

E. *The matter is treated by analogy to damage done in the category of tooth. Just as in the case of tooth we draw no distinction between a case in which the owner sent the beast out and it did damage and one in which the beast went along on its own, so in the case of foot, there is no distinction between a case in which the owner sent the beast out and one in which the beast went out on its own.*

14. A. *Then let the Scripture make reference to* "And he shall send forth" (Ex. 22:4) *and omit* "And it shall consume," *which would cover the classifications of both foot and tooth? It would cover foot in line with this verse:* "That send forth the feet of the ox and the ass," *and it would cover tooth, in line with this verse,* "And the teeth of beasts will I send upon them" (Dt. 32:24).

B. *Were it not for this apparently redundant statement, I might have imagined that the intent was either the one or the other, either foot, since damage done by the foot is commonplace, or tooth, since damage done by the tooth gives pleasure.*

C. *Well, we still have to include them both, since, after all, which one would you exclude anyhow [in favor of the other], their being equally balanced?*

D. *The additional clarification still is required, for you might otherwise have supposed that the liability pertains only where the damage is intentional, excluding a case in which the cattle went on its own; so we are informed that that is not the case.*

15. A. *What is the derivative of the generative category of tooth?*

B. If for its own pleasure the cow rubbed itself

against a wall and broke it, or spoiled produce by rolling around in it.

C. *What distinguishes damage done by the tooth* [as a generative category] is that it is a form of damage that gives pleasure to the one that does it, it derives from what is your own property, and you are responsible to take care of it? *Well, in these cases too, one may say the same thing, namely, here we have* a form of damage that gives pleasure to the one that does it, it derives from what is your own property, and you are responsible to take care of it.

D. *It must follow that the derivative classes of the generative category of tooth are equivalent to the generative category itself, and when R. Pappa made his statement, he must have referred to the generative category of foot.*

16. A. *What is the derivative of the generative category of foot?*

B. If the beast while moving did damage with its body or hair or with a load on it or with a bit in its mouth or with a bell around its neck.

C. *What distinguishes damage done by the foot* [as a generative category] is that it is a form of damage that is very common, it derives from what is your own property, and you are responsible to take care of it. *Well, in these cases too, one may say the same thing, namely, here we have* a form of damage that is very common, it derives from what is your own property, and you are responsible to take care of it.

D. *It must follow that the derivative classes of the generative category of foot are equivalent to the generative category itself, and when R. Pappa made his statement, he must have referred to the generative category of pit.*

17. A. *Then what would be derivatives of the generative category of pit?*

B. *Should I say that the generative category is a pit ten handbreadths deep, but a derive is one nine handbreadths deed, Scripture does not make explicit reference to either one ten handbreadths deep nor to one nine handbreadths deep!*

C. *In point of fact that is not a problem, since the All-Merciful has said,* "And the dead beast shall be his" (Ex. 21:34). *And, for their part, rabbis established that a pit ten handbreadths deed will case death, one only nine handbreadths*

deep *will cause only injury, but will not cause death.*
D. *So what difference does that make? The one is a generative classification of pit when it comes to yielding death, the other an equally generative classification yielding injury.*
E. *So R. Papa's statement must speak of a stone, knife, or luggage, left in the public domain, that did damage.*
F. *How then can we imagine damage of this kind? If they were declared ownerless and abandoned in the public domain, then from the perspective of both Rab and Samuel, they fall into the classification of pit.* **[3B]** *And if they were not declared ownerless and abandoned in the public domain, then from the perspective of Samuel,* who has said, "All public nuisances are derived by analogy to the generative classification of pit," *they fall into the classification of pit, and from the perspective of Rab, who has held,* "All of them do we derive by analogy to ox," *they fall under the classification of ox.*
G. *What is it that characterizes the pit? It is that* to begin with it is made as a possible cause of damage, it is your property, and your are responsible to watch out for it. *So of these too it may be said,* to begin with it is made as a possible cause of damage, it is your property, and your are responsible to watch out for it. *It therefore follows that the derivatives of pit are the same as the pit itself, and when R. Pappa made his statement, it was with reference to the derivatives of the crop-destroying beast.*
18. A. *So what can these derivatives of the crop-destroying beast be anyhow? From the perspective of Samuel, who has said,* "The crop destroying beast is the same as tooth [that is, trespassing cattle]," *lo, the derivative of tooth is in the same classification as tooth [as we have already shown], and from the perspective of Rab, who has said,* "The crop-destroying beast is in fact the human being," *then what generative categories and what derivatives therefrom are to be identified with a human being! Should you allege that a human being when awake is the generative classification, and the human being when asleep is a derivative, have we not learned in the Mishnah:* **Man is perpetually an attested danger [M. B.Q. 2:6A]**— *whether awake or asleep!*
B. *So when R. Pappa made his statement, he must have referred to a human being's phlegm or snot.*
C. *Yeah, well, then, under what conditions? If the damage*

was done while in motion, it comes about through man's direct action, and if it does its damage after it comes to rest, then, whether from Rab's or Samuel's perspective, it falls into the classification of pit. And, it must follow, the offspring of the crop-destroying beast is in the same classification as the crop destroying beast, so when R. Pappa made his statement, he must have been talking about the derivatives of fire.

19. A. *So what are derivatives of fire? Shall we say that such would be a stone, knife, or luggage, that one left on one's roof and were blown off by an ordinary wind and caused damage? Then here too, under what conditions? If the damage was done while in motion, then they fall into the category of fire itself. For what characterizes fire is that it derives from an external force, is your property, and is yours to guard, and these too are to be described in the same way, since each derives from an external force, is your property, and is yours to guard. And, it must follow, the offspring of fire are in the same classification as fire, so when R. Pappa made his statement, he must have been talking about the derivatives of foot.*

20. A. *Foot? Surely you're joking! Have we not already established the fact that the derivative of foot is in the same classification as the generative classification of foot itself.*

B. *At issue is the payment of half damages done by pebbles kicked by an animal's foot, which we have learned by tradition.*

C. *And why is such damage classified as a derivative of foot?*

D. *So that compensation should be paid only from property of the highest class possessed by the defendant.*

E. *But did not Raba raised the question on this very matter? For Raba raised this question,* "Is the half-damage to be paid for damage caused by pebbles to be paid only from the body of the beast itself or from the beast property of the owner of the beast?"

F. *Well, that was a problem for Raba, but R. Pappa was quite positive about the matter.*

G. *Well, if it's a problem to Raba, then from his perspective, why would pebbles kicked by an animal's foot be classified as a derivative of foot?*

H. *So that the owner in such a case may be exempted from having to pay compensation where the damage was done in the* public domain [just as damage caused by the generative category, foot, is not to be compensated if it was done in the public domain].

I have now set forth twenty distinct, well-crafted statements, which we might call "paragraphs." Many of these paragraphs use available materials, ready-made writing, but always, and only, for the purpose that the framer of the composite has in mind, that is, to make the point he wishes to make. Not only so, but the sequence of statements is so orderly and inexorable that if we removed one item, we should destroy the coherence of all that follows. Moreover, if we were to place the paragraphs into an order other than the one before us, the writing would be simply incomprehensible. So any notion that the Bavli is disorderly or fails to follow a discernible program and plan in expounding the Mishnah and the Halakhah (usually the Mishnah's Halakhah) derives from an uncomprehending and superficial examination of this and that, not a close and thoughtful reading of the whole. To show graphically how well-organized and wholly rational is this sizable composite, let me reproduce the whole in outline form. The primary propositions are at the left hand margin. The secondary developments are indented, and the tertiary amplifications indented once again.

I. MISHNAH-TRACTATE BABA QAMMA 1:1
A. **THERE ARE FOUR GENERATIVE CLASSIFICATIONS OF CAUSES OF DAMAGES: (1) OX (EX. 21:35-36), (2) PIT (EX. 21:33);**

1. I:1: Since the framer of the passages makes reference to generative causes, it is to be inferred that there are derivative ones as well. Are the derivative causes equivalent in effect to the generative causes or are they not equivalent to them in effect? What's the difference between an act that falls into the generative category and one that falls into the derivative category?

2. I:2: While a generative cause of uncleanness imparts uncleanness to a human being and utensils, a

derivative source of uncleanness imparts uncleanness to food and drink but not to a human being or utensils.

3. I:3: What is the upshot of the distinction at hand? Said R. Pappa, "There are some derivatives that are equivalent in effect to the generative cause, and there are some that are not equivalent in effect to the generative cause."

B. THE SCRIPTURAL FOUNDATIONS FOR THE DEFINITION OF GENERATIVE CAUSES OF DAMAGE; THE SUBSETS OF THE CLASSIFICATIONS

1. I:4: Three of the four generative causes of damage are stated with respect to the ox: horn, tooth, and foot.

2. I:5: How on the basis of Scripture do we know the case of the horn?

3. I:6: What are the derivatives of the horn?

   a. I:7: Why, when the Scripture refers to injury to a human being, does it say, "If it will gore" (Ex. 21:28), while when Scripture refers to an ox's injuring an animal, it uses the language, "if it will butt" (Ex. 21:35)?

   b. I:8: Biting: does this not fall into the classification of a derivative of tooth?

   c. I:9: Falling, and kicking: do these not fall into the classification of derivatives of foot?

I. I:10: Now, then, as to those derivatives that are not equivalent to the generative causes from which the derivatives come, to which R. Pappa made reference, what might they be?

4. I:11: Where in Scripture is reference made to tooth and foot?

   a. I:12: Gloss of the foregoing.

   b. I:13: As above.

   c. I:14: Continuation: Then let the Scripture make reference to "And he shall send forth" (Ex. 22:4) and omit "And it shall consume," which would cover the classifications of both foot and tooth? It would cover foot in line with this verse: "That send forth the feet of the ox and the ass," and it would cover tooth, in line with this verse, "And the teeth of beasts will I send upon them" (Deut. 32:24).

5. I:15: What is the derivative of the generative

category of tooth?
    6.   I:16: What is the derivative of the generative category of foot?
    7.   I:17: What would be derivatives of the generative category of pit?
    8.   I:18: What can these derivatives of the crop-destroying beast be anyhow?
    9.   I:19: What are derivatives of fire?
        a.   I:20: Secondary development of foregoing.

The outline leaves little doubt about how the whole holds together. Let us now review what is before us.

We open with a sizable exercise in explaining the language of our Mishnah-paragraph, in line with the same usage in other Mishnah-paragraphs, **I.1-3**. No. 4 then turns to the amplification of the Mishnah's statement by appeal to other Tannaite materials; we start with a complement that locates in Scripture the generative categories that are before us. This complement forms an integral part in the exposition of No. 3, and the entire composite goes from No. 3 through No. 20. That the whole is a continuous, beautifully crafted composite, shaped into a single coherent and unfolding statement, is beyond all doubt. When, we examine a miscellany, we shall see why the miscellany appears to form an anomaly in a writing of such remarkable power and determination as the one we have just now sampled.

IV.   The Composition and the Composite

Even my initial sample has shown the simple fact that the Talmud of Babylonia is made up of large-scale composites of already-completed compositions. To begin with, the document draws upon the already-completed writing, the Mishnah, being organized to present the appearance of a commentary to that writing. Second, it cites passages of another already-completed piece of writing, the Tosefta.[5] Third, very commonly we are able to identify a single cogent statement, with its own beginning, middle, and end (represented in my outline by unit I/B). Furthermore we readily distinguish that statement from a larger framework in which, whole and complete, it is set to serve some larger purpose.

When, therefore, I say that the Bavli is made up of composites themselves comprised by purposeful compositions, I mean that for the most part, the framers of the whole have made use of (some) already completed pieces of writing. They moreover set them out in such a way as to serve a purpose not necessarily contemplated by the author(s) of the original compositions but rather a purpose clearly dictated by the analytical and propositional program of the framers of the Bavli itself. The distinction between composition and composite is so fundamental that, before proceeding, I had best give a simple example of what I mean. Only then will the issue of this monograph be set forth in an intelligible context of literary analysis.

Let me explain to begin with how the materials that follow are meant to clarify the point at hand: what is a composition and what is a composite? A composition is a fully-articulated, cogent statement, which contains everything we need to understand what the author of the writing wishes to say to us. A composite is a collection of such completed pieces of writing, worked out in such a way as to make the point that the framer of the composite, not the authors of the compositions that he uses, wishes to make. As I have explained in *The Rules of Composition of the Talmud of Babylonia. The Cogency of the Bavli's Composite*,[6] the author of a composition sets forth a

---

[5] I omit reference to the baraita-corpus, which presents its own problems. These are to be dealt with in an appropriate setting.

[6] Atlanta, 1991: Scholars Press for South Florida Studies in the History of Judaism.

proposition of his own, while the framer of a composite may make use of a variety of such compositions to make the quite different point that he has in mind. The one paints the fragment of a framed picture, the other arranges a collage of such pictures.

I have chosen a passage to which we shall return later on. It is part of the exposition of Mishnah-tractate Abodah Zarah 1:1 by Bavli Abodah Zarah. We may signal the building blocks of a composite by visual means, indentation for example. Now, with this simple distinction in mind, we have, also, carefully to distinguish between glosses, such as — in the example to follow — are found at 2.B, D-E, and free-standing compositions that are utilized for a purpose other than that for which, on the face of it, they were written. What illustrates the classification, "composition," in the sample at hand? The statement of Hisda, F, has been set down in its own terms. It is adduced to prove the point of E. So F is a composition, E-F a composite put together to clarify D, itself a gloss of C.

> **2.** A. R. Hanina bar Pappa, and some say, R. Simlai, gave the following exposition [of the verse, "They that fashion a graven image are all of them vanity, and their delectable things shall not profit, and their own witnesses see not nor know" (Is. 44:9)]: "In the age to come the Holy One, blessed be he, will bring a scroll of the Torah and hold it in his bosom and say, 'Let him who has kept himself busy with it come and take his reward.' Then all the gentiles will crowd together: 'All of the nations are gathered together' (Is. 43:9). The Holy One, blessed be he, will say to them, 'Do not crowd together before me in a mob. But let each nation enter together with **[2B]** its scribes, 'and let the peoples be gathered together' (Is. 43:9), and the word 'people' means 'kingdom:' 'and one kingdom shall be stronger than the other' (Gen. 25:23)."
>
> B. *But can there be a mob-scene before the Holy One, blessed be he? Rather, it is so that from their perspective they not*

form a mob, so that they will be able to hear what he says to them.

C. [Resuming the narrative of A:] "The kingdom of Rome comes in first."

D. *How come? Because they are the most important. How do we know on the basis of Scripture they are the most important? Because it is written,* "And he shall devour the whole earth and shall tread it down and break it into pieces" (Gen. 25:23), and said R. Yohanan, "This Rome is answerable, for its definition [of matters] has gone forth to the entire world [Mishcon: 'this refers to Rome, whose power is known to the whole world']."

E. *And how do we know that the one who is most important comes in first? It is in accord with that which R. Hisda said.*

F. For said R. Hisda, "When the king and the community [await judgment], the king enters in first for judgment: 'That he maintain the case of his servant [Solomon] and [then] the cause of his people Israel' (1 Kgs. 8:59)."...

We see therefore the traits of the composite over all. This brief snippet suffices to show the difference between compositions and composites.

Now, using the same materials, we turn to the massive miscellany, only a bit of which is given in the foregoing. Here we have one of the great composites of the Bavli. It is a fine example of the Bavli's purposive conglomeration and utilization of what appear to be autonomous compositions, lacking all indicative documentary traits in the context of the Bavli (or any other extant document).

V. The Rationality of a Major Massive Miscellany:
BAVLI ABODAH ZARAH CHAPTER ONE

Now we come to the heart of the matter, the documentary task undertaken by a miscellaneous composite set within the Bavli's primary construction, that made up of Mishnah-commentary and Halakhah-analysis and exposition. How, exactly, do the components of a massive miscellany cohere? What tasks are assigned to the Aggadic writing, whether narrative, sapiential, or exegetical of Scripture's own stories and prophecies? We come to the question, What validates my claim that the massive miscellany is purposive and coherent, carrying out a cogent program of exposition, in relationship with the work of Mishnah- and Halakhah-exegesis and amplification. I have chosen a single instance, which serves as a model for what is to be done.

In the context of this long and important chapter of Bavli Abodah Zarah, we have a variety of miscellanies. We shall address the chapter as a whole, first of all asking in context of the individual entries [1] how they hold together, and second, forming a theory, in the setting of the entire chapter, concerning [2] what place the miscellanies make for themselves in the context of the chapters in which they occur. I shall restrict my comments to the issue of how the miscellanies cohere, what principle has guided the compiler of discrete compositions in linking one with another, in the order before us and not in some other. A full exposition of the chapter as a whole is in my *The Talmud of Babylonia. An American Translation.* Atlanta, 1991: Scholars Press for Brown Judaic Studies. XXV.A. *Tractate Abodah Zarah. Chapters One and Two.* To highlight the composites that I regard as miscellanies, I indent those entirely at both margins, leaving at the normal margins both the Mishnah and the portion of the Talmud devoted to the exposition of the Mishnah and its principles. I further intent what I regard as footnotes or appendices to principal components of the Bavli's composite. This further clarifies the character of the document before us. As before, the Mishnah and the Tosefta are in bold face type, the voice of the Bavli in plain type when in Hebrew, in italics when in Aramaic.

BAVLI ABODAH ZARAH 1:1

A. [2A] Before the festivals of gentiles for three days it is forbidden to do business with them.

B. (1) to lend anything to them or to borrow anything from them.

C. (2) to lend money to them or to borrow money from them.

D. (3) to repay them or to be repaid by them.

E. R. Judah says, "They accept repayment from them, because it is distressing to him."

F. They said to him, "Even though it is distressing to him now, he will be happy about it later."

I.1 A. [2A] Rab and Samuel [in dealing with the reading of the key-word of the Mishnah, translated festival, the letters of which are 'aleph daled, rather than 'ayin daled, which means, calamity]:

B. *one repeated the formulation of the Mishnah as, "their festivals."*

C. *And the other repeated the formulation of the Mishnah as "their calamities."*

D. *The one who repeated the formulation of the Mishnah as "their festivals" made no mistake, and the one who repeated the formulation of the Mishnah as "their calamities" made no mistake.*

E. *For it is written,* "For the day of their calamity is at hand" (Dt. 32:15).

F. *The one who repeated the formulation of the Mishnah as "their festivals" made no mistake,, for it is written,* "Let them bring their testimonies that they may be justified" (Is. 43:9).

G. *And as to the position of him who repeats the formulation of the Mishnah as "their festivals," on what account does he not repeat the formulation of the Mishnah to yield, "their calamities"?*

H. *He will say to you, "'Calamity' is preferable [as the word choice when speaking of idolatry]."*

I. *And as to the position of whim who repeats the formulation of the Mishnah as "their calamities," on what account does* he not repeat the formulation of the Mishnah to yield "their festivals"?

J. He will say to you, 'What causes the calamity that befalls them if not their testimony, so testimony is preferable!"

K. *And as to the verse,* "Let them bring their testimonies that they may be justified" (Is. 43:9), *is this written with reference to gentiles? Lo, it is written in regard to Israel.*

L. For said R. Joshua b. Levi, "All of the religious duties that Israelites carry out in this world come and give testimony in their behalf in the world to come: 'Let them bring their witnesses that they may be justified' (Is. 43:9), that is, Israel; 'and let them hear and say, It is truth' (Is. 43:9) — this refers to gentiles."

M. Rather, said R. Huna b. R. Joshua, "He who formulates the Mishnah to refer to their calamities derives the reading from this verse: 'They that fashion a graven image are all of them vanity, and their delectable things shall not profit, and their own witnesses see not nor know' (Is. 44:9)."

The composite begins with a very long, but coherent exposition of a single theme, which is, God's judgment of the nations. No. 2 holds together rather well, once we realize that it is heavily footnoted. I further intend the footnoted materials of that glossed composition.

2. A. R. Hanina bar Pappa, and some say, R. Simlai, gave the following exposition [of the verse, "They that fashion a graven image are all of them vanity, and their delectable things shall not profit, and their own witnesses see not nor know" (Is. 44:9)]: "In the age to come the Holy One, blessed be he, will bring a scroll of the Torah and hold it in his bosom and say, 'Let him who has kept himself busy with it come and take his reward.' Then all the gentiles will crowd together: 'All of the nations are gathered together' (Is. 43:9). The Holy One, blessed be he, will say to them, 'Do not crowd together before me in a mob. But let each nation enter together with **[2B]** its scribes, 'and let the peoples be gathered together' (Is. 43:9), and the word 'people' means 'kingdom:' 'and one kingdom shall be stronger than the other' (Gen. 25:23)."

B. *But can there be a mob-scene before the Holy One, blessed be he? Rather, it is so that from their perspective they not form a mob, so that they will be able to hear what he says to them.*

C. [Resuming the narrative of A:] "The kingdom of Rome comes in first."

D. *How come? Because they are the most important. How do we know on the basis of Scripture they are the most important? Because it is written,* "And he shall devour the whole earth and shall tread it down and break it into pieces" (Gen. 25:23), and said R. Yohanan, "This Rome is answerable, for its definition [of matters] has gone forth to the entire world [Mishcon: 'this refers to Rome, whose power is known to the whole world']."

E. *And how do we know that the one who is most important comes in first? It is in accord with that which R. Hisda said.*

F. For said R. Hisda, "When the king and the community [await judgment], the king enters in first for judgment: 'That he maintain the case of his servant [Solomon] and [then] the cause of his people Israel' (1 Kgs. 8:59)."

G. *And how come? If you wish, I shall say it is not appropriate to keep the king sitting outside. And if you wish, I shall say that [the king is allowed to plea his case] before the anger of the Holy One is aroused.*

H. [Resuming the narrative of C:] "The Holy One, blessed be he, will say to them, 'How have defined your chief occupation?'

I. "They will say before him, 'Lord of the world, a vast number of marketplaces have we set up, a vast number of bath houses we have made, a vast amount of silver and gold have we accumulated. And all of these things we have done only in behalf of Israel, so that they may define as their chief occupation the study of the Torah.'

J. "The Holy One, blessed be he, will say to them, 'You complete idiots! Whatever you have done has been for your own convenience. You have set up a vast number of marketplaces to be sure, but that was so as to set up whore-houses in them. The bath-houses were for your own pleasure. Silver and gold belong to me anyhow: "Mine is the silver and mine is the gold, says the Lord of hosts" (Hag. 2:8). Are there any among you who have been telling of "this," and "this" is only the Torah: "And this is the Torah that Moses set before the children of Israel' (Dt. 4:44)." So they will make their exit, humiliated.

K. "When the kingdom of Rome has made its exit, the kingdom of Persia enters afterward."

L. *How come? Because they are second in importance. And how do we know it on the basis of Scripture? Because it is written,* "And behold, another beast, a second, like a bear" (Dan. 7:5), *and in this connection R. Joseph repeated as a Tannaite formulation,* "This refers to the Persians, who eat and drink like a bear, are obese like a bear, are shaggy like a bear, and are restless like a bear."

M. "The Holy One, blessed be he, will say to them, 'How have defined your chief occupation?'

N. "They will say before him, 'Lord of the world, We have thrown up a vast number of bridges, we have conquered a vast number of towns, we have made a vast number of wars, and all of them we did only for Israel, so that they may define as their chief occupation the study of the Torah.'

O. "The Holy One, blessed be he, will say to them, 'Whatever you have done has been for your own convenience. You have thrown up a vast number of bridges, to collect tolls, you have conquered a vast number of towns, to collect the corvée, and, as to making a vast number of wars, I am the one who makes wars: "The Lord is a man of war" (Ex. 19:17). Are there any among you who have been telling of "this," and "this" is only the Torah: "And this is the Torah that Moses set before the children of Israel" (Dt. 4:44).' So they will make their exit, humiliated.

P. *But if the kingdom of Persia has seen that such a claim issued by the kingdom of Rome did no good whatsoever, how come they go in at all?*

Q. *They will say to themselves,* 'These are the ones who destroyed the house of the sanctuary, but we are the ones who built it."

R. "And so it will go with each and every nation."

S. But if each one of them has seen that such a claim issued by the others did no good whatsoever, how come they go in at all?

T. They will say to themselves, "Those two subjugated Israel, but we never subjugated Israel."

U. And how come the two conquering nations are singled out as important and the others are not?

V. It is because the rule of these will continue until the Messiah comes.

W. "They will say to him, 'Lord of the world, in point of fact, did you actually give it to us and we did not accept it?'"

X. But how can they present such an argument, since it is written, "The Lord came from Sinai and rose from Seir to them, he shined forth from Mount Paran" (Dt. 33:2), and further, "God comes from Teman" (Hab. 3:3). *Now what in the world did he want in Seir, and what was he looking for in Paran?* Said R. Yohanan, "This teaches that the Holy One, blessed be he, made the rounds of each and every nation and language and none accepted it, until he came to Israel, and they accepted it."

Y. *Rather, this is what they say,* "Did we accept it but then not carry it out?"

Z. *But to this the rejoinder must be,* "Why did you not accept it anyhow!"

AA. Rather, "this is what they say before him, 'Lord of the world, Did you hold a mountain over us like a cask and then we refused to accept it as you did to Israel, as it is written, "And they stood beneath the mountain" (Ex. 19:17).'"

BB. And [in connection with the verse, "And they stood beneath the mountain" (Ex. 19:17),] said R. Dimi bar Hama, "This teaches that the Holy One, blessed be he, held the mountain over Israel like a cask and said to them, 'If you accept the Torah, well and good, and if not, then there is where your grave will be.'"

CC. "Then the Holy One, blessed be he, will say to them, 'Let us make known what happened first: "Let them announce to us former things" (Is. 43:9). As to the seven religious duties that you did accept, where have you actually carried them out?'"

DD. *And how do we know on the basis of Scripture that they did not carry them out?* R. Joseph formulated as a Tannaite statement, "'He stands and shakes the earth, he sees and makes the nations tremble' (Hab. 3:6): what did he see? He saw the seven religious duties that the children of Noah accepted upon themselves as obligations but never actually carried them out. Since they did not carry out those obligations, he went and remitted their obligation."

EE. *But then they benefited — so it pays to sin!*

FF. Said Mar b. Rabina, **[3A]** "What this really proves is that even they carry out those religious duties, they get no reward on that account."

GG. *And they don't, don't they? But has it not been taught on Tannaite authority:* R. Meir would say, "How on the basis of Scripture do we know that, even if it is a gentile, if he goes and takes up the study of the Torah as his occupation, he is equivalent to the high priest? Scripture states, 'You shall therefore keep my statues and my ordinances, which, if a human being does them, one shall gain life through them' (Lev. 18:5). What is written is not 'priests' or 'Levites' or 'Israelites,' but rather, 'a human being.' So you have learned the fact that, even if it is a gentile, if he goes and takes up the study of the Torah as his occupation, he is equivalent to the high priest."

HH. Rather, what you learn from this [DD] is that they will not receive that reward that is coming to those who are commanded to do them and who carry them out, but rather, the reward that they receive will be like that coming to the one who is not commanded to do them and who carries them out anyhow.

II. For said R. Hanina, "Greater is the one who is commanded and who carries out the religious obligations than the one who is not commanded but nonetheless carries out religious obligations."

JJ. [Reverting to AA:] "this is what the gentiles say before him, 'Lord of the world, Israel, who accepted it — where in the world have they actually carried it out?'

KK. "The Holy One, blessed be he, will say to

them, 'I shall bear witness concerning them, that they have carried out the whole of the Torah!'

LL. "They will say before him, 'Lord of the world, is there a father who is permitted to give testimony concerning his son? For it is written, "Israel is my son, my firstborn" (Ex. 4:22).'

MM. "The Holy One, blessed be he, will say to them, 'The heaven and the earth will give testimony in their behalf that they have carried out the entirety of the Torah.'

NN. "They will say before him, 'Lord of the world, The heaven and earth have a selfish interest in the testimony that they give: 'If not for my covenant with day and with night, I should not have appointed the ordinances of heaven and earth' (Jer. 33:25).'"

OO. *For said R. Simeon b. Laqish, "What is the meaning of the verse of Scripture,* 'And there was evening, and there was morning, the sixth day' (Gen. 1:31)? This teaches that the Holy One, blessed be he, made a stipulation with all of the works of creation, saying to them, 'If Israel accepts my Torah, well and good, but if not, I shall return you to chaos and void.' *That is in line with what is written:* 'You did cause sentence to be heard from heaven, the earth trembled and was still' (Ps. 76:9). If 'trembling' then where is the stillness, and if stillness, then where is the trembling? Rather, to begin with, trembling, but at the end, stillness."

PP. [Reverting to MM-NN:] "The Holy One, blessed be he, will say to them, 'Some of them may well come and give testimony concerning Israel that they have observed the entirety of the Torah. Let Nimrod come and give testimony in behalf of Abraham that he never worshipped idols. Let Laban come and give testimony in behalf of Jacob, that he never was suspect of thievery. Let the wife of Potiphar come and give testimony in behalf of Joseph, that he was never suspect of 'sin.' Let Nebuchadnessar come and give testimony in behalf of Hananiah, Mishael, and Azariah, that they never bowed down to the idol. Let Darius come and give testimony in behalf of Daniel, that he did not neglect even the optional prayers. Let Bildad the Shuhite and Zophar the Naamatite and Eliphaz the Temanite and Elihu son of Barachel the Buzite come and testify in behalf of Israel that they have observed the entirety of the Torah: "Let the nations bring their own witnesses, that they may be justified" (Is. 43:9).'

QQ. "They will say before him, 'Lord of the world, Give it to us to begin with, and let us carry it out.'

RR. "The Holy One, blessed be he, will say to them, 'World-class idiots! He who took the trouble to prepare on the eve of the Sabbath [Friday] will eat on the Sabbath, but he who took no trouble on the even of the Sabbath — what in the world is he going to eat on the Sabbath! Still, [I'll give you another chance.] I have a rather simple religious duty, which is called "the tabernacle." Go and do that one.'"

SS. *But can you say any such thing? Lo, R. Joshua b. Levi has said, 'What is the meaning of the verse of Scripture, 'The ordinances that I command you this day to do them' (Dt. 7:11)? Today is the day to do them, but not tomorrow; they are not to be done tomorrow; today is the day to do them, but not the day on which to receive a reward for doing them."*

TT. Rather, it is that the Holy One, blessed be he, does not exercise tyranny over his creatures.

UU. *And why does he refer to it as a simple religious duty? Because it does not involve enormous expense [to carry out that religious duty].*

VV. "Forthwith every one of them will take up the task and go and make a tabernacle on his roof. But then the Holy, One, blessed be he, will come and make the sun blaze over them as at the summer solstice, and every one of them will knock down his tabernacle and go his way: 'Let us break their bands asunder and cast away their cords from us' (Ps. 23:3)."

WW. But lo, you have just said, "it is that the Holy One, blessed be he, does not exercise tyranny over his creatures"!

XX. *It is because the Israelites too — sometimes* **[3B]** *the summer solstice goes on to the Festival of Tabernacles, and therefore they are bothered by the heat!*

YY. But has not Raba stated, "One who is bothered

[by the heat] is exempt from the obligation of dwelling in the tabernacle"?

ZZ. *Granting that one may be exempt from the duty, is he going to go and tear the thing down?*

AAA. [Continuing from UU:] "Then the Holy One, blessed be he, goes into session and laughs at them: 'He who sits in heaven laughs' (Ps. 2:4)."

BBB. Said R. Isaac, "Laughter before the Holy One, blessed be he, takes place only on that day alone."

CCC. *There are those who repeat as a Tannaite version this statement of R. Isaac in respect to that which has been taught on Tannaite authority:*

DDD. R. Yosé says, "In the coming age gentiles will come and convert."

EEE. *But will they be accepted? Has it not been taught on Tannaite authority:* Converts will not be accepted in the days of the Messiah, just as they did not accept proselytes either in the time of David or in the time of Solomon?

FFF. Rather, "they will make themselves converts, and they will put on phylacteries on their heads and arms and fringes on their garments and a mezuzah on their doors. But when they witness the war of Gog and Magog, he will say to them, 'How come you have come?' They will say, '"Against the Lord and against his Messiah."' For so it is said, 'Why are the nations in an uproar and why do the peoples mutter in vain' (Ps. 2:1). Then each one of them will rid himself of his religious duty and go his way: 'Let us break their bands asunder' (Ps. 2:3). Then the Holy One, blessed be he, goes into session and laughs at them: 'He who sits in heaven laughs' (Ps. 2:4)."

GGG. Said R. Isaac, "Laughter before the Holy One, blessed be he, takes place only on that day alone."

HHH. But is this really so? And has not R. Judah said Rab said, "The day is made up of twelve hours. In the first three the Holy One, blessed be he, goes into session and engages in study of the Torah; in the second he goes into session and judges the entire world. When he realizes that the world is liable to annihilation, he arises from the throne of justice and takes up a seat on the throne of mercy. In the third period he goes into session and nourishes the whole world from the horned buffalo to the brood of vermin. During the fourth quarter he laughs [and plays] with leviathan: 'There is leviathan, whom you have formed to play with' (Ps. 104:26)." [This proves that God does laugh more than on that one day alone.]

III. Said R. Nahman bar Isaac, "With his creatures he laughs [everyday], but at his creatures he laughs only on that day alone."

3. A. Said R. Aha to R. Nahman bar Isaac, "From the day on which the house of the sanctuary, the Holy One blessed be he has had no laughter.

B. *"And how on the basis of Scripture do we know that he has had none? If we say that it is because it is written,* 'And on that day did the Lord, the god of hosts, call to weeping and lamentation' (Is. 22:12), *that verse refers to that day in particular. Shall we then say that that fact derives from the verse,* 'If I forget you, Jerusalem, let my right hand forget her cunning, let my tongue cleave to the roof of my mouth if I do not remember you' (Ps. 137:5-6)? *That refers to forgetfulness, not laughter. Rather, the fact derives from this verse:* 'I have long held my peace, I have been still, I have kept in, now I will cry' (Is. 42:14)."

4. A. [Referring to the statement that during the fourth quarter he laughs [and plays] with leviathan,] *[nowadays] what does he do in the fourth quarter of the day?*

B. He sits and teaches Torah to kindergarten students: "Whom shall one teach knowledge, and whom shall one make understand the message? Those who are weaned from the milk? (Is. 28:19).

C. *And to begin with [prior to the destruction of the Temple, which ended his spending his time playing with leviathan], who taught them?*

D. *If you wish, I shall say it was Metatron, and if you wish, I shall say that he did both [but now does only one].*

E. And at night what does he do?

F. *If you wish, I shall say that it is the sort of thing he does by day;*

G. *and if you wish, I shall say,* he rides his light cherub and floats through eighteen thousand worlds:

"The chariots of God are myriads, even thousands and thousands [shinan] (Ps. 868:48). Read the letters translated as thousands, shinan, as though they were written, she-enan, meaning, that are not [thus: "the chariots are twice ten thousand less two thousand, eighteen thousand (Mishcon)].

H. *And if you wish, I shall say,* he sits and listens to the song of the Living Creatures [hayyot]: "By the day the Lord will command his loving kindness and in the night his song shall be with me" (Ps. 42:9).

Here is a fine case of my thesis that massive miscellanies undertake the tasks we assign in contemporary writing to footnotes or appendices: to bear the burden of information that is necessary to a proposition but tangential in the strategy of exposition of said proposition. If we regard the deeply indented materials as footnotes and appendices, attached for thematic reasons, then we can see Nos. 1-4 as an entirely coherent statement, a composite to be sure, but in no way a miscellany. Having examined that set and seen the clear connections between one composition and the next, on the one side, and the coherent character of the whole (with its footnotes and appendix), on the other, we are now ready to look at the miscellany that follows and to ask ourselves how each entry is linked to what is juxtaposed to it, fore and aft. If I had to find a rational explanation for putting No. 5 in at all, it is because it addresses the theme of study of Torah, to which No. 4 has made reference.

5. A. Said R. Levi, "To whoever stops studying the words of the Torah and instead takes up words of mere chatter they feed glowing coals of juniper: 'They pluck salt-wort with wormwood and the roots of juniper are their food' (Job 30:4)."

B. Said R. Simeon b. Laqish, "For whoever engages in study of the Torah by night — the Holy One, blessed be he, draws out the thread of grace by day: 'By day the Lord will command his loving kindness, and in the night his song shall be with me' (Ps. 42:9). Why is it that 'By day the Lord will command his loving kindness'? Because 'in the night his song shall be with me.'"

C. *Some say,* said R. Simeon b. Laqish, "For whoever engages in study of the Torah in this world, which is like the night, — the Holy One, blessed be he, draws out the thread of grace in the world to come, which is like the day: 'By day the Lord will command his loving kindness, and in the night his song shall be with me' (Ps. 42:9). [Supply: Why is it that 'By day the Lord will command his loving kindness'? Because 'in the night his song shall be with me.']"

The sustaining character of study of the Torah, No. 5, explains the relevance of the composition of No. 6.

6. A. Said R. Judah said Samuel, *"What is the meaning of the verse of Scripture,* 'And you make man as the fish of the sea and as the creeping things, that have no ruler over them' (Hab. 1:14)? Why are human beings compared to fish of the sea? To tell you, just as fish in the sea, when they come up on dry land, forthwith begin to die, so with human beings, when they take their leave of teachings of the Torah and religious deeds, forthwith they begin to die.

B. "Another matter: just as the fish of the sea, as soon as dried by the sun, die, so human beings, when struck by the sun, die."

C. *If you want, this refers to this world, and if you want, this refers to the world to come.*

D. *If you want, this refers to this world,, in line with that which R. Hanina [said],* for said R. Hanina, "Everything is in the hands of Heaven except cold and heat: 'colds and heat boils are in the way of the froward, he who keeps his soul holds himself far from them' (Prov. 22:5)."

E. *and if you want, this refers to the world to come, in accord with that which was stated by R. Simeon b. Laqish.* For said R. Simeon b. Laqish, "In the world to come, there is no Gehenna, but rather, the Holy One, blessed be he, brings the sun out of its sheathe and he heats the wicked but heals the righteous through it. The wicked are brought to judgment by **[4A]** it: 'For behold, the days comes, it burns as a furnace, and all the proud and all who do wicked things shall be stubble, and the day that comes shall set them ablaze, says the Lord of hosts, that it shall leave them neither root nor branch' (Mal. 3:19).

F. "'it shall leave them neither root' — in this world; 'nor branch' — in the world to come."

G. "'but heals the righteous through it:' 'But to you that fear my name shall the sun of righteousness arise with healing in its wings' (Mal. 3:19). They will revel in it: 'And you shall go forth and gambol as calves of the stall' (Mal. 3:20)."

H. [Continuing C, above:] "Another matter: just with as the fish of the sea, whoever is bigger than his fellow swallows his fellow, so in the case of human beings, were it not for fear of the government, whoever is bigger than his fellow would swallow his fellow."

I. *That is in line with what we have learned in the Mishnah:* **R. Hananiah, Prefect of the Priests, says, "Pray for the welfare of the government. For if it were not for fear of it, one man would swallow his fellow alive" [M. Abot 3:2A-B].**

The foregoing has mentioned the theme of Gehenna and the world to come, and we shall now pursue that theme, now the contrast between Gehenna and the world to come, the gentiles and Israel, God's anger and God's grace. No. 7 contrasts the time of judgment and the time of God's war against his enemies; No. 8 then deals with the anger of God with the gentiles; Nos. 9, 10 with God's destruction.

7. A. *R. Hinena bar Pappa contrasted verses of Scripture:* "It is written, 'As to the Almighty, we do not find him exercising plenteous power' (Job 37:23), but by contrast, 'Great is our Lord and of abundant power' (Ps. 147:5), and further, 'Your right hand, Lord, is glorious in power' (Ex. 15:6).

B. "But there is no contradiction between the first and second and third statements, for the former speaks of the time of judgment [when justice is tempered with mercy, so God does not do what he could] and the latter two statements refer to a time of war [of God against his enemies]."

8. A. *R. Hama bar Hanina contrasted verses of Scripture: "it is written,* 'Fury is not in me' (Is. 27:4) but also 'The Lord revenges and is furious' (Nah. 1:2).

B. *"But there is no contradiction between the first and second statements,* for the former speaks of Israel, the latter of the gentiles."

C. R. Hinena bar Pappa said, "'Fury is not in me' (Is. 54:9), for I have already taken an oath: 'would that I had not so vowed, then as the briars and thorns in flame would I with one step burn it altogether' (Is. 54:9)."

9. A. *That is in line with what R. Alexandri said, "What is the meaning of the verse,* 'And it shall come to pass on that day that I will seek to destroy all the nations' (Zech. 12:9) —

B. "'seek' — seek permission from whom?

C. "Said the Holy One, blessed be he, 'I shall seek in the records that deal with them, to see whether there is a cause of merit, on account of which I shall redeem them, but if not, I shall destroy them.'"

10. A. *That is in line with what Raba said, "What is the meaning of the verse,* 'Howbeit he will not stretch out a hand for a ruinous neap though they cry in his destruction' (Job 30:24)?

B. "Said the Holy One, blessed be he, to Israel, 'When I judge Israel, I shall not judge them as I do the gentiles, for it is written, "I will overturn, overturn, overturn it" (Ez. 21:32), rather, I shall exact punishment from them as a hen pecks.'

C. "Another matter: 'Even if the Israelites do not carry out a religious duty before me more than a hen pecking at a rubbish heap, I shall join together [all the little pecks] into a great sum: "although they pick little they are saved" (Job 30:24) [following Mishcon's rendering].'

D. "Another matter: 'As a reward for their crying

out to me, I shall help them' (Job 30:24) [following Mishcon's rendering]."

The sequence of compositions on the same theme, God' judgment, this world and the world to come, suffering in this world so as to enjoy the world to come, Israel's suffering in this world and its enjoyment of the world to come, goes on through Nos. 11, 12, 13, 14. Then we shall have a set on God's anger. The movement is imperceptible, since No. 15 simply refers to God's anger in the context of judgment. But forthwith, at No. 16, we move into the theme of divine anger, and that sets us off in a slightly different direction from the one that we have followed up to now.

11. A. *That is in line with what R. Abba said, "What is the meaning of the verse,* 'Though I would redeem them, yet they have spoken lies against me' (Hos. 7:23)? 'I said that I would redeem them through [inflicting a penalty] on their property in this world, so that they might have the merit of enjoying the world to come, "yet they have spoken lies against me" (Hos. 7:23).'"

12. A. *That is in line with what R. Pappi in the name of Raba said, "What is the meaning of the verse,* 'Though I have trained [and] strengthened their arms, yet they imagine mischief against me' (Hos. 7:15)?

B. Said the Holy One, blessed be he, I thought that I would punish them with suffering in this world, so that their arm might be strengthened in the world to come, "yet they have spoken lies against me" (Hos. 7:23).'"

13. A. R. *Abbahu praised R. Safra to the* minim [in context: Christian authorities of Caesarea], *saying that he was* a highly accomplished authority. *They therefore remitted his taxes for thirteen years.*

B. *One day they came upon him and said to him, "It is written,* 'You only have I known among all the families of the earth; therefore I will visit upon you all your iniquities' (Amos 3:2). *If one is angry, does he vent it on someone he loves?"*

C. *He fell silent and said nothing at all. They wrapped a scarf around his neck and tortured him. R. Abbahu came along and found them. He said to them, "Why are you torturing him?":*

D. *They said to him, "Didn't you tell us that he is* a highly accomplished authority, *but he does not know how to explain this verse!"*

E. *He said to them, "True enough, I told you that he was a master of Tannaite statements, but did I say anything at all to you about his knowledge of Scripture?"*

F. *They said to him, "So how come you know?"*

G. *He said to them, "Since we, for our part, spend a lot of time with you, we have taken the task of studying it thoroughly, while others [in Babylonia, Safra's place of origin] do not study [Scripture] that carefully."*

H. *They said to him, "So tell us."*

I. He said to them, "I shall tell you a parable. To what is the matter comparable? To the case of a man who lent money to two people, one a friend, the other an enemy. From the friend he collects the money little by little, from the enemy he collects all at once."

14. A. *Said R. Abba bar Kahana, "What is the meaning of the following verse of Scripture:* 'Far be it from you to do after this manner, to slay the righteous with the wicked' (Gen. 18:25).

B. "Said Abraham before the Holy One, blessed be he, 'Lord of the world! It is a profanation to act in such a way [a play on the Hebrew letters, shared by the words 'far be it' and 'profanation'], 'to slay the righteous with the wicked' (Gen. 18:25)."

C. But is it not [so that God might do just that]? And is it not written, "And I will cut off from you the righteous and the wicked" (Ez. 21:8)?

D. That speaks of one who is not completely righteous, but not of one who is completely righteous.

E. And will he not do so to one who is completely righteous? And is it not written, "And begin the slaughter with my sanctuary" (Ez. 9:6), in which connection R. Joseph repeated as a Tannaite version, "Read not 'with my sanctuary' but rather, 'with those who are holy to me,' namely, the ones who carried out the Torah beginning to end."

F. *There too,* since they had the power to protest against the wickedness of the others and did not do so, they were not regarded as completely righteous at all.

15. A. *R. Pappa contrasted verses of Scripture:* "It is written, 'God is angry every day' (Ps. 7:12) but also 'who could stand before his anger' (Nah. 1:6).

B. *"But there is no contradiction between the first and second statements,* for the former speaks of the individual, the latter of the community."

The reference to God's anger, No. 16, marks an imperceptible movement to a new theme, namely Balaam, the prophet of the gentiles. Balaam then forms the unifying theme for Nos. 17-19. Because I regard these as footnote-entries, I indent them.

16. A. *Our rabbis have taught on Tannaite authority:*

B. "God is angry every day" (Ps. 7:12), and how long is his anger? It is for a moment. And how long is a moment? The portion 1/53,848th of an hour is a moment.

C. And no creature can determine that moment, except for Balaam that wicked man, of whom it is written, **[5A]** "who knew the knowledge of the Most High" (Num. 24:16).

D. How can it be that a man who did not know the mind of his animal could have known the mind of the Most High?

17. A. *And what is the meaning of the statement that* he did not know the mind of his animal?

B. *When they saw him riding on his ass, they said to him, "How come you're not riding on a horse?"*

C. *He said to them, "I sent it to the meadow."*

D. Forthwith: "The ass said, Am I not your ass" (Num. 22:30).

E. *He said to it, "Just as a beast of burden in general."*

F. *She said to him,* "Upon whom you have ridden" (Num. 22:30).

G. *He said to it, "Only from time to time."*

H. *She said to him,* "ever since I was yours {Num. 22:30). And not only so, but I serve you for riding by day and fucking by night."

    I. For here the word "I was wont" is used, and the same letters bear the meaning of bed mate: "...and she served him as a bed-mate" (1 Kings 1:2).

18. A. *And what is the meaning of the statement that* he could have known the mind of the Most High?

    B. For he knew precisely that moment at which the Holy One, blessed be he, was angry.

    C. *That is in line with what the prophet had said to them,* "O my people, remember now what Balak king of Moab consulted and what Balaam son of Beor answered him from Shittim to Gilgal, that you may know the righteousness of the Lord" (Mic. 6:5).

19. A. ["O my people, remember now what Balak king of Moab consulted and what Balaam son of Beor answered him from Shittim to Gilgal, that you may know the righteousness of the Lord" (Mic 6:5)]:

    B. Said R. Eleazar, "Said R. Eleazar, "Said the Holy one blessed be he to Israel, 'My people, see how many acts of righteousness I carried out with you, for I did not grow angry with you during all those [perilous] days, for if I had grown angry with you, there would not have remained from Israel a remnant or a survivor.'

    C. "And that is in line with what Balaam says: 'How can I curse seeing that God does not curse, and how can I be wrathful, seeing that the Lord has not been wrathful' (Num. 23:8)."

We now realize that Nos. 17-19 form a protracted footnote to No.16, for No. 20 will return us to the theme broken off at No. 16, namely, God's anger. The composite that follows, No. 20- 23, is held together by that theme.

20. A. And how long is his wrath? It is for a moment. And how long is a moment? The portion 1/53,848th of an hour is a moment.

    B. And how long is a moment?

    C. Said Amemar — others say, Rabina — "So long as it takes to say the word 'moment.'"

    D. *And how on the basis of Scripture do we know that his*

wrath lasts for only a moment?

E. *As it is written,* "For his anger is for a moment, his favor is for a lifetime" (Ps. 30:6).

F. *If you prefer:* "Hide yourself for a brief moment, until the wrath be past" (Is. 26:20).

21. A. *When is he angry?*

B. *Said Abbayye, "In the first three hours of the day, when the comb of the cock is white."*

C. *Isn't it white all the rest of the day?*

D. *At other times it has red streaks, but then it has none.*

22. A. *R. Joshua b. Levi — a certain* min *would bother him about verses of Scripture. Once he took a chicken and put it between the legs of the bed and watched it. He reasoned, "When that hour comes, I shall curse him."*

B. *But when that hour came, he was dozing. He said, "What you learn from this experience is that it is not correct to act in such a way:* 'His tender mercies are over all his works' (Ps. 145:9), *'Neither is it good for the righteous to inflict punishment' (Prov. 17:26)."*

23. A. *It was taught as a Tannaite version in the name of R. Meir,* "[That time at which God gets angry comes] when the kings put on their crowns on their heads and prostrate themselves to the sun. Forthwith the Holy One, blessed be he, grows angry."

Once again we are at a border-line between one set and another, and once more, the movement is subtle. We have just now referred to times at which God is angry, and times at which he is merciful. God is particularly angry, No. 23, when the king's put their crowns on their heads and worship the sun; No. 24 completes this composite, a different but related distinction between the time to pray and the time not to pray.

24. A. *Said R. Joseph, "A person should not recite the Prayer of the Additional Service for the first day of the New Year [the Day of Judgment] during the first three hours of the day or in private, lest, since that is the time of judgment, his deeds may be examined, and his prayer rejected."*

B. *If so, then the prayer of the community also should not* be recited at that time?

C. The merit [accruing to the community as a whole] is greater.

D. If so, then that of the Morning Service also should not be recited in private?

E. Since at that time the community also will be engaged in reciting the Morning Prayer, the individual's recitation of the Prayer will not be rejected.

F. But have you not said, "In the first three the Holy One, blessed be he, goes into session and engages in study of the Torah; in the second he goes into session and judges the entire world"?

G. Reverse the order.

H. Or, if you prefer, actually do not reverse the order. For when God is occupied with study of the Torah, called by Scripture "truth" as in "buy the truth and do not sell it" (Prov. 23:23), the Holy One, blessed be he, in any event will not violate the strict rule of justice. But when engaged in judgment, which is not called "truth" by Scripture, the Holy One, blessed be he, may step across the line of strict justice [towards mercy].

No. 25 is going to direct our attention way back to 2.RR. What we have, then, is a massive appendix to that reference, once that was formed in its own terms and is coherent around its own theme. That theme is the religious deeds and duties carried out by Israel, and how these will be rewarded not now but in the world to come. No. 26 introduces David's sin in the context of this discussion, explicitly referring back to No. 25. Then, Nos. 26-27, we pursue a composite devoted to David.

25. A. Reverting to the body of the prior text:

B. R. Joshua b. Levi has said, "What is the meaning of the verse of Scripture, 'The ordinances that I command you this day to do them' (Dt. 7:11)? Today is the day to do them, but not tomorrow; they are not to be done tomorrow; today is the day to do them, but today is not the day on which to receive a reward for doing them:"

C. Said R. Joshua b. Levi, "All the religious duties

that Israelites do in this world come and give evidence in their behalf in the world to come: 'Let them bring their witnesses that they may be justified, let them hear and say it is truth."

D. "Let them bring their witnesses that they may be justified:" this is Israel.

E. "let them hear and say it is truth:" this refers to the gentiles.

F. And said R. Joshua b. Levi, "All the religious duties that Israelites do in this world come and flap about the faces of gentiles in the world to come: 'Keep therefore and do them, for this, your wisdom and understanding, will be in the eyes of the peoples' (Dt. 4:6).

G. "What is stated here is not 'in the presence of the peoples' but 'in the eyes of the peoples,' which teaches you that they will come and flap about the faces of gentiles in the world to come."

H. And said R. Joshua b. Levi, "The Israelites made the golden calf only to give an opening to penitents: 'O that they had such a heart as this always, to fear me and keep my commandments' (Dt. 5:26)."

26. A. That is in line with what R. Yohanan said in the name of R. Simeon b. Yohai: "David was really not so unfit as to do such a deed [as he did with Bath Sheva]: 'My heart is slain within me' (Ps. 109:22) [Mishcon: David's inclinations had been completely conquered by himself]. And the Israelites were hardly the kind of people to commit such an act: "O that they had such a heart as this always, to fear me and keep my commandments' (Dt. 5:26). So why did they do it?

B. "**[5A]** It was to show you that if an individual has sinned, they say to him, 'Go to the individual [such as David, and follow his example], and if the community as a whole has sinned, they say to them, 'Go to the community [such as Israel].'

C. *And it was necessary to give both examples. For had we been given the rule governing the individual, that might have been supposed to be because his personal sins were not broadly known, but in the case of the community, the sins of which will be broadly known, I might have said that that is not the case.*

D. *And if we had been given the rule governing the com-*

munity, that might have been supposed to be the case because they enjoy greater mercy, but an individual, who has not got such powerful *zekhut*, might have been thought not subject to the rule.

    E.   So both cases had to be made explicit.

27. A. That is in line with what R. Samuel bar. Nahmani said R. Jonathan said, "What is the meaning of the verse of Scripture, 'The saying of David, son of Jesse, and the saying of the man raised on high' (2 Sam. 23:1)?

    B.   "It means, 'The saying of David, son of Jesse, the man who raised up the yoke of repentance.'"

No. 28 brings us back to the general theme of doing a good deed in this world and enjoying the result in the world to come. That theme spills over into No. 29.

28. A. Said R. Samuel bar Nahmani said R. Jonathan, "Whoever does a religious duty in this world -- that deed goes before him to the world to come, as it is said, 'And your righteousness shall go before you' (Is. 58:8).

    B.   "And whoever commits a transgression in this world -- that act turns aside from him and goes before him on the Day of Judgment, as it is said, 'The paths of their way are turned aside, they go up into the waste and perish' (Job 6:18)."

    C.   R. Eliezer says, "It attaches to him like a dog, as it is said, 'He did not listen to her to lie by her or to be with her' (Gen. 39:10).

    D.   "'To lie by her' in this world

    E.   "'Or to be with her' in the world to come."

29. A. Said R. Simeon b. Laqish, "Come and let us express our gratitude to our ancestors, for if it were not for their having sinned, we for our part should never have been able to come into the world: 'I said you are gods and all of you sons of the Most High' (Ps. 82:6). Now that you have ruined things by what you have done: 'you shall indeed die like mortals' (Ps. 82:6)."

    B.   *Does that statement then bear the implication, therefore, that if they had not sinned, they would not have propagated? But has it not been written,* "And you, be fruitful and multiply" (Gen. 9:7)?

C. *That applies up to Sinai.*

D. *But in connection with Sinai it also is written,* "Go say to them, Go back to your tents" (Ex. 19:15), meaning, to marital relationships. *And is it not also written,* "that it might be well with them and with their children" (Dt. 5:26)?

E. That speaks only to those who were actually present at Mount Sinai.

F. *But has not R. Simeon b. Laqish stated, "What is the meaning of that which is written:* 'This is the book of the generations of Adam' (Gen. 5:1)? Now did the first Adam have a book? The statement, rather, teaches that the Holy One, blessed be he, showed to the first Adam each generation and its authoritative expositors, each generations and its sages, each generation and those that administered its affairs. When he came to the generation of R. Aqiba, he rejoiced in the master's Torah but he was saddened by the master's death.

G. "He said, 'How precious are your thoughts to me, O God' (Ps. 139:17)."

H. And said R. Yosé, "The son of David will come only when all of the souls that are stored up in the body will be used up: 'For I will not contend for ever, neither will I be always angry, for the spirit should fall before me and the spirits which I have made' (Is. 57:16)." [Mishcon: in the face of the foregoing teachings, how could it be stated that had it not been for the sin of the golden calf, we should not have come into the world?]

I. *Do not, therefore, imagine that the sense of the statement is,* we should have not come into the world [if our ancestors had not sinned], *but rather,* it would have been as though we had not come into the world.

J. *Does that then bear the implication that, if they had not sinned, they would never have died? But not been written the passages that deal with the deceased childless brother's widow and the chapters about inheritances [which take for granted that people die]?*

K. These passages are written conditionally [meaning, if people sin and so die, then the rules take effect, but it is not necessary that they take effect unless that stipulation is fulfilled].

L. *And are there then any verses of Scripture that are stated conditionally?*

M. *Indeed so, for said R. Simeon b. Laqish, "What is the meaning of that which has been written,* 'And it was evening and it was morning, the sixth day' (Gen. 1:31)? This teaches that the Holy One, blessed be he, made a stipulation with the works of creation and said, 'If the Israelites accept the Torah, well and good, but if not, I shall send you back to the condition of formlessness and void."

N. *An objection was raised:* "O that they had such a heart as this always, to fear me and keep my commandments, that it may be well with them and their children" (Dt. 5:26): it is not possible to maintain that the meaning here is that he would take away the angel of death from them, for the decree had already been made. It means that the Israelites accepted the Torah only so that no nation or tongue would rule over them: "that it might be well with them and their children after them" [Mishcon: how could R. Simeon b. Laqish hold that but for the golden calf worship Israel would have enjoyed physical deathlessness?]

O. *[R. Simeon b. Laqish] made his statement in accord with the position of this Tannaite authority, for it has been taught on Tannaite authority:*

P. R. Yosé says, "The Israelites accepted the Torah only so that the angel of death should not have power over them: 'I said you are gods and all of you sons of the Most High. Now that you have ruined things by what you have done 'you shall indeed die like mortals' (Ps. 82:6)."

Q. *But to R. Yosé also must be addressed the question, has it not been written,* "O that they had such a heart as this always, to fear me and keep my commandments, that it may be well with them and their children" (Dt. 5:26)? *Goodness is what is promised, but there still will be death!*

R. *R. Yosé will say to you, "If there is no death, what greater goodness can there ever be?"*

S. *And the other Tannaite authority — how does he read the phrase,* "You shall indeed die"?

T. *The sense of* "death" *here is* "poverty," for a master has said, "Four classifications of persons are equivalent to corpses, and these are they: the poor man, the blind man, the person afflicted with the skin disease [of Lev. 13], and the person who has no children.

U. "The poor man, as it is written: 'for all the men are dead who sought your life' (Ex. 4:129). *Now who were they? This refers to Dathan and Abiram, and they were certainly not then dead,* they had only lost all their money.

V. "The blind man, as it is written: 'He has made me dwell in darkness as those that have been long dead' (Lam. 3:6).

W. "The person afflicted with the skin disease, as it is written: 'Let her, I pray you, not be as one who is dead' (Num. 12;12).

X. "And the person who has no children, as it is written: 'Give me children or else I die' (Gen. 30:1)."

A new composite of compositions now commences. No. 30 begins with reference to Israel's sin. The connection to No. 29, so far as I can see, is simple. We have dealt with Israel's good deeds in this world, which yield the world to come. No. 29 also has referred to the penalties for sin, and how these are appropriate. Now we turn to Israel's bad deeds. The composite on Israel's sins will continue through Nos. 30-33.

30. A. *Our rabbis have taught on Tannaite authority:*

B. "If you walk in my statutes" (Lev. 26:3) — the word "if" is used in the sense of supplication, as in the verse, O that my people would hearken to me, that Israel would walk in my ways...I should soon subdue their enemies" (Ps. 81:14-15); "O that you had listened to my commandments, then my peace would have been as a river, your seed also would have been as the sand" (Is. 48:18).

31. A. *Our rabbis have taught on Tannaite authority:*

B. "O that they had such a heart as this always, to fear me and keep my commandments, that it may be well with them and their children" (Dt. 5:26)

C. Said Moses to the Israelites, "You are a bunch of ingrates, children of ingrates. When the Holy One, blessed be he, said to you, 'O that they had such a heart as this always, to fear me and keep my commandments, that it may be well with them and their children' (Dt. 5:26), they should have said, 'You give it.'

D. "They were ingrates, since it is written, 'Our soul loathes **[5B]** this light bread' (Num. 21:5).

E. "...the children of ingrates: 'The woman whom you gave to be with me, she gave me of the fruit of the tree and I ate it' (Gen. 3:12).

F. "So our rabbi, Moses, gave an indication of that fact to the Israelites only after forty years: 'And I have led you forty years in the wilderness...but the Lord has not give you a heart to know and eyes to see and ears to hear unto this day' (Dt. 29:3, 4)."

32. A. ["And I have led you forty years in the wilderness...but the Lord has not given you a heart to know and eyes to see and ears to hear unto this day" (Dt. 29:3, 4):]

B. Said Raba, "This proves that a person will fully grasp the mind of his master only after forty years have passed."

33. A. *Said R. Yohanan in the name of R. Benaah, "What is the meaning of the verse of Scripture,* 'Happy are you who sow beside all waters, that send forth the feet of the ox and the ass' (Is. 32:20)? 'Happy are you, O Israel, when you are devoted to the Torah and to doing deeds of grace, then their inclination to do evil is handed over to them, and they are not handed over into the power of their inclination to do evil.

B. "For it is said, 'Happy are you who sow beside all waters.' For what does the word 'sowing' mean, if not 'doing deeds of grace,' in line with the use of the word in this verse: 'Sow for yourselves in righteousness, reap according to mercy' (Hos. 10:12), and what is the meaning of 'water' if not Torah: 'Oh you who are thirsty, come to the water' (Is. 55:1)."

C. As to the phrase, "that send forth the feet of the ox and the ass:"

D. it has been taught by the Tannaite authority of

the household of Elijah:

E. "A person should always place upon himself the work of studying the Torah as an ox accepts the yoke, and as an ass, its burden."

That completes the miscellany. It certainly plays no role in Mishnah-exegesis. It also sets forth no proposition, in a way in which compositions of Mishnah-exegesis, and even composites thereof, commonly do. Rather, we have a set of compositions of a rather diverse quality, which are grouped by common themes; the points that they make jointly are at best commonplaces.

Before proceeding, let me once more present a reprise of the composite, again in outline form. This allows us to see how the several compositions hold together and relate to one another, e.g., as secondary expansions of a prior point and the like. The composite finds its place at I.B: the theology of the gentile idolatry that governs the Halakhah of relating to gentiles on their festival days.

I. MISHNAH-TRACTATE ABODAH ZARAH 1:1

A. BEFORE THE FESTIVALS OF GENTILES:

1. I:1: Rab and Samuel in dealing with the reading of the key word of the Mishnah, translated festival, the letters of which are 'aleph daled, rather than 'ayin daled, which means, calamity: one repeated the formulation of the Mishnah as, "their festivals." And the other repeated the formulation of the Mishnah as "their calamities."

B. A THEOLOGY OF GENTILE IDOLATRY: ITS ORIGINS AND ITS IMPLICATIONS FOR HOLY ISRAEL

1. I:2: Why the gentiles rejected the Torah. R. Hanina bar Pappa, and some say, R. Simlai, gave the following exposition of the verse, "They that fashion a graven image are all of them vanity, and their delectable things shall not profit, and their own witnesses see not

nor know" (Is. 44:9): "In the age to come the Holy One, blessed be He, will bring a scroll of the Torah and hold it in his bosom and say, 'Let him who has kept himself busy with it come and take his reward.' The kingdom of Rome comes in first. The Holy One, blessed be He, will say to them, 'How have you defined your chief occupation?' They will say before him, 'Lord of the world, a vast number of marketplaces have we set up, a vast number of bathhouses we have made, a vast amount of silver and gold have we accumulated. And all of these things we have done only in behalf of Israel, so that they may define as their chief occupation the study of the Torah.' The Holy One, blessed be He, will say to them, 'You complete idiots! Whatever you have done has been for your own convenience. You have set up a vast number of marketplaces to be sure, but that was so as to set up whorehouses in them. The bathhouses were for your own pleasure. Silver and gold belong to me anyhow: "Mine is the silver and mine is the gold, says the Lord of hosts" (Hag. 2:8). Are there any among you who have been telling of "this," and "this" is only the Torah: "And this is the Torah that Moses set before the children of Israel' (Dt. 4:44)." So they will make their exit, humiliated. When the kingdom of Rome has made its exit, the kingdom of Persia enters afterward...." ...They say before him, 'Lord of the world, did you hold a mountain over us like a cask and then we refused to accept it as you did to Israel, as it is written, "And they stood beneath the mountain" (Ex. 19:17).'" Then the Holy One, blessed be He, will say to them, 'Let us make known what happened first: "Let them announce to us former things" (Is. 43:9). As to the seven religious duties that you did accept, where have you actually carried them out?' "This is what the gentiles say before him, 'Lord of the world, Israel, who accepted it — where in the world have they actually carried it out?' The Holy One, blessed be He, will say to them, 'I shall bear witness concerning them, that they have carried out the whole of the Torah!' They will say before him, 'Lord of the world, is there a father who is permitted to give testimony concerning his son? For it is written, "Israel is my son, my firstborn" (Ex. 4:22).' The Holy One, blessed be He, will say to them, 'The Heaven and the earth will give testimony in their behalf that they have carried out the entirety of the Torah....'"

  a. I:3: Gloss of a tangential detail of the foregoing.

  b. I:4: As above.

C. THE CRITICAL IMPORTANCE OF TORAH-STUDY FOR THE SALVATION OF ISRAEL, INDIVIDUALLY AND COLLECTIVELY

  1. I:5: Said R. Levi, "To whoever stops studying the words of the Torah and instead takes up words of mere chatter they feed glowing coals of juniper." Said R. Simeon b. Laqish, "For whoever engages in study of the Torah by night — the Holy One, blessed be He, draws out the thread of grace by day."

  2. I:6: Said R. Judah said Samuel, "What is the meaning of the verse of Scripture, 'And you make man as the fish of the sea and as the creeping things, that have no ruler over them' (Hab. 1:14)? Why are human beings compared to fish of the sea? To tell you, just as fish in the sea, when they come up on dry land, forthwith begin to die, so with human beings, when they take their leave of teachings of the Torah and religious deeds, forthwith they begin to die."

D. GOD FAVORS HOLY ISRAEL OVER THE GENTILES, BECAUSE THE FORMER ACCEPT, STUDY, AND CARRY OUT THE TORAH AND THE LATTER DO NOT. THEREFORE AT THE END OF DAYS GOD WILL SAVE ISRAEL AND DESTROY IDOLATRY

  1. I:7: R. Hinena bar Pappa contrasted verses of Scripture: "It is written, 'As to the almighty, we do not find him exercising plenteous power' (Job 37:23), but by contrast, 'Great is our Lord and of abundant power' (Ps. 147:5), and further, 'Your right hand, Lord, is glorious in power' (Ex. 15:6). But there is no contradiction between the first and second and third statements, for the former speaks of the time of judgment when justice is tempered with mercy, so God does not do what he could and the latter two statements refer to a

time of war of God against his enemies."

2. I:8: R. Hama bar Hanina contrasted verses of Scripture: "It is written, 'Fury is not in me' (Is. 27:4) but also 'The Lord revenges and is furious' (Nah. 1:2). But there is no contradiction between the first and second statements, for the former speaks of Israel, the latter of the gentiles."

    a. I:9: Amplification of the foregoing.

3. I:10: Raba said, "What is the meaning of the verse, 'Howbeit he will not stretch out a hand for a ruinous heap though they cry in his destruction' (Job 30:24)? Said the Holy One, blessed be He, to Israel, 'When I judge Israel, I shall not judge them as I do the gentiles, for it is written, "I will overturn, overturn, overturn it" (Ezek. 21:32), rather, I shall exact punishment from them as a hen pecks.'"

4. I:11: R. Abba said, "What is the meaning of the verse, 'Though I would redeem them, yet they have spoken lies against me' (Hos. 7:23)? 'I said that I would redeem them through inflicting a penalty on their property in this world, so that they might have the merit of enjoying the world to come, "yet they have spoken lies against me" (Hos. 7:23).'"

5. I:12: R. Pappi in the name of Raba said, "What is the meaning of the verse, 'Though I have trained and strengthened their arms, yet they imagine mischief against me' (Hos. 7:15)? Said the Holy One, blessed be He, I thought that I would punish them with suffering in this world, so that their arm might be strengthened in the world to come, "yet they have spoken lies against me" (Hos. 7:23).'"

E. GOD'S JUDGMENT AND WRATH, GOD'S MERCY AND FORGIVENESS

1. I:13: "It is written, 'You only have I known among all the families of the earth; therefore I will visit upon you all your iniquities' (Amos 3:2). If one is angry, does he vent it on someone he loves?" He said to them, "I shall tell you a parable. To what is the matter comparable? To the case of a man who lent money to two people, one a friend, the other an enemy. From the friend he collects the money little by little, from the en-

emy he collects all at once."

2. I:14: Said R. Abba bar Kahana, "What is the meaning of the following verse of Scripture: 'Far be it from you to do after this manner, to slay the righteous with the wicked' (Gen. 18:25). Said Abraham before the Holy One, blessed be He, 'Lord of the world! It is a profanation to act in such a way a play on the Hebrew letters, shared by the words 'far be it' and 'profanation', 'to slay the righteous with the wicked' (Gen. 18:25)."

3. I:15: R. Pappa contrasted verses of Scripture: "It is written, 'God is angry every day' (Ps. 7:12) but also 'who could stand before his anger' (Nah. 1:6). But there is no contradiction between the first and second statements, for the former speaks of the individual, the latter of the community."

F. BALAAM, THE PROPHET OF THE GENTILES, AND ISRAEL; GOD'S ANGER WITH THE GENTILES AND WITH ISRAEL

1. I:16: Our rabbis have taught on Tannaite authority: "God is angry every day" (Ps. 7:12), and how long is his anger? It is for a moment. And how long is a moment? The portion 1/53,848th of an hour is a moment. And no creature can determine that moment, except for Balaam that wicked man, of whom it is written, "who knew the knowledge of the Most High" (Num. 24:16). How can it be that a man who did not know the mind of his animal could have known the mind of the Most High?

a. I:17: Gloss of foregoing: And what is the meaning of the statement that he did not know the mind of his animal?

b. I:18: Gloss of foregoing: And what is the meaning of the statement that he could have known the mind of the Most High?

2. I:19: "O my people, remember now what Balak king of Moab consulted and what Balaam son of Beor answered him from Shittim to Gilgal, that you may know the righteousness of the Lord" (Mic. 6:5): Said R. Eleazar, "Said the Holy One, blessed be He, to Israel, 'My people, see how many acts of righteousness I carried out with you, for I did not grow angry with you

during all those perilous days, for if I had grown angry with you, there would not have remained from Israel a remnant or a survivor.'

    a. I:20: Further gloss of I:16: And how long is his wrath? It is for a moment. And how long is a moment? The portion 1/53,848th of an hour is a moment. And how long is a moment?

    b. I:21: When is he angry? Said Abbayye, "In the first three hours of the day, when the comb of the cock is white."

    c. I:22: As above.

G. THE TIME OF GOD'S ANGER IN RELATIONSHIP TO THE GENTILES AND TO ISRAEL; THE ROLE OF IDOLATRY IN GOD'S WRATH AGAINST THE NATIONS

    1. I:23: It was taught as a Tannaite version in the name of R. Meir, "That time at which God gets angry comes when the kings put on their crowns on their heads and prostrate themselves to the sun. Forthwith the Holy One, blessed be He, grows angry."

    2. I:24: Said R. Joseph, "A person should not recite the Prayer of the Additional Service for the first day of the New Year the Day of Judgment during the first three hours of the day or in private, lest, since that is the time of judgment, his deeds may be examined, and his prayer rejected."

    3. I:25: R. Joshua b. Levi has said, "What is the meaning of the verse of Scripture, 'The ordinances that I command you this day to do them' (Dt. 7:11)? Today is the day to do them, but not tomorrow; they are not to be done tomorrow; today is the day to do them, but today is not the day on which to receive a reward for doing them": Said R. Joshua b. Levi, "All the religious duties that Israelites do in this world come and give evidence in their behalf in the world to come: 'Let them bring their witnesses that they may be justified, let them hear and say it is truth.'" And said R. Joshua b. Levi, "All the religious duties that Israelites do in this world come and flap about the faces of gentiles in the world to come: 'Keep them and do them, for this, your wisdom and understanding, will be in the eyes of the peoples'

(Dt. 4:6)."

H. THE SINFUL ANCESTOR OF THE MESSIAH AND GOD'S FORGIVENESS OF HIM AND OF ISRAEL

1. I:26: That is in line with what R. Yohanan said in the name of R. Simeon b. Yohai: "David was really not so unfit as to do such a deed as he did with Beth Sheva: 'My heart is slain within me' (Ps. 109:22) And the Israelites were hardly the kind of people to commit such an act: "O that they had such a heart as this always, to fear me and keep my commandments' (Dt. 5:26). So why did they do it? It was to show you that if an individual has sinned, they say to him, 'Go to the individual such as David, and follow his example, and if the community as a whole has sinned, they say to them, 'Go to the community such as Israel.'

2. I:27: That is in line with what R. Samuel bar Nahmani said R. Jonathan said, "What is the meaning of the verse of Scripture, 'The saying of David, son of Jesse, and the saying of the man raised on high' (2 Sam. 23:1)? It means, 'The saying of David, son of Jesse, the man who raised up the yoke of repentance.'"

3. I:28: Said R. Samuel bar Nahmani said R. Jonathan, "Whoever does a religious duty in this world — that deed goes before him to the world to come, as it is said, 'And your righteousness shall go before you' (Is. 58:8). And whoever commits a transgression in this world — that act turns aside from him and goes before him on the Day of Judgment, as it is said, 'The paths of their way are turned aside, they go up into the waste and perish' (Job 6:18)."

4. I:29: Said R. Simeon b. Laqish, "Come and let us express our gratitude to our ancestors, for if it were not for their having sinned, we for our part should never have been able to come into the world: 'I said you are gods and all of you sons of the Most High' (Ps. 82:6). Now that you have ruined things by what you have done, 'you shall indeed die like mortals' (Ps. 82:6)."

5. I:30: Our rabbis have taught on Tannaite authority: "If you walk in my statutes" (Lev. 26:3) — the word "if" is used in the sense of supplication, as in the verse, O that my people would hearken to me, that Is-

rael would walk in my ways...I should soon subdue their enemies" (Ps. 81:14-15); "O that you had listened to my commandments, then my peace would have been as a river, your seed also would have been as the sand" (Is. 48:18).

    6.   I:31: Our rabbis have taught on Tannaite authority: "O that they had such a heart as this always, to fear me and keep my commandments, that it may be well with them and their children" (Dt. 5:26). Said Moses to the Israelites, "You are a bunch of ingrates, children of ingrates. When the Holy One, blessed be He, said to you, 'O that they had such a heart as this always, to fear me and keep my commandments, that it may be well with them and their children' (Dt. 5:26), they should have said, 'You give it.'"

    a.   I:32: Gloss of foregoing.

    7.   I:33: Said R. Yohanan in the name of R. Benaah, "What is the meaning of the verse of Scripture, 'Happy are you who sow beside all waters, that send forth the feet of the ox and the ass' (Is. 32:20)? 'Happy are you, O Israel, when you are devoted to the Torah and to doing deeds of grace, then their inclination to do evil is handed over to them, and they are not handed over into the power of their inclination to do evil.'"

The outline has identified the principal propositions and how they are spelled out and instantiated (demonstrated). Let me make explicit my theory of how the whole holds together.

The grouping of the compositions into subcomposites is fairly easy to explain, and their further agglutination into the large-scale composite before us lays within the range of reasonable explanation. We have something more than a random scrapbook of this and that. The survey just now concluded leaves us with an impression somewhat different from what we expected at the outset. First of all, identifying the supplementary entries — footnotes, appendices — shows us that a fair amount of the miscellany in fact is made up of secondary expansions of a quite coherent text. Within the technical limitations of our authorship, who, after all, had no way of signifying footnotes and appendices, the framers of the whole had no choice but to gloss. Second, the rather sizable sequence of free-standing compositions in the aggregate is made up of conglomerates, the cogency of which we are able to explain. Third, the order of the conglomerates is not entirely beyond reason, since if we were to state the propositions not proved but illustrated by what is before us, we would have these simple statements:

1. study of the Torah on the part of a human being elicits in God a counterpart response, one of grace.
2. Israel lives through study of the torah.
3. God favors Israel, by reason of Israel's study of the Torah, and is angry with the gentiles.
4. Israel's good deeds in this world will be rewarded not now but in the world to come.

We then end with what is labeled as an appendix to materials introduced earlier. Now while we can hardly claim that the enormous composite made up of No. 2 through 33 is a sustained and well-crafted whole, we also cannot settle for the characterization of the set as a mere miscellany. It is made up of clearly-identifiable composites, each of them comprising already-made up compositions. Where there is a movement from one to the next, there is ordinarily a clear connection, e.g., a reference to a sub-theme now given principal place as a main theme; an allusion to a person, now formed into the focus of a set of compositions. What holds the parts together, one to the next, is a connection of a formal, generally a thematic character. What holds the whole together is a sequence of unfolding themes. It would claim far too much to allege that we have a demonstration of a single proposition, e.g., God hates and is angry with idolaters and loves and rewards Israel. But it would be obtuse not to observe that that theme, remarkably coherent with the Mishnah-tractate overall and with the opening paragraph of the Mishnah in particular, is present and is treated.

Let me now summarize the whole. **I.1** begins with a systematic inquiry into the correct reading of the Mishnah's word-choices. The dispute is fully articulated in balance, beginning to end. No. 2 then forms a footnote to No. 1. No. 3 then provides a footnote to the leitmotif of No. 2, the conception of God's not laughing. and No. 4 returns us to the exposition of No. 2, at III. Nos. 5, 6 are tacked on — a Torah-study anthology — because they continue the general theme of Torah-study every day, which formed the main motif of No. 2 — the gentiles did not accept the Torah, study it, or carry it out. So that theme accounts for the accumulation of sayings on Torah-study in general, a kind of appendix on the theme. Then — so far as I can see, because of the reference to God's power — No. 7 begins with a complement to 6.I. The compositions, Nos. 7, 8, then are strung together because of a point that is deemed to link each to its predecessor. No. 7 is linked to the foregoing because of the theme of God's power; but it also intersects with 2.III and complements that reference; the entire sequence beyond No. 2 then in one way or another relates to either No. 2, theme or proposition, or to an item that is tacked on to No. 2 as a complement. Thus No. 8 is joined to No. 7 because of the shared method of contrasting verses. Then No. 9 is tacked on because it continues the proposition of No. 8. No. 10 continues the foregoing. No. 11 is tacked on to No. 10 for the reason made explicit: it continues what has gone before. The same is so for No. 12.

No. 13 continues the theme, but not the form or the proposition, of the prior compositions, namely, punishment little by little, e.g., in this world, in exchange for a great reward later on. The established theme then is divine punishment and how it is inflicted: gently to Israel, harshly to the gentiles; the preferred form is the contrast among two verses. That overall principle of conglomeration — form & theme — explains the inclusion of Nos. 14, 15+16, which is tacked on to 15. But then the introduction of Balaam, taken as the prototype for the min, accounts for the inclusion of a variety of further sayings on the same theme, specifically, No. 17, a gloss on the foregoing; No. 18, a continuation of the foregoing process of glossing, No. 19, an amplification on the now-dominant theme; No. 20, a reversion to No. 16; No. 21, a story on the theme of how difficult it is to define precisely the matter dealt with in the foregoing.

No. 21, 22, 23 complete the discussion of that particular time at which God is angry, a brief moment but one that is marked by a just cause. No. 23 then introduces the theme of choosing the right time — that is not the moment of divine wrath — for prayer. This seems to me a rather miscellaneous item, and it marks the conclusion of the systematic expansion begun much earlier. That that is the fact is shown by the character of No. 24, which cites 2.HHH, and by No. 25, which explicitly reverts to 2.RR, which justifies my insistence that the entire corpus of materials that follow No. 2 simply amplify and augment No. 2, and that is done in a very systematic way. Some of the sets, as we have seen, were formed into conglomerates prior to insertion here, but once we recognize that all of the sets serve the single task at hand, we see the coherent of what on the surface appears to be run on and miscellaneous. These materials serve No. 2, some as footnotes, some as appendices, and some as footnotes or appendices to footnotes or appendices.

No. 26 is a fine case in point. It complements 25.H, and is tacked on for that reason. Then No. 27 complements No. 26's statements concerning David. Bearing a formal tie to No. 27, with the same authority, No. 28 fits in also because it reverts to the theme of No. 25, the power of the religious duties that one carries out. No. 29 continues the theme of No. 28, that is, death and the day of judgment. Simeon's statement defines the center of gravity of the passage, which obviously was complete prior to its inclusion here. The reason it has been added is its general congruence to the discussions of sin, penitence, death and forgiveness. No. 30 is attached to No. 31, and No. 31 is tacked on because it refers to the proof-text in the prior composition. No. 32 takes up the proof-text of No. 31. No. 33 writes a solid conclusion to the whole, addressing as it does the basic theme that Israel's actions define their fate, and that study of the Torah is what determines everything else. That is a thematic conclusion to a composite largely devoted, one way or another, to that one theme.

What then leads us to see as a miscellany Nos. 2 through 33? It is the contrast between that composite and the amazingly coherent character of the Talmud's Mishnah-commentary. And since the Talmud is made up mostly of Mishnah-commentary, what holds together its thematic sets, and what accounts for their relationship to the Mishnah, are considerations that are easy to miss. So much for first impressions. They prove superficial. For in the case of what is before us, we can readily see both what holds the several composites together, what links one composite to the next, and what defines the relationship of the entire group of composites to the Mishnah-paragraph that stands at the head.

The upshot may be easily stated. The miscellanies really are not at all miscellaneous. They form an integral part of the Talmud's program of Mishnah-commentary. But they are made up of materials that, on their own, do not address the language or propositions of the Mishnah, only its (implicit) themes. As a result, they do not exhibit the literary cogency that makes the bulk of the Talmud so remarkably coherent. Viewed in their own terms, however, the materials we have examined answer the question the Mishnah-paragraph raises and respond to its topical program: gentiles observe holy days in the service of idols. Israel should have nothing to do with such things. God loves Israel, who study the Torah, forgives their sins, and in the world to come will give them their lasting, and just reward. In light of the propositions of the Mishnah, we can hardly have asked for a more appropriate set of compositions than those selected and arranged in the massive "miscellany" at hand.

VI. THE PROBLEM OF AGGLUTINATIVE DISCOURSE

With these sizable examples in hand, we are ready to turn to the main issue: the challenge to the documentary reading of the Rabbinic canon that is presented by miscellanies. What, precisely, are the documentary traits that are violated by the miscellany, and does the Bavli (otherwise) conform to formal conventions at all? To answer that question, me now set forth the traits of the document that, over all, classify the writing as anything but miscellaneous. Then the problem of the literary formations treated in this pages will become entirely clear. For until I have established that most of the Bavli follows easily discerned rules of composition and the formation of composites, and that these rules dictate the character of the document as a whole — a commentary to the Mishnah — my claim to identify and differentiate writing of a quite different character will not be fully understood. Since I propose not only to identify this other kind of writing, but also to define and explain the rules that dictate the making of those composites of the Bavli that serve a different purpose from Mishnah-commentary, I had best begin with the norms of the document, and only then to turn to what is different from the normal but also, in its way, governed by reasons we can uncover.

The writers of the Talmud spoke in a single voice.

Whatever its writers wished to say, they said in a single way. Viewed as a whole, the Talmud of Babylonia covers thirty-seven of the Mishnah's sixty-three tractates, and, in discussing these thirty-seven Mishnah-tractates, the authorship of the Talmud speaks in a single way. A fixed rhetorical pattern and a limited program of logical inquiry governs throughout. Whatever authors wish to say, they say within a severely restricted repertoire of rhetorical choices, and the intellectual initiatives they are free to explore everywhere dictate one set of questions and problems and not any other. The document's "voice," then, comprises that monotonous and repetitious language, which conveys a recurrent and single melody. In the ancient and great centers of learning in which the Talmud of Babylonia is studied today, masters and their disciples — studying out loud and in dialogue with one another and with the text — commonly and correctly say, "the Talmud says...," (Yiddish: *zogt die gemora;* Hebrew: *hattalmud omeret*), meaning, the anonymous, uniform, ubiquitous voice of the document, speaking in the name of no one in particular and within an indeterminate context of space and time, makes a given statement or point. Through years of encounter with the document, within the conventions of centuries of study in continuing circles of learning, by reference to "the Talmud says," the masters express the result of innumerable observations of coherence, uniformity, and cogency. I represent their usage when I speak of "the Talmud's one voice."

Why do I claim that the document may be read as a single coherent statement? The reason is that the document as a whole is cogent, doing some few things over and over again; it conforms to a few simple rules of rhetoric, including choice of languages for discrete purposes,[7] and that fact attests to the

---

[7] I refer to *Language as Taxonomy. The Rules for Using Hebrew and Aramaic in the Babylonian Talmud.* Atlanta, 1990: Scholars Press for South Florida Studies in the History of Judaism. This work is made possible by my translation,

coherent viewpoint of the authorship at the end — the people who put it all together as we have it — because it speaks, over all, in a single way, in a uniform voice. It is not merely an encyclopaedia of information, but a sustained, remarkably protracted, uniform inquiry into the logical traits of passages of the Mishnah or of Scripture. Most of the Talmud deals with the exegesis and amplification of the Mishnah's rules or of passages of Scripture. Wherever we turn, that labor of exegesis and amplification, without differentiation in topics or tractates, conforms to a few simple rules in inquiry, repeatedly phrased, implicitly or explicitly, in a few simple rhetorical forms or patterns.

The Bavli's one voice governs throughout, about a considerably repertoire of topics speaking within a single restricted rhetorical vocabulary. In the pages of *The Bavli's One Voice: Types and Forms of Analytical Discourse and their Fixed Order of Appearance*,[8] that vocabulary — the limited repertoire of speech — is set forth through an inductive process, hence "the Bavli's one voice" refers to a remarkably limited set of intellectual initiatives, only this and that, initiatives that moreover always adhere to a single sequence or order: this first, then that — but never the other thing. I can identify the Bavli's authorships' rules of composition,. These are not many. Not only so, but the order of types of compositions (written in accord with a determinate set of rules) itself follows a fixed pattern, so that a composition written in obedience to a given rule as to form will always appear in the same point in a sequence of compositions that are written in obedience to two or more

---

which distinguishes between Hebrew and Aramaic by the use of plain and italic type. Then, quite graphically, how each language serves its own distinct, taxonomic purpose, that is, identifying the status and purpose of what is said in that language, is easily portrayed.

[8] Atlanta, 1991: Scholars Press for South Florida Studies in the History of Judaism.

rules: type A first, type B next, in fixed sequence. The Talmud's one voice then represents the outcome of the work of the following:

[1] an author preparing a composition for inclusion in the Bavli would conform to one of a very few rules of thought and expression; and, more to the point,

[2] a framer of a cogent composite, often encompassing a set of compositions, for presentation as the Bavli would follow a fixed order in selecting and arranging the types of consequential forms that authors had made available for his use.[9]

With a clear and specific account of the facts yielding that anticipated result, I shall be well justified in asking about the message of the rhetorical and logical method of the Bavli. The Talmud of Babylonia is made up of large-scale composites — completed units of discourse, with a beginning, middle, and end, which supply all of the data a reader (or listener) requires to understand the point that the framer of that composite wishes to make. A composite commonly draws upon available information, made available in part by prior and completed composites, e.g., Scripture, the Mishnah, the Tosefta, and in part by compositions worked out entirely within their own limits, which we might compare with a paragraph of a chapter; or a free-standing composition of a few lines. By "rules of composition" I mean the laws that dictated to the framers of a cogent and coherent composites — such as I allege comprise

---

[9]The distinction between composition and composite, which is fundamental to all that follows, is explained in *The Rules of Composition of the Talmud of Babylonia. The Cogency of the Bavli's Composite.* And that distinction begins with my development of an analytical reference system, which makes possible the division of columns of undifferentiated words into much more than sentences, paragraphs, chapters, but the analytical re-presentation of undifferentiated words into their functional components: principal and subordinate. Here again, it would serve no useful purpose to go over familiar results.

the whole of the Talmud of Babylonia — precisely how to put together whatever they wished to say, together with the supporting evidence as well as argument, in the composition that they proposed to write. Here, then, "rules of composition" govern how people formed composites that comprise the Bavli: how they are classified, how they are ordered.

Now to set forth the results of the analysis of eleven tractates systematically treated in *The Bavli's One Voice*. It is the simple fact that the Bavli throughout speaks in a single and singular voice. It is single because it is a voice that expresses the same limited set of notes everywhere. It is singular because these notes are arranged in one and the same way throughout. The Bavli's one voice, sounding through all tractates, is the voice of exegetes of the Mishnah. The document is organized around the Mishnah, and that is not a merely formal, but a substantive order. At every point, if the framers have chosen a passage of Mishnah-exegesis, that passage will stand at the head of all further discussion. Every turning point brings the editors back to the Mishnah, always read in its own order and sequence.

So the Bavli's speaks in a single way about some few things, and that is the upshot of my sustained inquiry. It follows that well-crafted and orderly rules governed the character of the sustained discourse that the writing in the Bavli sets forth. All framers of composites and editors of sequences of composites found guidance in the same limited repertoire of rules of analytical rhetoric: some few questions or procedures, directed always toward one and the same prior writing. Not only so, but a fixed order of discourse dictated that a composition of one sort, A, always come prior to a composite of another type, B. A simple logic instructed framers of composites, who sometimes also were authors of compositions, and who sometimes drew upon available compositions in the making of their cogent composites. So we have now to see the Bavli as entirely of a piece, cogent and coherent, made up of well-composed large-scale constructions. It is coherent not only in its rules of the use of Hebrew and Aramaic, it is even more coherent in its rhetorical laws.

The Bavli's one voice utilizes only a few, well-modulated tones: a scale of not many notes. When we classify more than three thousand composites, spread over eleven tractates, we find that nearly 90% of the whole comprises Mishnah-commentary of various kinds; not only so, but the variety of the types of Mishnah-commentary is limited, as a review of the representation of Temurah in detail, and of the ten tractates of our sample in brief characterization, has shown. Cogent composites are further devoted to Scripture or to topics of a moral or theological character not closely tied to the exegesis of verses of Scripture; these form in the aggregate approximately 10% of the whole number of composites, but, of tractates to begin with not concerned with scriptural or theological topics (in our sample these are Sanhedrin and Berakhot), they make up scarcely 3% of the whole. So the Bavli has one voice, and it is the voice of a person or persons who propose to speak about one document and to do so in some few ways. Let me spell out precisely what I mean. The results of the survey of eleven tractates and classification of all of the composites of each one of them yields firm and one-sided results.

First, we are able to classify all composites in three principal categories: [1] exegesis and amplification of the law of the Mishnah; [2] exegesis and exposition of verses of, or topics in, Scripture; [3] free-standing composites devoted to topics other than those defined by the Mishnah or Scripture. That means that my initial proposal of a taxonomic system left no lacunae.

Second, with the classification in place, we see that much more than four-fifths of all composites of the Bavli address the Mishnah and systematically expound that document. These composites are subject to sub-classification in two ways: Mishnah-exegesis and speculation and abstract theorizing about the implications of the Mishnah's statements. The former type of composite, further, is to be classified in a few and simple taxa, for example, composites organized around [1] clarification of the statements of the Mishnah, [2] identification of the authority behind an anonymous statement in the Mishnah, [3] scriptural foundation for the Mishnah's rules; [4] citation and not seldom systematic exposition of the Tosefta's amplification of the Mishnah. That means that most of the Bavli is a systematic exposition of the Mishnah.

Third, the other fifth (or less) of a given tractate will comprise composites that take shape around [1] Scripture or [2] themes or topics of a generally theological or moral character. Distinguishing the latter from the former, of course, is merely formal; very often a scriptural topic will be set forth in a theological or moral framework, and very seldom does a composite on a topic omit all reference to the amplification of a verse or topic of Scripture. The proportion of a given tractate devoted to other-than-Mishnah-exegesis and amplification is generally not more than 10%. My figure is distorted by the special problems of tractates Sanhedrin and Berakhot, and, in the former, Chapter Eleven in particular.

These two tractates prove anomalous for the categories I have invented, because both of them contain important components that are devoted to begin with to scriptural or theological topics. And it is these anomalies that called my attention to the necessity of a closer look at what I here call "miscellanies." Tractate Sanhedrin Chapter Eleven, lists various scriptural figures in catalogues of those who do, or do not, inherit the world to come; it further specifies certain doctrines that define the norms of the community of Israel that inherits the world to come. It will therefore prove quite natural that numerous composites will attend to scriptural or theological topics. Tractate Berakhot addresses matters of prayer and other forms of virtue, with the same consequence. In the analysis that follows, therefore, I calculate the averages of proportions of various types of composites both with and without these anomalous tractates. The upshot is that a rather inconsequential proportion of most tractates, and a small proportion of the whole, of the Bavli, is devoted to the systematic exposition of either verses of Scripture or topics of a theological or moral character. But even though the miscellanies prove anomalous within the Bavli, we are going to see that, in their own setting, viewed in relationship to one another, there are quite clear rules that govern throughout.

Someone who had in hand a variety of compositions that were candidates for a composite of a miscellaneous character knew precisely what to choose for his work and exactly how to string together these composites. The one thing that he knew to begin with is that these composites would not serve the purpose of Mishnah-commentary. I cannot point to a single miscellaneous composite that intersects with the Mishnah's propositions in any detailed way, and where the composite shares a topic with the Mishnah, the topical congruence plays no role in the framing of said composite. So, up front, we must recognize that the miscellany addresses a problem other than the exegesis and amplification of the Mishnah. The people who made it up then obeyed one rule that is clear at the outset: their "miscellany" would not address the Mishnah in any way at all. But then, if that rule of formation is sound, then the miscellanies look considerably less miscellaneous than they did at the outset. Let us now consider in detail the eleven tractates' proportions of types of composites, to see the foundation for these generalizations.

Temurah

		Number	Percent
1.	Exegesis of the Mishnah	58	75%
2.	Exegesis of Mishnah-law	8	10%
3.	Speculation and Abstract Thought on Law	8	10%
4.	Scripture	3	4%
4.	Free-standing Composites	-	-
6.	Miscellanies	0	-
Total		77	

Sukkah

		Number	Percent
1.	Exegesis of the Mishnah	141	89%
2.	Exegesis of the Mishnah's Law	8	5%
3.	Speculation and Abstract Thought on Law	4	2%
4.	Scripture	1	-%

5.	Miscellanies 3%	<u>5</u>
Total		159

KERITOT

1.	Exegesis of the Mishnah 94%	80
2.	Exegesis of the Mishnah's Law 4%	4
3.	Speculation and Abstract Thought on Law -	8
4.	Scripture 1%	1
5.	Free-standing Composites -	0
6.	Miscellanies -	<u>0</u>
Total		85

ARAKHIN

1.	Exegesis of the Mishnah 91%	127
2.	Exegesis of the Mishnah's Law 6%	8
3.	Speculation and Abstract Thought on Law 1.5%	2
4.	Scripture -	0
5.	Free-standing Composites 1.5%	2
6.	Miscellanies -	<u>0</u>

Total   139

The importance of the free-standing composites is not reflected by the count, since both items are enormous and the first of the two serves as the prologue to the tractate as a whole.

NIDDAH

1.	Exegesis of the Mishnah	290	97%
2.	Exegesis of the Mishnah's Law	6	2%
3.	Speculation and Abstract Thought on Law	0	-
4.	Scripture	0	-
5.	Free-standing Composites	3	1%
6.	Miscellanies	0	-

Total   299

ABODAH ZARAH

1.	Exegesis of the Mishnah	244	85%
2.	Exegesis of the Mishnah's Law	3	1%
3.	Speculation and Abstract Thought on Law	0	-
4.	Scripture	28	10%
5.	Free-standing Composites	12	4%

6.	Miscellanies	<u>0</u>
Total		287

SOTAH

1.	Exegesis of the Mishnah 91%	193
2.	Exegesis of the Mishnah's Law -	0
3.	Speculation and Abstract Thought on Law -	0
4.	Scripture 5%	10
5.	Free-standing Composites 4%	8
6.	Miscellanies 0.5%.	<u>1</u>
Total		212

BABA MESIA

1.	Exegesis of the Mishnah 86%	334
2.	Exegesis of the Mishnah's Law 11%	42
3.	Speculation and Abstract Thought on Law -	0
4.	Scripture 0.5%	2
5.	Free-standing Composites 3%	10
6.	Miscellanies	<u>0</u>

Total   388

BEKHOROT

1.	Exegesis of the Mishnah 98%	281	
2.	Exegesis of the Mishnah's Law 1%	2	
3.	Speculation and Abstract Thought on Law	0	-
4.	Scripture	0	-
5.	Free-standing Composites 1%	2	
6.	Miscellanies	=	

Total   285

BERAKHOT

1.	Exegesis of the Mishnah 59%	330	
2.	Exegesis of the Mishnah's Law 0.5%	3	
3.	Speculation and Abstract Thought on Law	0	-
4.	Scripture 6%	34	
5.	Free-standing Composites 34%	187	
6.	Miscellanies	<u>2</u>	

	0.4%
Total	556

SANHEDRIN

1.	Exegesis of the Mishnah 45%	313
2.	Exegesis of the Mishnah's Law 0.8%	6
3.	Speculation and Abstract Thought on Law 0.8%	6
4.	Scripture 23%	163
5.	Free-standing Composites 30%	214
6.	Miscellanies	0 —
Total		702

When the eleven tractates are seen in the aggregate, the proportions of them that are devoted solely to Mishnah-exegesis average 83%. If we omit reference to the two clearly-anomalous tractates, Berakhot and Sanhedrin, the proportion of Mishnah-exegesis rises to 89.5%. If, then, we combine exegesis of the Mishnah and exegesis of the broader implications of the Mishnah's law — and in the process of classification, it was not always easy to keep these items apart in a consistent way — we see a still more striking result. More than 86% of the whole of the surveyed tractates is devoted to the exegesis of the Mishnah and the amplification of the implications of its law; without the anomalous tractates, the proportion is close to 94-95%.

We dismiss as a taxon that did not serve any useful purpose the one that was supposed to identify "speculation and abstract thought on law." As a matter of fact, nearly all speculative or abstract thought on law, measured by the number of composites devoted to that purpose, treats the Mishnah's concrete laws; nearly all speculation is precipitated by an inquiry into the premises of those laws. There is virtually no abstract thought on law that does not aim at the clarification of the Mishnah's laws in particular. That result is as stunning as the foregoing.

Composites devoted to Scripture, not the Mishnah, are calculated in two ways. In the first nine tractates, I counted each composite as one entry, just as, overall, I counted each composite devoted to the Mishnah as one entry. On the surface such a mode of counting understated the proportions of the anomalous tractates that are devoted to Scripture-exegesis, or to topics drawn from Scripture. Overall, we should expect to find something on the order of 4% of a given tractate made up of Scripture-composites. If we eliminate the two anomalous tractates, the anticipated proportion would be 2%. Free-standing composites, formed in general around themes, rather than passages of the Mishnah or sequences of verses of Scripture or topics provided by Scripture, average 10% for eight tractates (omitted: Temurah, Sukkah, Keritot, where I found none), and, without the anomalous ones, 1.5-3%. The latter figure seems to me more probable than the former.

So I have demonstrated beyond any reasonable doubt that the Bavli is a cogent, well-planned, coherent document. Stated simply: the Talmud speaks through one voice, that voice of logic that with vast assurance reaches into our own minds and by asking the logical and urgent next question tells us what we should be thinking. Fixing our attention upon the Mishnah, the Talmud's rhetoric seduces us into joining its analytical inquiry, always raising precisely the question that should trouble us (and that would trouble us if we knew all of the pertinent details as well as the Talmud does). The Bavli speaks about the Mishnah in essentially a single voice, about fundamentally few things. Its mode of speech as much as of thought is uniform throughout. Diverse topics produce slight differentiation in modes of analysis. The same sorts of questions phrased in the same rhetoric — a moving, or dialectical, argument, composed of questions and answers — turn out to pertain equally well to every subject and problem. The Talmud's discourse forms a closed system, in which people say the same thing about everything. The fact that the Talmud speaks in a single voice supplies striking evidence (1) that the Talmud does speak in particular for the age in which its units of discourse took shape, and (2) that that work was done toward the end of that long period of Mishnah-reception that began at the end of the second century and came to an end at the conclusion of the sixth century.

When I speak of the Bavli's one voice, its formally-cogent character, as now is clear, I mean to say it everywhere speaks uniformly, consistently, and predictably. The voice is the voice of a book. The message is one deriving from a community, the collectivity of sages for whom and to whom the book speaks. The document seems, in the main, to intend to provide notes, an abbreviated script which anyone may use to reconstruct and reenact formal discussions of problems: about this, one says that. Curt and often arcane, these notes can be translated only with immense bodies of inserted explanation. All of this script of information is public and undifferentiated, not individual and idiosyncratic. We must assume people took for granted that, out of the signs of speech, it would be possible for anyone to reconstruct speech, doing so in accurate and fully conventional ways. So the literary traits of the document presuppose a uniform code of communication:

a single voice.

So it is time to ask the purpose of that composition: what the authors, authorships, or framers of the document wished to say through the writing that they have given us. If there is a single governing method, then what can we expect to learn about the single, repeated message? The evidence before us indicates that the purpose of the Talmud is to clarify and amplify selected passages of the Mishnah. We may say very simply that the Mishnah is about life, and the Talmud is about the Mishnah. That is to say, while the Mishnah records rules governing the conduct of the holy life of Israel, the holy people, the Talmud concerns itself with the details of the Mishnah. The one is descriptive and free-standing, the other analytical and contingent. Were there no Mishnah, there would be no Talmud. But what is the message of the method, which is to insist upon the Mishnah's near-monopoly over serious discourse?

To begin with, the very character of the Talmud tells us the sages' view of the Mishnah. The Mishnah presented itself to them as constitutive, the text of ultimate concern. So, in our instance, the Mishnah speaks of a quarrel over a coat, the Talmud, of the Mishnah's provision of an oath as a means of settling the quarrel in a fair way: substance transformed into process. What the framers of the Bavli wished to say about the Mishnah will guide us toward the definition of the message of their method, but it will not tell us what that message was, or why it was important. A long process of close study of texts is required to guide us toward the center of matters. The upshot is simple. We may speak about "the Talmud," its voice, its purposes, its mode of constructing a view of the Israelite world. The reason is that, when we claim "the Talmud" speaks, we replicate both the main lines of chronology and the literary character of the document. These point toward the formation of the bulk of materials — its units of discourse — in a process lasting (to take a guess) about half a century, prior to the ultimate arrangement of these units of discourse around passages of the Mishnah and the closure and redaction of the whole into the document we now know.

VII. TRAITS OF AGGLUTINATIVE DISCOURSE IN THE BAVLI

We are now able to state matters in a simple way. The Talmud of Babylonia makes use of two distinct principles for the formation of large-scale composites of distinct compositions, and the framers of the document very rarely set forth a composition on its own, standing without clear ties to a larger context. One is the assembly of compositions that serve for Mishnah-exegesis; the other, what I call "agglutinative discourse," as I shall now explain.

Ordinarily, first, they brought together distinct and free-standing compositions in the service of Mishnah-exegesis and amplification of law originating in a Mishnah-paragraph under analysis. For that purpose they would then draw upon already-written compositions, which would be adduced as cases, statements of principles, fully-exposed analyses, inclusive of debate and argument, in the service of that analysis. So all of the compositions in a given composite would serve the governing analytical or propositional purpose of the framer of the composite. Where a composition appears to shade over into a direction of its own, that very quickly is seen to serve as a footnote or even an appendix to the composite at hand.

We have now seen that, second, in addition to propositional and even analytical composites, the framers of the Bavli also formed compositions into thematic composites, and on the face of it, this second type of composite presents the appearance of a miscellany. But, far from forming a mere rubbish heap of this and that, this other type of composite proves not at all miscellaneous. Clear, governing, and entirely predictable principles allow us to explain how one composition is joined to another. Ordinarily, a sizable miscellany forms a topical appendix, or a protracted footnote to a subject. It will tell us more about a subject that the Mishnah addresses. Or it will richly illustrate a principle that the Mishnah means to set forth through its cases and examples. In that sense, the miscellaneous kind of composite is set forth as Mishnah-commentary of a particular kind.

As we have seen, an agglutinative composite may be formed by appeal to a common theme, ordinarily stated by the Mishnah or at least suggested by its contents, and several closely-related themes will then come under exposition in a massive miscellany. One common theme will be a passage of Scripture, systematically examined. A subordinate principle of agglutination will join composites attributed to the same authority or tradent, though it would be unusual for the compositions so joined to deal with entirely unrelated topics. So the principal point of differentiation between propositional composites and agglutinative ones is that the form analyze a problem, the latter illustrate a theme or even a proposition.

It follows that two modes of forming composites serve the framers of the Bavli, the paramount, propositional and analytical mode, and the subordinate, agglutinative sort. The one joins together a variety of distinct compositions into a propositional statement, commonly enriched with analytical initiatives, and frequently bearing a burden of footnotes and appendices. The other combines distinct compositions into a thematic composite, the proposition of which is ordinarily rather general and commonplace.

A second principle of agglutinative composite-making appeals to common attributions, though when two or more compositions are joined into a composite because they are assigned to the same authority or tradental chain, they very likely will also bear in common an interest in a single theme, if not in a uniform proposition in connection with that theme.

One might be tempted to propose that agglutinative discourse governs the treatment of one type of subject matter, theology or exegesis, but not another, the more prominent, and generally held, normative one, of law. To demonstrate that the distinction between lore and law (*Aggadah* and *Halakhah*) makes no difference in whether or not compositions will be linked into composites by appeal to propositional-analytical or merely agglutinative principles of formation, let me give a fine example of an agglutinative legal ("Halakhic") passage, which shows beyond any doubt that there is no important point of distinction, so far as agglutinative discourse is concerned, between compositions and sub-composites of one kind and of the other. We find in both types of subject-matter, Halakhic and Aggadic, precisely the same literary traits of composite-making. Here the compositions are joined agglutinatively, by reference to a common subject-matter; but the composite that results does not make a point, e.g. of proposition, analysis, or argument. Rather, it serves to illustrate a theme, very much the way the massive miscellanies in tractates Berakhot and Sanhedrin illustrate a theme. We deal with Bavli Baba Batra chapter Five.

BAVLI BABA BATRA 5:11

A. Said Rabban Simeon b. Gamaliel, "Under what circumstances?

B. "In the case of liquid measures.

C. "But in the case of dry measures, it is not necessary"

D. [88B] And [a shopkeeper] is liable to let the scales go down by a handbreadth [to the buyer's advantage].

E. [If] he was measuring out for him exactly, he has to give him an overweight —

F. one part in ten for liquid measure,

G. one part in twenty for dry measure.

H. In a place in which they are accustomed to measure with small measures, one must not measure with large measures;

I. with large ones, one must not measure with small;

J. [in a place in which it is customary] to smooth down [what is in the measure], one should not heap it up;

K. to heap it up, one should not smooth it down.

III.1 A. In a place in which they are accustomed to measure with small measures, one must not measure with large measures; with large ones, one must not measure with small; in a place in which it is customary to smooth down what is in the measure, one should not heap it up; to heap it up, one should not smooth it down:

B. *Our rabbis have taught on Tannaite authority:*

C. How on the basis of Scripture do we know that in a place in which it is customary to smooth down what is in the measure, one should not heap it up; to heap it up, one should not smooth it down? Scripture says, "A perfect measure" (Dt. 25:15). [Slotki: deviating from the usual practice the buyer or the seller may defraud or mislead others.]

D. And how do we know that if one said, "Lo, where it is customary to heap up, I will level it off, and reduce the price,' or, in a place where they level, I will heap it up, and raise the price," they do not listen to him [he may not do so]?

E. Scripture says, "A perfect and just measure you shall have" (Dt. 25:15).

2. A. *Our rabbis have taught on Tannaite authority:*

B. How on the basis of Scripture do we know that in a place where the practice is to allow an overweight, they do not give the exact weight, and in a place in which they give an exact weight, they do not give an overweight?

C. Scripture says, "A perfect weight" (Dt. 25:15).

D. And how on the basis of Scripture do we know that if one said in a place in which they give an overweight, "Lo, I shall give an exact weight and charge him less," or in a place in which they give an exact weight, "Lo, I shall give him an overweight and add to the price," they do not listen to him?

E. Scripture says, "A perfect weight and a just one" (Dt. 25:15).

F. Said R. Judah of Sura, "'You shall not have anything in your house' (Dt. 25:14). Why? Because of your 'diverse weights' (Dt. 25:13). But if you keep 'a perfect and just weight,' you shall have' (Dt. 25:15) things, 'if a perfect and just measure, you shall have....'"

There is no problem in explaining why No. 2 is tacked on to No. 1. The proposition is the same, so is the form. But what follows is another matter, since we are now going to entertain a different proposition altogether.

3. A. *Our rabbis have taught on Tannaite authority:*

B. "You shall have...:" this teaches that they appoint market supervisors to oversee measures, but they do not appoint market supervisors to control prices.

No. 4 will now illustrate the foregoing.

4. A. *The household of the patriarch appointed market supervisors to oversee measures and to control prices. Said Samuel to Qarna, 'Go, repeat the Tannaite rule to them:* they appoint market supervisors to oversee measures, but they do not appoint market supervisors to control prices.

B. He went out and instructed them: "They appoint market supervisors to oversee measures and to control prices."

C. He said to him, "What do they call you? Qarna [horn]? Let a horn grow out of your eye." A horn grew out of his eye.

D. And as for Qarna, in accord with what authority did he reach this conclusion?

E. It was in accord with what Rammi bar Hama said R.

Isaac said, "They appoint market supervisors to oversee measures and to control prices, on account of crooks."

Now we have a miscellany, meaning, a set of compositions, each standing on its own foundation, all making clearly-articulated points, none related except in a shared theme to what stands fore or aft. What we shall also observe is sub-sets, clearly joined to one another, but connected to the larger context only by the general theme. These subsets do not require explicit specification, being obvious on the face of it.

5. A. *Our rabbis have taught on Tannaite authority:*
B. If somebody ordered a litra, he should measure out a litra; if he ordered a half-litra, he should measure out for him a half litra; a quarter-litra, he should measure out a quarter.
C. *So what does that passage tell us?*
D. *It is that we provide weights in these denominations.*

6. A. *Our rabbis have taught on Tannaite authority:*
B. If someone ordered three quarters of a litra, he should not say to him, "Weigh out for me three quarters of a litra one by one," but he should say to him, "Weight out a litra for me but leave out a quarter-litra with the meat" [Slotki: on the other scale].

7 A. *Our rabbis have taught on Tannaite authority:*
B. If someone wanted to order ten litras, he should not say to him, "Weigh them out for me one by one and allow an overweight for each," but all of them are weighed together, with one overweight covering the whole order [cf. T. B.B. 5:9B-I]

8. A. *Our rabbis have taught on Tannaite authority:*
B. [Slotki:] The hollow handle in which the tongue of the balance rests must be suspended in the air three handbreadths [removed from the roof from which the balance hangs], and it must be three handbreadths above the ground.
C. The beam and the rope that goes with it should be twelve handbreadths, and the balances of wool dealers and glass ware dealers must be suspended two hand-

breadths in the air from the ceiling and two above the ground. The beams and ropes that go with them must be nine handbreadths in length. The balance of a shopkeeper and a householder must be suspended a handbreadth in the air from above and a handbreadth above the ground. The beam and ropes that go with them must be six handbreadths. A gold balance must be suspended three fingerbreadths in the air from above and three above the ground. I don't know the length of the beam and the cords.

D. *What kind of balance is the one mentioned first [before the specific rulings for those of the wool dealers, glass ware dealers, and so on]?*

E. **[89B]** *Said R. Pappa, "The one used for heavy pieces of metal."*

9. A. Said R. Mani bar Patish, "Just as they have specified certain restrictions with regard to disqualifying balances for commercial purposes, so they have laid down disqualifications with regard to their constituting utensils for the purpose of receiving cultic uncleanness."

B. *What does he tell us that we do not learn from the following:* **The cord of the scales of the storekeepers and [or] of householders — [to be susceptible to uncleanness must be in length at least] a handbreadth. A handle of the ax at its front — a handbreadth. The projection of the shaft of a pair of compasses — a handbreadth. The shaft of a stonemason's chisel — a handbreadth A cord of the balances of wool dealers and of glass weighers — two handbreadths. The shaft of a millstone chisel — two handbreadths. The battle ax of the legions — two handbreadths. The goldsmith's hammer — two handbreadths. And of the carpenters — three handbreadths] [M. Kel. 29:5-6]***!* [Slotki: since this restriction has been applied to one kind of balance, are not the other kinds of balance to be implied?]

C. The statement that he made is necessary to deal with the sizes of the beam and cords [that are not dealt with at the parallel].

A subset now follows, Nos. 10-13, glossed by No. 14.

10. A. *Our rabbis have taught on Tannaite authority:*

B. They make weights out of neither tin or led or alloy but of stone or glass.

11. A. *Our rabbis have taught on Tannaite authority:*

B. They make the strike not out of a board, because it is light, nor out of metal, because it is heavy, but out of olive, nut, sycamore, or box wood.

12. A. *Our rabbis have taught on Tannaite authority:*

B. They do not make the strike thick on one side and thin on the other.

C. They do not make the strike with a single quick movement, because striking in that way brings loss to the seller and advantage to the buyer, nor very slowly, since this is a loss to the buyer but a benefit to the seller.

D. In regard to all of these shady practices, said Rabban Yohanan b. Zakkai, "Woe is me if I speak, woe is me if I do not speak. If I speak, then sharpies will learn from me, and if I don't speak, then the sharpers will say, 'The disciples of sages haven't got the slightest idea what we are doing.'"

13. A. *The question was raised: "So did he speak of them or didn't he?"*

B. Said R. Samuel bar R. Isaac, "He did speak of them: 'For the ways of the Lord are right, and the just walk in them; but transgressors stumble therein' (Hos. 14:10)."

14. A. *Our rabbis have taught on Tannaite authority:*

B. "You shall do no unrighteousness in judgment, in surveying, weight, or in measure" (Lev. 19:35):

C. "in surveying:" these refers to surveying the real estate, meaning, one should not measure for one party in the dry season and another in the rainy season.

D. "weight:" one should not keep one's weights in salt.

E. "in measure" (Lev. 19:35): one should not make the liquid form a head.

F. And that yields an argument a fortiori: if with reference to a mere "measure" [Lev. 19:35), which is merely one sixth of a log, the Torah demanded meticulous attention, how much the more so must one give meticulous case in measuring out a hin, half a hin, a third of a hin, a quarter of a hin, a log, a half a log, a quarter of a log, a toman, half a toman, and an uqla.

15. A. Said R. Judah said Rab, "It is forbidden for someone to keep in his house a measure that is either smaller or larger than the norm, even for the purpose of a piss pot."

B. *Said R. Pappa, "But we have stated that rule only in a place where measures are not properly marked with a seal, but where they are properly sealed, they are permitted, since, if the purchaser sees no mark, he is not going to accept their use. And even in a place where measures are not properly marked with a seal, we have stated that rule only in a case in which they are not supervised [by administrative officers of the market], but if they are ordinarily supervised, we should have no objection."*

C. *But that is not the case, for sometimes the buyer may come by at twilight and may happen to take a faulty measure. And so too that has been taught on Tannaite authority:* It is forbidden for someone to keep in his house a measure that is either smaller or larger than the norm, even for the purpose of a piss pot. But he may make a seah measure, a tarqab, a half tarqab, a qab, a half qab, a quarter qab, a toman, **[90B]** and an ukla measure. How much is an uqla-measure? It is a fifth of a quarter of a qab. In the case of liquid measures, one may make a hin, a half hin, third hin, quarter hin, log, half log, quarter log, eighth log, and eight of an eighth, which is a qortob.

D. *So why shouldn't someone also make a double-qab measure?*

E. *It might be confused with a tarqab.*

F. *Therefore people may err by as much as a third.*

G. *If so, then a qab also people should not make, since they might confused it with a half-tarqab. Rather, as to a double qab, this is the reason that one is not to make it, specifically, that one will confused it with a half tarqab.*

H. *And this proves that one may err by a quarter.*

I. *If so, a half toman and an ukla measure are things people should not make.* [Slotki: the difference between a half toman, a sixteen qab, and an ukla, a twentieth qab, is only one eightieth of a qab, which is a fifth of the half toman, less than a quarter, so that these two measures could certainly be mistaken for one another.]

J. *Said R. Pappa, "With small measures people are quite expert."*

K. *What about a third of a hin and a fourth of a hin — shouldn't people be forbidden to make these?*

L. *Since these were utilized in the sanctuary, rabbis made no decree in their regard.*

M. *Well, shouldn't there be a precautionary decree with respect to the sanctuary?*

N. *The priests are meticulous in their work.*

16. A. Said Samuel, "They may not increase the size of the measures [whether or not people concur] by more than a sixth, nor the coins by more than a sixth, and he who makes a profit must not profit by more than a sixth."

B. What is the operative consideration for the first of these three rulings?

C. *If we say that it is because the market prices will rise, then for that same consideration, it should not be permitted to increase the size of the measures even by a sixth. And if the operative consideration is overreaching, so that the transaction should not have to be annulled, did not* Raba say, "One can retract from an agreement that involves fraud in measure, weight, or number, even though it is less than the standard, a sixth, of overreaching." *And if the operative consideration is that the dealer may not incur any loss, then is the whole purpose of the law to guard him from loss? Is he not entitled to make a profit? But* "buy and sell at no profit, merely to be called a merchant!"

D. *Rather, said R. Hisda, "Samuel identified a verse of Scripture and interpreted it,* 'And the shekel shall be twenty gerahs, twenty sheqels, twenty-five sheqels, ten and five sheqels shall be your maneh' (Ez. 45:12). **[90B]** *Now was the maneh to be two hundred forty denars?* [But it is supposed to be twenty five sheqels or a hundred denars (Cashdan).] *But three facts are to be inferred from this statement:* [1] the maneh used in the sanctuary is worth double what the maneh is usually worth; [2] they may not increase the size of the measures [whether or not people concur] by more than a sixth, and [3] the sixth is added over and above the original [so to add a sixth, the original is divided into five parts and another part of equal value, making a sixth one, then is added to it, so the maneh consisted of 240 denars (Cashdan, *Menahot*)]."

17. A. *R. Pappa bar Samuel ordained a measure of three qepizi. They said to him,* "Lo, said Samuel, 'They may not increase the size of the measures [whether or not people concur] by more than a sixth'!"

B. *He said to them, "What I am ordaining is an entirely new measure." He sent it to Pumbedita, and they did not adopt it. He sent it to Papunia and they adopted it, naming it the Pappa-measure.*

Any doubt that we are dealing with a miscellany is removed by what follows, which in no way pertains to the foregoing in any detail. And yet it is introduced for a very clear purpose, which is to make a point about a common theme and proposition: fair-dealing in the market, giving and getting true value.

18. A. *Our rabbis have taught on Tannaite authority:*

B. Concerning those who store up produce, lend money on usury, falsify measures, and price-gouge, Scripture says, "Saying, when will the new moon be gone, that we may sell grain, and the Sabbath, that we may set forth grain? Making the ephah small and the shekel great and falsifying the balances of deceit" (Amos 8:5). And in their regard, Scripture states, "The Lord has sworn by the pride of Jacob, surely I will never forget any of their works" (Amos 8:7).

C. *What would be an example of those who store up produce?*

D. *Said R. Yohanan, "Like Shabbetai the produce-hoarder."*

19. A. *The father of Samuel would sell produce at the early market price when the early market price prevailed [that is, cheap, so keeping prices down through the year (Slotki)]. Samuel his son held the produce back and sold it when the late market prices prevailed, but at the early market price.*

F. *They sent word from there, "The father is better than the son. How come? Prices that have been held down remain down."*

20. A. Said Rab, "Someone may store up his own

produce" [but may not hoard for trading purposes (Slotki)].

B. *So too it has been taught on Tannaite authority:*

C. [Following Tosefta's version:] They do not hoard in the Land of Israel things upon which life depends, for example, wine, oil, fine flour, and produce. But things upon which life does not depend, for instance, cummin and spice, lo, this is permitted. And they put things in storage for three years, the eve of the seventh year, the seventh year itself, and the year after the seventh year.

D. Under what circumstances.

E. In the case of that which one purchases in the market.

F. But in the case of what one puts aside from what he himself has grown, even for a period of ten years it is permitted.

G. But in a year of famine even a qab of carobs one should not put into storage, because he brings a curse on the prices [by forcing them upward through artificial demand] [T. A.Z. 4:1A-G].

21. A. *Said R. Yosé b. R. Hanina to Puga his servant, "Go, store up fruit for me for the next three years: the eve of the Sabbatical year, the Sabbatical year, and the year after the Sabbatical year."*

22. A. *Our rabbis have taught on Tannaite authority:*

B. They do not export from the Land of Israel to Syria things upon which life depends, for example, wine, oil, and fine flour.

C. R. Judah b. Batera says, "I say that they export wine to Syria, because in doing so, one diminishes silliness [in the Land of Israel]."

D. Just as they do not export to Syria, so they do not export from one hyparchy to another.

E. And R. Judah permits doing so [91A] from one hyparchy to another [T. A.Z. 4:2].

23. A. *Our rabbis have taught on Tannaite authority:*

B. They are not to make a profit in the land of Israel from the necessities of life, for instance, wine, oil, and flour.

C. They said concerning R. Eleazar b. Azariah

that he would make a profit from wine and oil all his life [T. A.Z. 4:1H-J].

D. *In the matter of wine, he concurred with the view of R. Judah [b. Batera], and in the matter of oil, as it happens, in the place where R. Eleazar b. Azariah lived, oil was abundant.*

24. A. Our rabbis have taught on Tannaite authority:

B. People are not to profit from eggs twice.

C. *Said Mari bar Mari, "There was a dispute between Rab and Samuel. One says, 'Two for one' [selling for two what was bought for one], and the other said, 'Selling by a dealer to a dealer' [making two profits on the same object]."*

25. A. Our rabbis have taught on Tannaite authority:

B. They sound the alarm on account of a collapse in the market in trading goods even on the Sabbath.

C. Said R. Yohanan, "For instance, linen clothing in Babylonia and wine and oil in the Land of Israel."

D. *Said R. Joseph, "But that is the case when these are so cheap that ten go for the price of six."*

26. A. Our rabbis have taught on Tannaite authority:

B. A person is not allowed to emigrate from the Land of Israel unless wheat goes at the price of two seahs for a sela.

C. Said R. Simeon, "Under what circumstances? Only in a case in which he does not find any to buy even at that price. But if he finds some to buy at that price, even if a seah of grain goes for a sela, he should not emigrate."

D. And so did R. Simeon bar Yohai say, "Elimelech, Machlon and Kilion were the great men of his time, and one of those who sustained the generation. But because he went abroad, he and his sons died in famine. But all the Israelites were able to survive on their own land, as it is said, 'and when they came to Bethlehem, the whole town was stirred because of them' (Ruth 1:19). This teaches that all of the town had survived, but he and his sons had died in the famine" [T. A.Z. 4:4A-H].

27. A. "and when they came to Bethlehem, the whole town was stirred because of them, and the women said, 'Is this Naomi'" (Ruth 1:19):

B. *What is the meaning of the phrase, "Is this Naomi"?*

C. Said R. Isaac, "They said, 'Did you see what happened to Naomi, who emigrated from the Land for a foreign country?'"

28. A. And said R. Isaac, "The day that Ruth the Moabite emigrated from the Land to a foreign land, the wife of Boaz died. *That is in line with what people say: 'Before a person dies, his successor as master of the house is appointed.'"*

29. A. Said Rabbah bar R. Huna said Rab, "Isban is the same as Boaz."

B. *So what in the world does that mean?*

C. *It is in line with what Rabbah b. R. Huna further said, for* said Rabbah bar R. Huna said Rab, "Boaz made for his sons a hundred and twenty wedding banquets: 'And Isban had thirty sons and thirty daughters he sent abroad, and thirty daughters he brought from abroad for his sons, and he judged Israel seven years' (Judges 12:9). For each one of them he made two wedding feasts, one in the household of the father, the other in the household of the father in law. But to none of them did he invite Manoah, for he said, 'How will that barren mule ever repay my hospitality?' And all of them died in his lifetime. That is in line with what people say, *'In your lifetime you begot sixty? What good are the sixty? Marry again and get another one, brighter than all sixty.'"*

30. A. Said R. Hanan bar Raba said Rab, "Elimelech and Salmon and 'such a one' [Ruth 4:1] and the father of Naomi were all sons of Nahshon b. Amminadab [Ex. 6:23, Num. 10:14]."

B. *So what in the world does that mean?*

C. It is that even one who has a substantial store of unearned merit gained from his answers, it will serve him no good when he emigrates from the Land to a foreign land."

31. A. And said R. Hanan bar Raba said Rab, *"The mother of Abraham was named Amathelai, daughter of Karnebo; the name of the mother of Haman was Amatehilai, daughter of Orabti; and the mnemonic will be, 'unclean to the unclean, clean to the clean.' The mother of David was Nizbeth daughter of Adael, the mother of Samson was Zlelponit, and his sister was Nasyan."*

B. *So what?*

C. For answering heretics.

32. A. And said R. Hanan bar Raba said Rab, "For ten years our father, Abraham, was kept in prison, three in Kuta, seven in Kardu."

B. *And R. Dimi of Nehardea repeats the matter in reverse order.*

C. *Said R. Hisda, "The lesser Kuta is the same as Ur of the Chaldees [Gen. 11:31]."*

33. A. And said R. Hanan bar Raba said Rab, "The day on which our father, Abraham, died, all of the principal authorities of the nations of the world formed a line and said, 'Woe is the world that has lost **[91B]** its leader, woe to the ship that has lost its helmsman.'"

34. A. "And you are exalted as head above all" (1 Chr. 29:11):

B. *Said R. Hanan bar Raba said Rab, "Even the superintendent of the water supply is appointed by Heaven."*

35. A. Said R. Hiyya bar Abin said R. Joshua b. Qorhah, "God forbid! Even if [Elimelech and his family] had found bran, they would never have emigrated. So why were they punished? Because they should have besought mercy for their generation but filed to do so: 'When you cry, let them that you have gathered deliver you' (Is. 57:13)."

36. A. Said Rabbah bar bar Hannah said R. Yohanan, "This [prohibition against emigration] has been taught only when money is cheap [and abundant] and produce expensive, but when money is expensive [and not to be found, there being no capital], even if four seahs cost only a sela, it is permitted to emigration."

B. *Said R. Yohanan, "I remember when four seahs of grain cost a sela and many died of starvation in Tiberias, not having an issar for bread."*

C. *And said R. Yohanan, "I remember when workmen wouldn't agree to work on the east side of town, where workers were dying because of the scent of bread [which they could not afford to buy]."*

37. A. *And said R. Yohanan, "I remember when a child would break open a carob pod and a line of honey would run over both his arms."*

B. *And said R. Eleazar, "I remember when a raven would grab a piece of meat and a line of oil would run down from* the top of the wall to the ground."

C. And said R. Yohanan, "I remember when boys and girls would promenade in the market at the each of sixteen or seventeen and not sin."

D. And said R. Yohanan, "I remember when they would say in the house of study, 'Who agrees with them falls into their power, who trusts in them — what is his becomes theirs.'"

38. A. It is written, "Mahlon and Chilion" (Ruth 1:2) and it is written "Joash and Saraph" (1 Chr. 4:22)!

B. Rab and Samuel —

C. One said, "Their names really were Mahlon and Chilion, and why were they called Joash? Because they despaired hope of redemption [the words for Joash and despair using the same letters], and Saraph? because they become liable by the decree of the Omnipresent to be burned."

D. And the other said, "Their names really were Joash and Saraph, but they were called Mahlon and Chilion, Mahlon, because they profaned their bodies [the words for Mahlon and profane using the same letters], and Chilion, because they were condemned by the Omnipresent to destruction [the words for destruction and Chilion using the same letters]."

E. *It has been taught on Tannaite authority in accord with the view of him who said that their names really were Mahlon and Chilion. For it has been taught on Tannaite authority:* What is the meaning of the verse, "And Jokim and the men of Cozeba and Joash and Saraph, who had dominion in Moab, and Jashubilehem, and the things are ancient"?1 Chr. 4:22)?

F. "Jokim:" this refers to Joshua, who kept his oath to the men of Gibeon [Josh. 9:15, 26].

G. "and the men of Cozeba:" these are the men of Gibeon who lied to Joshua [the words for lie and Cozeba using the same letters] [Josh. 9:4].

H. "and Joash and Saraph:" Their names really were Mahlon and Chilion, and why were they called Joash? Because they despaired hope of redemption [the words for Joash and despair using the same letters], and Saraph? because they become liable by the decree of the Omnipresent to be burned.

The Bavli's Massive Miscellanies 97

I. "who had dominion in Moab:" they married wives of the women of Moab.

J. "and Jashubilehem:" this refers to Ruth of Moab, who had returned [using letters that are shared with Jashub] and remained in Bethlehem of Judah.

K. "and the things are ancient:" these things were stated by the Ancient of Days.

39. A. "These were the potters and those that dwelt among plantations and hedges; there they dwelt occupied in the kings work" (1 Chr. 4:23):

B. "These were the potters:" this refers to the sons of Jonadab, son of Rahab, who kept the oath of their father [Jer. 35:6].

C. "and those that dwelt among plantations:" this speaks of Solomon, who in his rule was like a fecund plant.

D. "and hedges:" this refers to the Sanhedrin, who hedged in the breaches in Israel.

E. "there they dwelt occupied in the kings work:" this speaks of Ruth of Moab, who lived to see the rule of Solomon, her grandson's grandson: "And Solomon caused a throne to be set up for the king's mother" (1 Kgs. 2:19), in which connection R. Eleazar said, "For the mother of the dynasty."

40. A. *Our rabbis have taught on Tannaite authority:*

B. "And you shall eat of the produce, the old store" (Lev. 25:22) — without requiring preservatives.

C. *What is the meaning of* without requiring preservatives?

D. R. Nahman said, "Without grain worms."

E. And R. Sheshet said, "Without blast."

F. *It has been taught on Tannaite authority in accord with the view of R. Sheshet, and it has been taught on Tannaite authority in accord with the view of R. Nahman.*

G. *It has been taught on Tannaite authority in accord with the view of R. Nahman:*

H. "And you shall eat the old store" (Lev. 25:22) — might one suppose that the sense is that the Israelites will be eager for the new produce because last year's has been destroyed [by the grain worm]? Scripture says, "until her produce came in," that is, until the produce will come on its own [without an early, forced harvest (Slotki)].

I. *It has been taught on Tannaite authority in accord with the view of R. Sheshet:*

J. "And you shall eat of the produce, the old store" (Lev. 25:22) — might one suppose that the sense is that the Israelites will be eager for the new produce because last year's has been spoiled [Slotki: by the blast]? Scripture states, "until her produce came in," that is, until the new crop will come in the natural way.

41. A. *Our rabbis have taught on Tannaite authority:*

B. "And you shall eat old store long kept" (Lev. 26:10) — whatever is of an older vintage than its fellow is better in quality than its fellow.

C. I know that that is so only of things that are ordinarily aged. What about things that are not ordinarily aged?

D. Scripture is explicit: "old store long kept" (Lev. 26:10) — in all cases.

42. A. "And you shall bring forth the old from before the new" (Lev. 26:10) —

B. this teaches that the storehouses will be full of last year's crop, and the threshing floors, this year's crop, and the Israelites will say, "How are we going to remove the one before the other?"

C. *Said R. Pappa, "Everything is better when aged, except for dates, beer, and fish-hash."*

III.1, 2 provide a scriptural basis for the rule and principle of the Mishnah. The key-verse of No. 2 accounts for the inclusion of No. 3, which carries in its wake No. 4. Further Tannaite thematic supplements are at Nos. 5-8. No. 8 is glossed by No. 9, and then Nos. 10-12+13, 14 continue the Tannaite supplement. Carrying forward the general theme at hand, Nos. 15-42 form a miscellany built around the general theme before us. I see no formal differences between the miscellany at hand and those we have already examined. The only difference is subject-matter — but not *classification of subject-matter*. Is it possible, then, to state the propositions of the sub-

The Bavli's Massive Miscellanies 99

sets of the miscellany? These seem to me to state the paramount proposals:

1. People are to employ honest measures and when selling, to give accurate and honest measures: Nos. 5-17.

2. People are not to take advantage of shortages nor create shortages: Nos. 18-25.

3. If there are shortages, people are to try to remain in the Land of Israel if they possibly can: Nos. 26-28+29-36, 37-40.

One might argue that the combination of the set yields the syllogism that honesty in buying and selling the necessities of life is what makes possible Israel's possession of the Holy Land, but that does not seem to me a plausible proposal. I see here only a thematic composite, all the numbered items addressed to that single theme, perhaps, furthermore, with a number of cogent propositions joining some of compositions as well.

Let us now examine a reprise of the whole, once more in outline form. This underscores the rationality of the selection and arrangement of the composite. I underline passages of the Mishnah that are not taken up in the Talmud.

L. MISHNAH-TRACTATE BABA BATRA 5:10-11

A. <u>A WHOLESALER MUST CLEAN OFF HIS MEASURES ONCE EVERY THIRTY DAYS, AND A HOUSEHOLDER ONCE EVERY TWELVE MONTHS. RABBAN SIMEON B. GAMALIEL SAYS, "MATTERS ARE JUST THE OPPOSITE."</u> THE STOREKEEPER CLEANS OFF HIS MEASURES TWICE A WEEK, POLISHES HIS WEIGHTS ONCE A WEEK, AND CLEANS HIS SCALES AFTER EACH AND EVERY WEIGHING. <u>SAID RABBAN SIMEON B. GAMALIEL, "UNDER WHAT CIRCUMSTANCES? IN THE CASE OF LIQUID MEASURES. BUT IN THE CASE OF DRY MEASURES, IT IS NOT NECESSARY."</u>

AND A SHOPKEEPER IS LIABLE TO LET THE

SCALES GO DOWN BY A HANDBREADTH TO THE BUYER'S ADVANTAGE.

1. I:1: What is the source of this law in Scripture? Said R. Simeon b. Laqish, "Said Scripture, 'A perfect and just measure shall you have' (Deut. 25:15) — justify your weight by giving something of your own."

2. I:2: How much must be added to the weight?

B. IF HE WAS MEASURING OUT FOR HIM EXACTLY, HE HAS TO GIVE HIM AN OVERWEIGHT — ONE PART IN TEN FOR LIQUID MEASURE, ONE PART IN TWENTY FOR DRY MEASURE.

1. II:1: The question was raised, What is the sense of this statement? One part in ten for every ten units of liquid measure, one part in twenty for every twenty dry measure, or does it mean, one part in ten for every ten units of liquid and a tenth unit for every twenty units of dry?

C. THE PENALTY FOR FALSIFYING MEASURES COMPARED WITH PENALTIES FOR OTHER TRANSGRESSIONS

2. II:2: Said R. Levi, "The punishment for falsifying measures is more stringent than that for consanguineous relationships. In the latter case at Lev. 18:6 we find 'this,' while in the former, 'these,' with additional letters signifying additional penalty.

3. II:3: And said R. Levi, "Robbing a commoner is worse than robbing the Most High, for in the former case, 'sin' comes before 'trespass' 'If any one sin and commit a trespass' (Lev. 5:20) refers to robbing from a common person, while in the latter, trespass comes before sin 'if one commit a trespass and sin through error,' (Lev. 5:15) meaning one is guilty of sin only after he has committed the sacrilege."

4. II:4: And said R. Levi, "Come and see that the quality of the Holy One, blessed be He, is not like the quality of a mortal. The Holy One, blessed be He, blessed Israel using twenty-two letters of the Hebrew alphabet, while he curses them only with eight."

D. IN A PLACE IN WHICH THEY ARE AC-

CUSTOMED TO MEASURE WITH SMALL MEASURES, ONE MUST NOT MEASURE WITH LARGE MEASURES; WITH LARGE ONES, ONE MUST NOT MEASURE WITH SMALL; IN A PLACE IN WHICH IT IS CUSTOMARY TO SMOOTH DOWN WHAT IS IN THE MEASURE, ONE SHOULD NOT HEAP IT UP; TO HEAP IT UP, ONE SHOULD NOT SMOOTH IT DOWN.

1. III:1: How on the basis of Scripture do we know that in a place in which it is customary to smooth down what is in the measure, one should not heap it up; to heap it up, one should not smooth it down? Scripture says, "A perfect measure" (Deut. 25:15). Deviating from the usual practice the buyer or the seller may defraud or mislead others.

2. III:2: How on the basis of Scripture do we know that in a place where the practice is to allow an overweight, they do not give the exact weight, and in a place in which they give an exact weight, they do not give an overweight?

   a. III:3: "You shall have...": this teaches that they appoint market supervisors to oversee measures, but they do not appoint market supervisors to control prices.

   b. III:4: The household of the patriarch appointed market supervisors to oversee measures and to control prices. Said Samuel to Qarna, "Go, repeat the Tannaite rule to them: They appoint market supervisors to oversee measures, but they do not appoint market supervisors to control prices.

3. III:5: If somebody ordered a litra, he should measure out a litra; if he ordered a half-litra, he should measure out for him a half-litra; a quarter-litra, he should measure out a quarter.

4. III:6: If someone ordered three-quarters of a litra, he should not say to him, "Weigh out for me three-quarters of a litra one by one," but he should say to him, "Weight out a litra for me but leave out a quarter-litra with the meat" on the other scale.

5. III:7: If someone wanted to order ten litras, he should not say to him, "Weigh them out for me

one by one and allow an overweight for each," but all of them are weighed together, with one overweight covering the whole order cf. T. B.B. 5:9B-I.

E. THE CORRECT WEIGHTS AND MEASURES: DEFINITIONS

1. III:8: The hollow handle in which the tongue of the balance rests must be suspended in the air three handbreadths removed from the roof from which the balance hangs, and it must be three handbreadths above the ground.

2. III:9: Said R. Mani bar Patish, "Just as they have specified certain restrictions with regard to disqualifying balances for commercial purposes, so they have laid down disqualifications with regard to their constituting utensils for the purpose of receiving cultic uncleanness."

3. III:10: They make weights out of neither tin or lead or alloy but of stone or glass.

4. III:11: They make the strike not out of a board, because it is light, nor out of metal, because it is heavy, but out of olive, nut, sycamore, or box wood.

5. III:12: They do not make the strike thick on one side and thin on the other.

    a. III:13: Gloss of foregoing.

F. FALSIFYING WEIGHTS AND MEASURES

1. III:14: "You shall do no unrighteousness in judgment, in surveying, weight, or in measure" (Lev. 19:35): "In surveying": these refers to surveying the real estate, meaning, one should not measure for one party in the dry season and another in the rainy season. "Weight": one should not keep one's weights in salt.

2. III:15: Said R. Judah said Rab, "It is forbidden for someone to keep in his house a measure that is either smaller or larger than the norm, even for the purpose of a piss pot."

3. III:16: Said Samuel, "They may not increase the size of the measures whether or not people concur by more than a sixth, nor the coins by more than a sixth, and he who makes a profit must not profit by more than a sixth."

    a. III:17: R. Pappa bar Samuel ordained

a measure of three qepizi. They said to him, "Lo, said Samuel, 'They may not increase the size of the measures whether or not people concur by more than a sixth'!"

G. HOARDING; MANIPULATING THE MARKET PRICES

1. III:18: Concerning those who store up produce, lend money on usury, falsify measures, and price gouge, Scripture says, "Saying, when will the new moon be gone, that we may sell grain, and the Sabbath, that we may set forth grain? Making the ephah small and the shekel great and falsifying the balances of deceit" (Amos 8:5). And in their regard, Scripture states, "The Lord has sworn by the pride of Jacob, surely I will never forget any of their works" (Amos 8:7).

   a. III:19: The father of Samuel would sell produce at the early market price when the early market price prevailed that is, cheap, so keeping prices down through the year. Samuel his son held the produce back and sold it when the late market prices prevailed, but at the early market price.

2. III:20: Said Rab, "Someone may store up his own produce" but may not hoard for trading purposes."

   a. III:21: Said R. Yosé b. R. Hanina to Puga his servant, "Go, store up fruit for me for the next three years: the eve of the Sabbatical Year, the Sabbatical Year, and the year after the Sabbatical Year."

3. III:22: They do not export from the Land of Israel to Syria things upon which life depends, for example, wine, oil, and fine flour.

4. III:23 They are not to make a profit in the Land of Israel from the necessities of life, for instance, wine, oil, and flour.

5. III:24: People are not to profit from eggs twice.

6. III:25: They sound the alarm on account of a collapse in the market in trading goods even on the Sabbath.

H. MIGRATION FROM THE LAND OF ISRAEL BY REASON OF FAMINE. THE CASE OF RUTH'S FAMILY

1. III:26: A person is not allowed to emigrate from the Land of Israel unless wheat goes at the price of two seahs for a sela.

2. III:27: "And when they came to Bethlehem, the whole town was stirred because of them, and the women said, 'Is this Naomi'" (Ruth 1:19): What is the meaning of the phrase, "Is this Naomi"?

3. III:28: And said R. Isaac, "The day that Ruth the Moabite emigrated from the Land to a foreign land, the wife of Boaz died. That is in line with what people say: 'Before a person dies, his successor as master of the house is appointed.'"

4. III:29: Said Rabbah bar R. Huna said Rab, "Isban is the same as Boaz."

5. III:30: Said R. Hanan bar Raba said Rab, "Elimelech and Salmon and 'such a one' (Ruth 4:1) and the father of Naomi were all sons of Nahshon b. Amminadab (Ex. 6:23, Num. 10:14)."

   a. III:31: And said R. Hanan bar Raba said Rab, "The mother of Abraham was named Amathelai, daughter of Karnebo; the name of the mother of Haman was Amatehilai, daughter of Orabti; and the mnemonic will be, 'unclean to the unclean, clean to the clean.' The mother of David was Nizbeth daughter of Adael, the mother of Samson was Zlelponit, and his sister was Nasyan."

   b. III:32: And said R. Hanan bar Raba said Rab, "For ten years our father, Abraham, was kept in prison, three in Kuta, seven in Kardu."

   c. III:33: And said R. Hanan bar Raba said Rab, "The day on which our father, Abraham, died, all of the principal authorities of the nations of the world formed a line and said, 'Woe is the world that has lost its leader, woe to the ship that has lost its helmsman.'"

   d. III:34: "And you are exalted as head above all" (1 Chr. 29:11): Said R. Hanan bar Raba said Rab, "Even the superintendent of the water supply is appointed by Heaven."

6. III:35: Said R. Hiyya bar Abin said R. Joshua b. Qorhah, "God forbid! Even if Elimelech and

his family had found bran, they would never have emigrated. So why were they punished? Because they should have besought mercy for their generation but failed to do so: 'When you cry, let them that you have gathered deliver you' (Is. 57:13)."

7. III:36: Said Rabbah bar bar Hannah said R. Yohanan, "This prohibition against emigration has been taught only when money is cheap and abundant and produce expensive, but when money is expensive and not to be found, there being no capital, even if four seahs cost only a sela, it is permitted to emigration."

a. III:37: And said R. Yohanan, "I remember when a child would break open a carob pod and a line of honey would run over both his arms."

8. III:38: It is written, "Mahlon and Chilion" (Ruth 1:2) and it is written "Joash and Saraph" (1 Chr. 4:22)! Rab and Samuel — One said, "Their names really were Mahlon and Chilion, and why were they called Joash? Because they despaired hope of redemption the words for Joash and despair using the same letters, and Saraph? Because they become liable by the decree of the Omnipresent to be burned."

9. III:39: "These were the potters and those that dwelt among plantations and hedges; there they dwelt occupied in the king's work" (1 Chr. 4:23): "These were the potters": this refers to the sons of Jonadab, son of Rahab, who kept the oath of their father (Jer. 35:6).

I. THE BLESSINGS OF PLENTY

1. III:40: "And you shall eat of the produce, the old store" (Lev. 25:22) — without requiring preservatives.

2. III:41: "And you shall eat old store long kept" (Lev. 26:10) — whatever is of an older vintage than its fellow is better in quality than its fellow.

3. III:42: "And you shall bring forth the old from before the new" (Lev. 26:10) — This teaches that the storehouses will be full of last year's crop, and the threshing floors, this year's crop, and the Israelites will say, "How are we going to remove the one before the other?"

What the case instantiates is a single conclusion. That conclusion may be stated very simply. Massive miscellanies, each with its own focus, will be formed into a composite on the basis of one of three theories of linkage:

[1] topic,

[2] attribution, or

[3] sequence of verses of a passage of Scripture.

The agglutination of topically-coherent compositions predominates. And this leads to a further theory on the miscellany. The conglomerates of random compositions formed into topical composites ordinarily serve as an amplification of a topic treated in the Mishnah, or are joined to a composite that serves in that way, so that, over all, the miscellanies are made to extend and amplify the statements of the Mishnah, as much as, though in a different way from, the commonplace propositional, analytical, and syllogistic composite.

On the basis of that hypothesis, which has to be tested against the evidence of all of the other miscellanies of the Bavli, I should be prepared to propose the further hypothesis that the Bavli contains no important or sizable sequences of compositions that are entirely unrelated to one another, that is, nothing we should classify as a mere miscellany at all. What appears to be a random hodgepodge of this and that and the other thing in fact forms a considered and even crafted composite, the agglutinative principles of which we may readily discern. In fact what we have in the miscellany is nothing more than a Mishnah-commentary of a peculiar sort, itself extended and spun out, as the more conventional Mishnah-commentaries of the Bavli tend to be extended and spun out.

The agglutinative composite or miscellany may be defined, therefore, in a very simple way: it is, specifically, a composite that has been compiled so as to present for the Mishnah a commentary intending to provide information on topics introduced by the Mishnah, — that, and not much more than that. True, the miscellany is not propositional, and it is certainly not analytical. But it is very much a composite in the sense in which I have defined that literary structure in the present context: purposeful, coherent, and I think, elegant. What appears to be odd, incoherent, pointless, rambling, on the contrary attests in its own way to the single and definitive program of the Bavli's framers. Whatever those framers wished to say on their own account they insisted on setting forth within the framework of that received document upon the structure of which they made everything to depend. The importance of these propositions for the documentary hypothesis of the Rabbinic canon cannot be overstated.

Now we turn to the prior documents and ask two simple questions: what proportion of a given sample-chapter is comprised by non-documentary writing, and how important a role does that non-documentary writing play in accomplishing the document's goals? What we shall see is now readily predicted. Unlike the Bavli, the prior documents are comprised by a negligible component of non-documentary writing. And, unlike the Bavli's miscellanies, the non-documentary writing in the prior documents takes a tangential position in those documents. That serves to establish that the so-called "parallels" — writing that finds a place in two or more documents — form a paltry part of the whole. They establish a contrast to the distinctive traits that characterize the writing — the traits of rhetoric, topic, and logic — of the respective documents, viewed whole.

Part Two

Extra- and Non-Documentary Writing in Proportion and Position

Quantitative:
Showing that a Miniscule Proportion of Rabbinic Documents Is Comprised by Free-Standing Stories

AND

Qualitative:
Showing that These Few Free-Standing Stories Are Tangential in the Compositions Where They Do Occur

2.

Proportion And Position: Evidence of Shared, Autonomous Traditions in a Sample of the Mishnah and the Tosefta

I. When a Later Document Cites an Earlier One

Now, with the Bavli in hand, we are ready to begin our inquiry into samples of principal documents of the Rabbinic canon. We commence with the Halakhic tradition, represented by the Mishnah and Tosefta. We continue, in Chapter Three, with the Halakhic tradition represented by exegesis, *Midrash-Halakhah*, with Sifra in view. Then we proceed, in Chapter Four, to the Aggadic tradition in a sequence of principal Midrash-compilations, focusing upon Genesis Rabbah as a case of the Aggadic tradition, *Midrash-Aggadah*. There, as we shall see, the free-standing composition is proportionately more common than it is in the Halakhic documents. That fact demands attention within the nascent theory of the course of Rabbinic writing.

To begin with, what we mean by free-standing compositions requires a refinement. Merely because a passage occurs in more than a single document, that passage need not be classified as extra- or non-documentary. The passage may be lifted whole, cited from a completed document by a nascent, later one. Everyone understands that, beginning with the Mishnah in Halakhic exposition and starting with Scripture in Aggadic exposition, later documents utilize formulations, including compositions and composites, that are primary and particular to earlier ones. The distinctive, indicative formal traits of the prior document can be shown to characterize that cited composition. In no way can the recurring passage be classified as extra- or non-documentary. Not free-standing, it simply belongs to the document the conventions of which it replicates. It is utilized in a subsequent compilation. That fact sustains no hypothesis concerning the nullity of documentary lines; rather, articulated citation of an earlier document by a later one confirms the importance of the documentary venue of a piece of writing.[10]

What follows? Since we focus on free-standing stories and sayings, we immediately remove from consideration the citation and gloss of a composition originating in the foundation document by a continuation-document later on, e.g., a passage in the Mishnah cited and glossed by the Tosefta, or one originating in the Tosefta that is cited and glossed by the Yerushalmi or the Bavli. Such passages are integral to the document where they initially occur. They do not qualify as free-standing stories or sayings. They form part of a continuous, unfolding, linear literary-Halakhic tradition of citation, gloss, and amplification, and that is not at issue in the allegation under consideration in these pages. Proponents of the anti-documentary reading of matters do not extend their do-

---

[10] The same is so when a completed composite of Leviticus Rabbah is taken over by Pesiqta deRab Kahana, as I showed in *Extra- and Non-Documentary Writing in the Canon of Formative Judaism. I. The Pointless Parallel: Hans-Jürgen Becker and the Myth of the Autonomous Tradition in Rabbinic Documents*, Chapter Two.

main to citation of Scripture or the Mishnah in successor-compilations.[11]

The documentary reading of the Rabbinic canon insists upon the distinctive traits of the several compilations, and among these definitive qualities, a particular trait of the Tosefta, Yerushalmi, and Bavli is to cite the Mishnah, and of the Yerushalmi and Bavli to cite the Tosefta. Hence such citations form part of the distinctive traits of the documents that do the citing; they do not signify the presence of an autonomous, extra- and non-documentary tradition at all, but confirm the very opposite.

II. The Special Situation of the Mishnah

Like Scripture, in canonical context the Mishnah is *hors de combat*, because it is cited by later documents, but, being first in line, itself cites only Scripture. And the Mishnah imposes on nearly the entirety of its contents a distinctive documentary program.

By definition, the Mishnah contains no shared, autonomous traditions. That is because after Scripture, the Mishnah is the first document of Rabbinic Judaism. It occasionally cites Scripture, but no other writing. It therefore is quoted by, but it does not quote, other documents. The Mishnah contains compositions and composites cited by later documents. But its repertoire of definitive documentary traits

---

[11] That is not to suggest the fixedness of Mishnah- or Scripture-citation does not pose a question to the Goldberg-Schaefer-Becker school and its counterparts. I suspect that to this point they simply have not recognized the question; as we see, their theoretical apparatus is by no means fully formed and well crafted as yet.

characterizes nearly the whole of its contents.¹² Apart from Eduyyot, Tamid and Middot, I cannot point to entire tractates that diverge from the formal program(s) particular to the document. To be sure, for its part the Mishnah on occasion may allude to facts of Scripture without citing particular verses, but that does not change the picture one iota, as, e.g., in the following famous passage:

MISHNAH-TRACTATE BABA QAMMA 1:1

A. [There are] four generative causes of damages: (1) ox [Ex. 21:35-36], (2) pit [Ex. 21:33], (3) crop-destroying beast [Ex. 22:4], and (4) conflagration [Ex. 22:5].

B. [The definitive characteristic] of the ox is not equivalent to that of the crop- destroying beast;

C. nor is that of the crop-destroying beast equivalent to that of the ox;

D. nor are this one and that one, which are animate, equivalent to fire, which is not animate;

E. nor are this one and that one, which usually [get up and] go and do damage, equivalent to a pit, which does not usually [get up and] go and do damage.

F What they have in common is that they customarily do damage and taking care of them is your responsibility

G. And when one [of them] has caused damage, the [owner] of that which causes the damage is liable to pay compensation for damage out of the best of his land [Ex. 22:4].

MISHNAH-TRACTATE BABA QAMMA 1:2

---

¹² I see "repertoire" to take account of not only the principal indicative traits of the Mishnah's writing but also compositions that follow other formal plans than the main ones; these too are formally particular to the Mishnah, e.g., the narrative form used for the description of Temple rites. We need not be detained by these minor refinements.

> A. In the case of anything of which I am liable to take care, I am deemed to render possible whatever damage it may do.
>
> B. [If] I am deemed to have rendered possible part of the damage it may do,
>
> C. I am liable for compensation as if [I have] made possible all of the damage it may do.
>
> D. (1) Property which is not subject to the law of Sacrilege, (2) property belonging to members of the covenant [Israelites], (3) property that is held in ownership,
>
> E. and that is located in any place other than in the domain which is in the ownership of the one who has caused the damage,
>
> F or in the domain which is shared by the one who suffers injury and the one who causes injury —
>
> G. when one has caused damage [under any of the afore-listed circumstances],
>
> H. [the owner of] that one which has caused the damage is liable to pay compensation for damage out of the best of his land [= M. 1:1G] .

Here is a typical passage. The pertinent facts invoke Scripture's provisions. M. B.Q. 1:1 reviews the generative causes of damages that Scripture's laws and narratives define. M. B.Q. 1:2 states laws out of all relationship to Scripture. These two passages stand for the Mishnah throughout: where Scripture pertains, it is sometimes cited but always present in substance. Where no Scriptural laws pertain, the Mishnah provides its own laws; Little effort goes into differentiating law of the one type from that of the other.

Not only does the Mishnah not utilize extra-documentary writing, that is, free-standing compositions and peripatetic composites, other than the specified tractates the document also contains no material corpus of non-documentary writing.[13] The Mishnah is a document formulated in accord with a few, determinate rules of composition, which govern nearly everywhere in the document, if not throughout. The compositions of the Mishnah resort to a remarkably limited repertoire of formulary patterns, and the document as a whole exhibits remarkable formal uniformity. For the authorship of the Mishnah manages to say whatever it wants in one of the following ways:

1. the simple declarative sentence, in which the subject, verb, and predicate are syntactically tightly joined to one another, e.g., he who does so and so is such and such;

2. the duplicated subject, in which the subject of the sentence is stated twice, e.g., He who does so and so, lo, he is such and such;

3. mild apocopation, in which the subject of the sentence is cut off from the verb, which refers to its own subject, and not the one with which the sentence commences, e.g., He who does so and so..., it [the thing he has done] is such and such;

4. extreme apocopation, in which a series of clauses is presented, none of them tightly joined to what pre-

---

[13] But the formal repertoire of the Mishnah is not restricted or narrowly uniform. Rather, fixed conventions govern. For example, the Mishnah adopts a narrative style when dealing with the laws for Temple rites, preferring to tell the story of how thing were done over providing generalized rules to govern the rites. That generalization encompasses Tamid, and, in its model, such cultic narratives as Negaim Chapters Thirteen and Fourteen, the cutting of the omer-narrative of Menahot, the manner in which the bitter water is administered set forth in Sotah Chapter Three, the narrative of the preparation of the red cow of Num. 20 in Parah Chapter Three, recapitulated as rules in Chapter Four, and so on. These represent a decision to deal in this way with material of this classification. Organizing rules around the names of authorities, as at Kelim Chapter Twenty-Four or all of Eduyyot, represents a less commonly-elected option as well.

cedes or follows, and all of them cut off from the predicate of the sentence, e.g., He who does so and so..., it [the thing he has done] is such and such..., it is a matter of doubt whether...or whether...lo, it [referring to nothing in the antecedent, apocopated clauses of the subject of the sentence] is so and so...

5. In addition to these formulary patterns, in which the distinctive formulary traits are effected through variations in the relationship between the subject and the predicate of the sentence, or in which the subject itself is given a distinctive development, there is yet a fifth. In this last one we have a contrastive complex predicate, in which case we may have two sentences, independent of one another, yet clearly formulated so as to stand in acute balance with one another in the predicate, thus, He who does...is unclean, and he who does not...is clean.

It naturally will be objected, is it possible that "a simple declarative sentence" may be asked to serve as a formulary pattern, alongside the rather distinctive and unusual constructions which follow? True, by itself, a tightly constructed sentence consisting of subject, verb, and complement, in which the verb refers to the subject, and the complement to the verb, hardly exhibits traits of particular formal interest. Yet a sequence of such sentences, built along the same gross grammatical lines, may well exhibit a clear-cut and distinctive pattern. And here the mnemonics of the document enter into consideration. The Mishnah is not a generalizing document; it makes its points by repeating several cases that yield the same, ordinarily unarticulated, general principle. Accordingly, the Mishnah, as I said, utilizes sets of three or five repetitions of cases to make a single point. Now when we see that three or five "simple declarative sentences" take up one principle or problem, and then, when the principle or problem shifts, a quite distinctive formal pattern will be utilized, we realize that the "simple declarative sentence" has served the formulator of the unit of thought as aptly as did apocopation, a dispute, or another more obviously distinctive form or formal pattern. The contrastive predicate is one example; the Mishnah contains many more.

    The important point of differentiation, particularly for the simple declarative sentence, therefore appears in the intermediate or the whole cognitive unit, thus in the interplay between theme and form. It is there that we see a single pattern recurring in a long sequence of sentences, e.g., the X which has lost its Y is unclean because of its Z. The Z which has lost its Y is unclean because of its X. Another example will be a long sequence of highly developed sentences, laden with relative clauses and other explanatory matter, in which a single syntactical pattern will govern the articulation of three or six or nine exempla. That sequence will be followed by one repeated terse sentence pattern, e.g., X is so and so, Y is such and such, Z is thus and so. The former group will treat one principle or theme, the latter some other. There can be no doubt, therefore, that the declarative sentence in recurrent patterns is, in its way, just as carefully formalized as a sequence of severely apocopated sentences or of contrastive predicates or duplicated subjects. None of the Mishnah's secondary and amplificatory companions, e.g., the Tosefta, the Talmud of the Land of Israel or Yerushalmi, the Talmud of Babylonia or Bavli, exhibits the same tight and rigidly-adhered-to rhetorical cogency.

    The reason for the patterning of rhetoric becomes apparent when we appreciate the effect of doing so. It is vastly to facilitate memorizing the document. Exactly how does the formulation of the document facilitate remembering its exact words? The answer to that question derives from the smallest whole units of discourse, the cognitive units, defined as groups of sentences that make a point completely and entirely on their own, become intelligible on three bases: logical, topical, and rhetorical. It is the confluence of logic, topic, and rhetoric that generates at the deepest structure of the Mishnah's language a set of mnemonic patterns. These mnemonics serve by definition to facilitate the easy memorization of the text of the Mishnah. First to define the matter: what marks the smallest whole unit of discourse — a handful of sentences — is that the several sentences of which it is composed are unintelligible or not wholly intelligible by themselves but are entirely intelligible when seen as a group. The smallest whole unit of discourse in the Mishnah invariably constitutes a syllogism, that is, a statement of a proposition, in which a condition or question, constituting a protasis, finds resolution in a rule or answer, the apodosis. "If such and such is the case, then so and so is the rule" — that is the characteristic cognitive structure of the Mishnah's smallest whole unit of thought or discourse. Even if that statement were made up of two or three or even five declarative sentences, it is only when the proposition is fully exposed, both protasis and apodosis, that the declarative sentences reach the level of full and complete expression, that is, sense and intelligibility.

The patterns of language, e.g., syntactic structures, of the apodosis and protasis of the Mishnah's smallest whole units of discourse are framed in formal, mnemonic patterns. They follow a few simple rules. These rules, once known, apply nearly everywhere and form stunning evidence for the document's cogency. They permit anyone to reconstruct, out of a few key phrases, an entire cognitive unit, and even complete intermediate units of discourse. Working downward from the surface, therefore, anyone can penetrate into the deeper layers of meaning of the Mishnah. Then and at the same time, while discovering the principle behind the cases, one can easily memorize the whole by mastering the recurrent rhetorical pattern dictating the expression of the cogent set of cases. For it is easy to note the shift from one rhetorical pattern to another and to follow the repeated cases, articulated in the new pattern downward to its logical substrate. So syllogistic propositions, in the Mishnah's authors' hands, come to full expression not only in what people wish to state but also in how they choose to say it. The limits of rhetoric define the arena of topical articulation. Once we ask what three or five joined topical propositions have in common, we state the logic and can therefore propose the syllogism that is shared among them all.

    The contrast with the materials set forth in Chapter One demands attention. The Mishnah and the Bavli stand at opposite extremes, the former made up pretty much all at once, the latter cobbled together and formed — though purposefully — as much of non- or extra-documentary writing as of the documentary kind. The Mishnah's formal traits of rhetoric indicate that the document has been formulated all at once, and not in an incremental, linear process extending into a remote (mythic) past, (to Sinai) is one fact. It is that these traits, common to a series of distinct cognitive units, are redactional, because they are imposed at that point at which someone intended to join together discrete (finished) units on a given theme. The varieties of traits particular to the discrete units and the diversity of authorities cited therein, including masters of two or three or even four strata from the turn of the first century to the end of the second, make it highly improbable that the several units were formulated in a common pattern and then preserved, until, later on, still further units, on the same theme and in the same pattern, were worked out and added. The entire indifference, moreover, to historical order of authorities and concentration on the logical unfolding of a given theme or problem without reference to the sequence of authorities, confirm the supposition that the work of formulation and that of redaction go forward together.

The principal framework of formulation and formalization in the Mishnah is the intermediate division ("chapter") rather than the cognitive unit ("paragraph"). The least-formalized formulary pattern, the simple declarative sentence, turns out to yield many examples of acute formalization, in which a single distinctive pattern is imposed upon two or more (very commonly, groups of three or groups of five) cognitive units. While an intermediate division of a tractate may be composed of several such conglomerates of cognitive units, it is rare indeed for cognitive units formally to stand wholly by themselves. Normally, cognitive units share formal or formulary traits with others to which they are juxtaposed and the theme of which they share. It follows that the principal unit of formulary formalization is the intermediate division and not the cognitive unit. So much for the form-analysis of the Mishnah, a document that affords a position to a miniscule number of free-standing compositions and assigns to those compositions no documentary task whatsoever. Now on to the Tosefta.

III. THE FREE-STANDING COMPOSITION IN THE TOSEFTA. TOSEFTA HULLIN 2:21-24

The Tosefta relates to the Mishnah, sometimes citing the language of the Mishnah in so many words, sometimes alluding to the rule of the Mishnah without verbatim citation.[14]

---

[14] Compare the view of Alberdina Houtman, set forth in my *The Place of the Tosefta in the Halakhah of Formative Judaism. What Alberdina Houtman Didn't Notice*. Atlanta, 1998: Scholars Press for South Florida Studies in the History of Judaism. Another student of Schaefer, Houtman argues that the Tosefta can be read autonomous of the Mishnah. That is sometimes so, sometimes not so. But she does not demonstrate that the Tosefta as a complete document is framed out of all intersection with the Mishnah. And her cases — Shebiit, for example — completely ignore the Halakhic contents of the texts. Had the substance of matters engaged her

To show that that is so, I present in bold face type the citation of the Mishnah by the Tosefta, and in that way we see how the two documents relate. What we see is systematic citation and gloss of the Mishnah. That surely is not what people mean who invoke the presence of free-standing traditions to call into question the importance of documentary boundaries in the Rabbinic canon.

TOSEFTA BABA QAMMA 1:1

A. **In the case of anything for which I am liable to take care, I am deemed to render possible damage it may do [M. B.Q. 1:2A]** —

B. this refers to an ox or a pit.

C. **[If] I am deemed to have rendered possible part of the damage it may do, I am liable for compensation as if [I have] made possible all of the damage it may do [M. B.Q. 1:2B-C].**

D. This refers to a pit.

E. **I am liable for compensation ... for all of the damage it may do** —

F. this teaches that the owner has to take care of the disposition of the carcass.

G. **Property which is not subject to the law of Sacrilege [M. B.Q. 1:2D]** —

H. this is meant to exclude an ox belonging to an Israelite which gored an ox belonging to the sanctuary, or an ox belonging to the sanctuary which gored an ox belonging to an Israelite.

---

attention, she would have noticed that the Tosefta very commonly takes for granted and builds upon the logic initially embodied in the Mishnah's corresponding Halakhic ruling. That is what she did not notice in her dissertation, which relied for analysis entirely on computer-programming. That is another result of what I regard as the desiccated formalism and the nihilism of the German school of Rabbinic studies.

I. **Property belonging to members of the covenant {Israelites] [M. B.Q. I :2D]** —

J. THIS IS MEANT TO EXCLUDE AN OX BELONGING TO AN ISRAELITE WHICH GORED AN OX BELONGING TO A GENTILE.

K. **Property that is held in ownership [M. B.Q. 1:2D]** —

L. this is meant to exclude property which is ownerless;

M. **and that is located in any place other than the domain which is in the ownership of the one who has caused the damage [M. B.Q. 1:2E]** —

N. this is meant to exclude a case in which an ox caused damage in his [the owner's] own domain;

0. **and domain which is shared by the one who suffers injury and the one who causes injury [M. B.Q. 1:2F]** —

P. for example, a courtyard belonging to partners, or a valley;

Q. property which is subject to ownership which is located outside of the domain which is subject to the ownership of the one who has caused the injury and the domain of the one who has suffered the injury [cf. M. B.Q. 1 :2F],

R. and a case in which the one who has caused the injury is an uncompensated bailee,

5. one who has borrowed,

T. a paid bailee, or one who pays a rental, the ox of [any one of] whom has caused injury in the domain of the owner [of the ox, who receives the rental-payment]. **pays the whole value of the damage which has been caused [M. B.Q. 1:4N].**

V. **[If] that which is deemed harmless [causes damage], [the owner] pays half of the value of the damage which has been caused [M. B.Q. I:4L].**

W. All the same are damages caused by man and damages caused by beast:

X. they assess [the compensation for the damages and pay it] out of the best sort of property [M. B.Q. 1:2H],

Y. SINCE IT IS SAID, "HE SHALL MAKE RES-TITUTION FROM THE BEST OF HIS OWN FIELDS AND OF HIS OWN VINEYARD" (EX. 22:5).

The Mishnah is cited as a separate compilation, its documentary autonomy is underscored. The present classification of Tosefta-passage, accordingly, is to be classified as a construction of citation and gloss of the Mishnah. It does not take over and make its own the Mishnah's laws and language. When we come to passages of the Mishnah cited by the Tosefta, therefore, we cannot treat them as examples of "parallels," utilization in two or more documents of free-standing traditions bearing no indicative documentary traits. On the contrary, we must regard such citation-form as evidence of the recognition of the distinct standing of the Mishnah on the part of the Tosefta's framers.

The formal patterns of the Tosefta in the aggregate correspond with those of the Mishnah. But the Tosefta's formal traits present a wider selection of possibilities. It utilizes narrative, for example, for other-than-Temple rites, and it contains stories that are parachuted down and scarcely acknowledge the documentary setting in which they occur. A single instance serves to validate the claim that some small proportion of the Tosefta consists of extra- or non-documentary writing.

TOSEFTA HULLIN 2:21

A. People are not to sell anything to them or buy anything from them.

B. And they do not take wives from them or give children in marriage to them.

C. And they do not teach their sons a craft.

D. And they do not seek assistance from them, either financial assistance or medical assistance.

The foregoing could occur in the Mishnah as readily as in the Tosefta. It is a simple set of declarative sentences of Halakhah. Not uncommonly in the Mishnah occur illustrative, brief stories, *ma'asim,* which follow a clear form: a named authority, a sparse description of a case or event, and a ruling or outcome:

TOSEFTA HULLIN 2:22
A. STORY: R. ELEAZAR B. DAMAH WAS BITTEN BY A SNAKE.

B. And Jacob of Kefar Sama came to heal him in the name of Jesus son of Pantera.

C. And R. Ishmael did not allow him [to accept the healing].

The continuation of the story goes beyond the strict limits of the conventional *ma'aseh*.

D. They said to him, "You are not permitted [to accept healing from him], Ben Dama."

E. He said to him, "I shall bring you proof that he may heal me."

F. But he did not have time to bring the [promised] proof before he dropped dead.

Tosefta Hullin 2:23

A. Said R. Ishmael, "Happy are you, Ben Dama. For you have expired in peace, but you did not break down the hedge erected by sages.

B. "FOR WHOEVER BREAKS DOWN THE HEDGE ERECTED BY SAGES EVENTUALLY SUFFERS PUNISHMENT, AS IT IS SAID, 'HE WHO BREAKS DOWN A HEDGE IS BITTEN BY A SNAKE' (QOH. 10:8)."

What follows is inserted for obvious reasons, since it carries forward the general theme of learning traditions from the minim, here meaning, Christians. Not the law at hand, but the principle, comes to realization in the story, which is freestanding, entirely comprehensible out of the setting of T. Hul. 2:22-3. It is a story of a much more elaborate character, not formalized and conventional but nuanced and particular.

TOSEFTA HULLIN 2:24

A. Story: R. Eliezer was arrested on account of *minut*. They brought him to court for judgment.

B. That *hegemon* said to him, "Should an elder of your standing get involved in such things?"

C. He said to him, "The Judge is reliable in my view" [I rely upon the Judge]."

D. That *hegemon* supposed that he referred only to him, but he referred only to his Father in heaven.

E. He [the *hegemon*] said to him, "Since you have deemed me reliable for yourself, so thus I have ruled: Is it possible that these gray hairs should err in such matters? *[Obviously not, therefore]* Dimissus [you are pardoned]. Lo, you are free of liability."

F. And when he left court, he was distressed to have been arrested on account of matters of *minut*.

G. His disciples came to comfort him, but he did not accept their words of comfort.

H. R. 'Aqiba came and said to him, "Rabbi, May I say something to you so that you will not be distressed?"

I. He said to him, "Go ahead."

J. He said to him, "Perhaps some one of the *minim* told you something of *minut* which pleased you."

K. He said to him, "By Heaven! You remind me. Once I was strolling in the camp of Sepphoris. I bumped into Jacob of Kefar Sikhnin, and he told me a teaching of *minut* in the name of Jesus ben Pantiri, and it pleased me. So I was arrested on account of matters of *minut*, for I transgressed the teachings of Torah:

'Keep your way far from her and do not go near the door of her house' [Prov. 5:8]."

L. For R. Eliezer did teach, "One should always flee from what is disreputable and from whatever appears to be disreputable."

The upshot is to show us what a free-standing composition in the Tosefta looks like. The story (*ma'aseh*), T. Hul. 2:22, represents a familiar form of the Mishnah and the Tosefta. It is a brief illustration, a realization of an abstract law. Here it is tightly joined to T. Hul. 2:21.. But the elaborate account, T. Hul. 2:24 does not serve the documentary program of Mishnah- and Halakhah-exegesis. It stands for compositions not tightly linked to the exegetical program of the Tosefta. Now the question is, what proportion of the Tosefta is comprised by free-standing writing as against documentary compositions along the lines of the Mishnah's Halakhic presentations, and what role does free-standing writing effect in the Tosefta?

IV. THE NEGLIGIBLE PROPORTION AND PERIPHERAL ROLE OF FREE-STANDING STORIES: TOSEFTA MOED QATAN CHAPTER TWO

We therefore find ourselves required to examine a sample of the Tosefta, to determine the proportion of such free-standing compositions in a given tractate and the role — important or tangential — assigned to them. For that purpose I address the Tosefta tractate Moed Qatan, Chapter Two. I follow the cross references given by Saul Lieberman in his *Tosefta Moed* (N.Y., 1962: The Jewish Theological Seminary of America) for that tractate.

For the reasons given at the outset, I do not treat as a free-standing or autonomous saying or story a passage of the

Tosefta that is cited and glossed by the Yerushalmi or the Bavli, any more than I regard a passage of the Mishnah glossed by the Tosefta as an autonomous tradition. It is the very opposite.

In the following, I underline citations of the Mishnah. Further, I set in bold face type a Tosefta-passage that occurs other than in the Yerushalmi or the Bavli.

Tosefta Moed Qatan Chapter Two

2:1 A. <u>All those for whom they have ruled that they may cut their hair on the intermediate days of a festival [M. M.Q. 3:1]</u> —

B. It is permitted [for people in these same categories] to get a haircut within thirty days of the occurrence of a bereavement.

C. Even though they have permitted such a one to get a haircut, he should not get a haircut in public.

D. But he gets a haircut discreetly, in his own house.

2:2 A. <u>All those for whom they have ruled that they may wash their clothes on the intermediate days of a festival [M. M.Q. 3:2]</u> —

B. IT IS PERMITTED [FOR PEOPLE IN THESE SAME CATEGORIES] TO WASH THEIR CLOTHES WITHIN THIRTY DAYS OF THE OCCURRENCE OF A BEREAVEMENT.

C. Even though they have permitted such a one to wash clothing, he should not take his clothing to a laundry man.

D. But he washes his clothing discreetly, in his own house.

E. "And just as it is prohibited to get a haircut, it also is prohibited to cut one's fingernails," the words of R. Judah.

F. But R. Yosé permits [doing so].

G. And so did R. Judah rule, "Those who come [home] from the seashore or from overseas are prohibited to get a haircut and to wash their clothing" [vs. M. M.Q. 3:1-2].

H. But sages permit [their doing so].

1. Said Rabbi, "The opinion of R. Judah makes more sense in a case in which one has not gotten permission [from sages to go abroad],

"and that of sages makes more sense in a case in which one has gotten permission [from sages to go abroad]."

2:3 A. They do not prepare deeds for share-cropping land or receipts on the intermediate days of a festival.

B. R. Judah permits, for someone else might get there first.

2:4 A. A person writes out his accounts on the intermediate days of a festival.

B. And a person reckons up his expenses on the intermediate days of a festival.

2:5 A. They undertake contracts on the intermediate days of a festival [for work to be done] after the festival,

B. on condition that one not count up, weigh, or measure as one does on ordinary days.

2:6 A. He who buries his dead two days before the festival [cf. M. M.Q. 3 :5A]

B. interrupts [his mourning rites] for the festival,

C. and counts five [supplementary days of mourning] after the festival.

D. And the public takes care of him.

E. And his work is done by other people.

F. His male-slaves and female-slaves work in private for other people.

2:7 A. [If he buries his dead] with three days left of the festival week itself, he counts seven [days of mourning] after the festival.

B. For the first four, the public takes care of him. For the other three, the public does not take care of him.

C. For they have said that the days of mourning which took place on the festival so affect him that the public must take care of him.

D. And his work is done by others.

E. His male-slaves and female-slaves work in private for other people.

2:8 A. [If he buries his dead] eight days before a festival, he may get a haircut on the eve of the festival.

B. If he did not get a haircut on the eve of the festival, it is prohibited for him to get a haircut until the thirty days of the mourning period will have passed.

C. Even though the festival does not go to his credit for the counting of the seven days of mourning,

D. it does go to his credit for the counting of the thirty days of the mourning period [cf. M. M.Q. 3:5].

2:9 A. He who has fulfilled the rite of turning over the bed for three days before the festival does not have to turn over the bed after the festival.

B. R. Eliezer b. Jacob says, "Even one day."

C. R. Eleazar b. R. Simeon says, "The House of Shammai say, 'Three days.'

D. "And the House of Hillel say, 'Even one hour.'"

E. On Friday one sets his bed upright.

F. And at the end of the Sabbath he turns it over [again, resuming the mourning rite],

G. even though there remained for him only one day alone.

H. But one is not permitted to observe mourning during the festival.

I. But he mourns discreetly, in his own house.

2:10 A. They drink manure-water, palm-water, and a cup of root-water on the festival.

B. For at first they would rule, They do not drink manure-water, palmwater, and a cup of root-water on a festival,

C. UNTIL R. 'AQIBA CAME AND TAUGHT THAT THEY DRINK MANURE-WATER, PALM-

WATER, AND A CUP OF ROOT-WATER ON THE FESTIVAL.

2:11 A. They draw blood for a domesticated beast, a wild beast, and fowl.

B. And they do not hold back any sort of healing from a beast on the intermediate days of a festival.

C. A female domestic beast which goes into heat — they do not cover her.

D. But they bring her down to the corral.

E. R. Judah says, "A female ass who goes into heat — they cover her, so that she should not grow cold.

F. "But as to all other beasts, they bring them down to the corral."

G. And they do not arrange for insemination on the intermediate days of a festival.

H. And they do not [at any time] arrange for insemination in the case of a firstling or in the case of consecrated beasts which have been invalidated.

    1. They judge capital cases, property cases, and cases involving fines [cf. M. M.Q. 3:3].

J. And they burn a red cow.

K. And they break the neck of a heifer [in the case of a derelict corpse].

L. And they pierce the ear of a Hebrew slave [who wishes to remain with his master].

M. And they effect redemption for pledges of personal valuation, for things declared *Herem,* for things declared consecrated, and for second tithe [through coins to be taken up to Jerusalem].

N. And they untie a shoe from the last,

O. So long as one not put it back.

2:12 A. A press of laundry men which they untied before the intermediate day of a festival — one takes [clothing] from it, but does not put it back into it

B. As to a press belonging to householders, one puts [clothing] back into it.

C. And, it goes without saying, one takes [clothing] out of it [cf. M. Shab. 20:5].

2:13 A. In the case of stalls open to the stoa one opens and closes in the normal way.

B. [If they open out] onto the public way, one opens one and closes one.

C. On the eve of the last day of the Festival [of Tabernacles], one goes out and decorates the market place,

D. in honor of the last day of the Festival.

What follows is a set of three entries, matched stories making the single point that when it will give offense, one refrains from doing what is permitted. The trilogy, T. 2:15-16, does not intersect with the topical program of the composite where it is used. On the contrary, the point of T. 2:14, to which T. 2:15 is joined by reason of the common Halakhic ruling, is contradicted by the story. People thought taking seats by the chair of gentiles on the Sabbath is forbidden. Aqiba taught that it is permitted to do so, even though it gives the impression of improper transactions on the Sabbath. Then T. 2:15 has Gamaliel do just that; when corrected by the locals, he refrains from doing what is licit, rather than offend local opinion. To that story are two further stories, also involving Gamaliel's family, in which the same principle is illustrated. The three stories clearly form a distinct unit, joined together as a set before being inserted into the Tosefta-context in which they now occur. But they do not fit very well, with the jarring disjuncture between T. 2:15-16 and T. 2:14.

2:14 A. They take seats by the chair of gentiles [at which they do business] on the Sabbath.

B. For in the beginning they ruled that they do not take seats by the chair of gentiles on the Sabbath,

C. until R. 'Aqiba came and taught that they take seats by the chair of gentiles on the Sabbath.

2:15 A. WM'SH B: Rabban Gamaliel took a seat by the chair of gentiles on the Sabbath in Akko.

B. They said to him, "They were not accustomed to take seats at the chair of gentiles on the Sabbath."

C. But he did not want to say, "You are permitted to do so."

D. So he got up and went on his way.

E. A STORY: JUDAH AND HILLEL, SONS OF RABBAN GAMALIEL, WENT IN TO TAKE A BATH IN KABUL.

F. They said to him, "They were not accustomed to have two brothers take a bath together."

G. They did not want to say, "You are permitted to do so."

H. So they went in and took a bath one after the other.

2:16 A. SWB M'SH B: Judah and Hillel, sons of Rabban Gamaliel would go out in golden slippers on the Sabbath in Biri.

B. They said to them, "They were not accustomed to go out in golden slippers on the Sabbath."

C. They did not want to say to them, "You are permitted."

D. So they sent them along with their servants.

2:17 A. A sage who died —

B. all are deemed his relations [cf. M. M.Q. 3:7A].

C. All tear their garments.

D. And all bare [their shoulders].

E. AND ALL LAMENT.

F. And all receive a mourner's meal on his account,

G. even in the street of the town.

H. They do not bring wailing pipes to the house of mourning but to the banquet-house,

1. and to the house of rejoicing, in the place in which that was the custom.

J. What is a lamentation [M. M.Q. 3:8A-B]?

K. This is one which is upon the heart,

L. as it is said, *Beat upon your breasts* (Is. 32:12).

M. Clapping is with the hands.

N. A gesture of praise [QYLWS] — this is the spreading open of the arms.

Much of the composite is comprised by glosses of cited, or alluded-to, Mishnah-rulings. The rest, with the exception in bold face type, states Halakhic rulings in the manner of the Mishnah.

The indicated passage, T. 2:15-16, occupies six lines of the 54 lines of Lieberman's Tosefta Moed Chapter Two, that is, 11% of the chapter, not a significant part of the whole. Here is a passage that, on the face of it, is non- and extra-documentary writing, comparable to the counterpart in Tosefta Hullin.[15]

But there is another reason that T. 2:15-2:16 capture our attention, since they take their leave from the program of the Tosefta-exposition. They form an other-than-Halakhic exposition, a set of stories on the common theme of Rabbinic restraint in ruling on local practice. Even though the law permitted the conduct under discussion, the local custom prohibited it, and the sages, who knew the law, respected that custom. We can explain the inclusion of the stories. These items join to T. 2:14, because of the theme that joins T. 2:15 to T. 2:14, taking a seat by the chair of gentiles on the Sabbath. Aqiba permitted doing so. Then T. 2:15 addresses the same Halakhic issue but not the same problem. The story that

---

[15] That is not to suggest all protracted or developed stories fall into the classification of non- and extra-documentary writing. Were our problem the documentary analysis of the forms of the Mishnah or the Tosefta or the Yerushalmi or the Bavli, a systematic account of the documentary forms, such as I gave for the Mishnah, would be called for. In the present context, what is required is only the identification of what is unconventional in the sample, and its proportion and position within that sample.

pertains carries in its wake the two more stories, not about not Gamaliel but Gamaliel's sons. Clearly, the set, T. 2:14, 15, 16, does not works together especially well. That is because the problem of T. 2:14, the chair of the gentiles on the Sabbath, is left behind, and the focus of the story accounts for the joining of the trilogy. The whole was then inserted, ready-made, by reason of the intersection with Aqiba's ruling.

Here, then, is a trilogy that took shape within a program of agglutination other than that that prevails in the Mishnah and the Tosefta. That is to say, the three stories, two of them matched, are joined because, in shared formal patterns, all three illustrate the common principle that under the indicated circumstance one should refrain from doing what is permitted. But the Mishnah and in its wake the Tosefta form topical expositions, not presentations of principles that apply to a variety of topics. The tractates and chapters and paragraphs of the Mishnah and of the Tosefta are organized within category-formations defined by subject-matter, not by abstract legal principle.

As to the position of the extra-documentary writing — primary or peripheral — there is no doubt. The extra-documentary composite ignores the topical exposition of the chapter. It changes the subject and introduces a principle that does not quite accord with the rule that intersects with the first of the three stories of the composite. So we may not regard the extra- and non-documentary composite as primary to the documentary purpose; indeed, it is scarcely tangential. That is in two aspects. First, were we to remove the composite, nothing whatsoever is lost in the Tosefta's exposition of the rules corresponding to those of the Mishnah or otherwise. Second, if we examine the trilogy on its own, we fully understand it, beginning to end, without reference to the Tosefta-setting in which it is preserved. This non-documentary composite, then, forms a paltry proportion of the chapter in which it occurs and stands in a marginal position in that same context. But what we now realize is, non-documentary writing is preserved in the documents without much effort at accommodating that writing to the documentary requirements.

V. The Reception by the Yerushalmi and the Bavli of the Non-Documentary Composite of Tosefta Moed Qatan Chapter Two

A further question awaits: What about the later utilization of the non-documentary composite of Tosefta Moed Qatan Chapter Two? The set recurs at Y. Pes. 4:1 and B. Pes. 51a, in the following. The indentations move from what is primary to the Talmud's discussion — the Mishnah, then the exposition of the Mishnah — to what is secondary and onward to tangential glosses of glosses. As we shall now see, the freestanding stories take no part in the primary discussion of either Talmud. But the stories are not marginal to the Talmuds as they are to the Tosefta. The principle they enunciate does pertain, finding illustration in the point of those stories about respecting local custom. Stating the matter simply: writing that is non-documentary in the Mishnah and the Tosefta may be cited for a clear documentary purpose in some later compilation. When we take account of that fact, we see that the framers of the Yerushalmi and the Bavli have a clear purpose in citing the stories. While they do not fit comfortably in Tosefta Moed Qatan, they do work well in Yerushalmi Pesahim and in the Bavli counterpart.

YERUSHALMI PESAHIM 4:1
[A] Where people are accustomed to do work on the eve of Passover prior to noon — they do [so]. Where they are accustomed not to do [so] — they do not do [so]

[B] One who goes from a place where they [people] do to a place where they do not do [so], or from where they do not to where they do — they impose on him the stringencies of the place which he has left and the stringencies of the place to which he has gone

[C] But a person should not vary [from the local custom] so as [to avoid, contentiousness

[I:4A] [Regarding] all the matters [that follow] they made it contingent upon an actual custom:

[B] *Women who are accustomed not to work: on the departure of the Sabbath* — this does not comprise a custom; until the synagogue' lets out [on Saturday night, which is likely to be a little later than the precise end of the Sabbath because in synagogues people include additional prayers] — [this is] a custom; on Mondays and Thursdays [the days on which the Torah is read] — [it is] not a custom; until the fast-meeting [or "fast-prayer session"] lets out [for one of the Monday and Thursday fasts, accepted by the pious, when penitential and other special prayers were recited] — [this is] a custom; on the Sabbath eves — [it is] not a custom; from *afternoon prayer* time onwards [on Sabbath eves] — [this is] a custom; on the day of the [New] Moon — [this is] a custom.

[C] *Said R. Zeira, 'Women who are accustomed not to start a loom from the beginning of [the month of] Ab and onward — [this is] a custom,* for in it [Ab] the foundation stone [a stone from which the world was women] ceased [functioning]. What is the [scriptural] reason [for this association]? 'When the foundations are destroyed' (Ps. 11:3)." [It is assumed that this Psalm to David referring to a destruction alludes to the Temple's destruction, which is mourned in the month of Ab.]

[D] Said R. Hinena, "All the matters [above, whether or not based on actual customs] are [in effect] a custom [and should not be disregarded]."

[E] *Acacia trees [which were used in the holy ark's construction and hence venerated] were in Magdala of the Dyers.*

138 *Paltry Parallels*

> They came and asked R. Haninah the associate of the rabbis, "Is it permitted to work them?"
>
> [F] He said to them, "Since your ancestors were accustomed to treat them as prohibited, do not change the custom of your ancestors, whose souls are at peace."
>
> [G] R. Eleazar [said] in the name of R. Abin, "[Regarding] every matter that one does not know is permitted and in error [treats] as prohibited, one appears before sages and they permit him; and [regarding] every matter that one knows is permitted but treats as prohibited, one appears before sages and 1_ they do not permit him."

The trilogy is now introduced, a direct citation of the Tosefta's version, which then includes both what is needed, the three cases of Gamaliel and his family and their respect for local custom (in line with "a person should not vary from the local custom), and what is not pertinent, which is T. 2:14 = Y. I:5A.

> [I:5A] They sit on a Gentile's bench [on which a Gentile merchant sells wares] on the Sabbath [even though it might appear as if they were engaged in business] [T. M.Q. 2:14A].
>
> [B] A case (M'SH B) regarding Rabban Gamaliel who sat on a Gentile's bench on the Sabbath in Akko.
>
> [Locals] said to him, "They are not accustomed here to sit on a Gentile's bench on the Sabbath," and he did not want to tell them that it is permitted to act thus, but rather he got up and left.
>
> [C] A case concerning Judah and Hillel, the sons of Rabban Gamaliel, who went in to bathe in the baths of Kabul.
>
> They said to them, "Two brothers are not accustomed here to bathe together [out of mod-

esty]," and they did not want to say that it is permitted, but rather they entered one at a time.

[D] And moreover [there was a case concerning them] that they went out to walk with gilded bark [apparently loosely fitted] sandals on Sabbath night in Beri.

[Locals] said to them, "They are not accustomed here to walk with gilded bark sandals on the Sabbath [lest the sandals fall off and be carried home]." And they did not want to tell them that it is permitted thus, but rather they sent them home with their servants [T. M.Q. 2:15-16].

[I:6 A] Not only regarding Passover [e.g., not working prior to noon on the day on which the offering was brought, on the eve of Passover,] but also regarding a custom [people are to accept and maintain stringencies]:

[B] The net-fishers of Tiberias, and the grist-makers of Sepphoris, [and] the grain crushers of Akko accepted upon themselves not to work on the intermediate days of the festival [cf. M. M.Q. 2:5].

[C] It is understandable regarding the grist-makers of Sepphoris [and] the grain crushers of Akko [as R. Yosé reports in M. M.Q. 2:5, they imposed a stringency upon themselves]; regarding the net-fishers of Tiberias [not mentioned in M. M.Q. 2:5], however, do they not diminish the joy of the festival [by decreasing the availability of fish]?

[D] [The angler] fishes with a hook, [and] he fishes with a small net.

[E] Even thus, do they not diminish the joy of the festival [for their catch would be smaller than needed]?

[F] *R. Ammi cursed them because they diminished the joy of the holiday.*

The story is cited in the context of respecting local custom, but now the local custom pertains to working on the eve of the Passover rite. The story, at Y. 1:5, is cited verbatim, but the story is not integrated into the Halakhic setting at hand. It simply illustrates the basic principle, realized in the two distinct rules. But that suffices for Yerushalmi (and Bavli), which take as their task the discovery of the principle, pertinent to a variety of Halakhic topics, that sustains all of them all together. That is the principle of avoiding contentiousness and honoring local custom, which applies to the Sabbath, to the festival, and to brothers' taking baths together.

BAVLI PESAHIM 4:1

A. Where they are accustomed to do work on the eve of Passover up to noon, they do so.

B. Where they are accustomed not to do so, they do not do so.

C. He who goes from a place in which they do work to a place in which they do not do work,

D. or from a place in which they do not do work to a place in which they do work —

E. they lay upon him the strict rules followed in the place from which he has gone forth and the strict rules followed in the place to which he has gone.

F. [50B] **But a person should not vary [from the local custom] so as [to avoid] contentiousness.**

I.11 A. *The people of Beisan had the custom of not going from Tyre to Sidon on the eve of the Sabbath. Their children came before R. Yohanan. They said to him, "Our fathers — they could refrain, but we can't refrain."*

B. He said to them, "Your fathers have already accepted that discipline upon themselves [for you]: 'Hear, my son, the instruction of your father and don't abandon the teaching of your mother' (Prov. 1:8)."

I.12 A. *The people of Khuzistan had the custom of separating dough-offering for bread made of rice. They came and told R. Joseph. He said to them, "Let a non-priest eat it in their presence."*

B. Objected Abbayye, "...in respect to things that are permitted, treated by others as prohibited, [51A] you are not permitted to treat as permitted in the presence of those who regard them as prohibited, in line with the verse, 'he shall not break his word' (Num. 30:3)."

C. *He said to him, "But wasn't it said in this connection, 'said R. Hisda, "This refers to the Samaritans"'? How so with regard to the Samaritans? It is because they confuse one thing with something else. And these people, too, will confuse one thing with something else!"*

D. *Rather, said R. Ashi, "We see: If most of them eat rice bread, then a non-priest must not eat the dough-offering in their presence, lest the Torah of dough-offering be forgotten from among them; but if most of them eat bread from grain, then let a non-priest eat it in their presence, lest they turn out to separate dough-offering from what is liable in behalf of what is exempt and from what is exempt in behalf of what is liable."*

I.13 A. *Reverting to the body of the foregoing:*

B. In respect to things that are permitted, treated by others as prohibited, you are not permitted to treat as permitted in the presence of those who regard them as prohibited, in line with the verse, "he shall not break his word" (Num. 30:3). Said R. Hisda, "This refers to the Samaritans" –

C. *So doesn't it refer to everybody in general? And hasn't it been taught on Tannaite authority:*

D. Two brothers may bathe together, but in Kabul two brothers may not bathe together.

E. **There was the case involving Judah and Hillel, Rabban Gamaliel's sons, who bathed together in Kabul, and everyone in town ridiculed them, saying, "We have never seen such a thing in all our lives." Hillel withdrew and went to the outer chamber of the bath but didn't tell them, "You are permitted to do what we did."**

F. **People are permitted to go out in slippers on the Sabbath [Freedman: though they fit loosely, we don't fear that they may fall off and one will turn out to carry them in the street, which is forbidden]. But people do not go out in slippers on the Sabbath in Biri.**

G. **There was the case involving Judah and Hillel, Rabban Gamaliel's sons, who went out in** slippers on the Sabbath in Biri, and everyone in town ridiculed them, saying, "We have never seen such a thing in all our lives." They took them off and handed them over to their servants, but they didn't want to tell them, "You are permitted to do what we did."

H. They may sit on gentiles' chairs on the Sabbath, but they don't sit on gentiles' chairs on the Sabbath in Akko.

I. There was the case of Rabban Simeon b. Gamaliel, who sat on gentiles' chairs on the Sabbath in Akko, and everyone in town ridiculed him, saying, "We have never seen such a thing in all our lives." He slipped off, down to the ground, but he didn't want to tell them, "You are permitted to do what I did" [T. Moed 2:15-16].

J. *Since rabbis are not commonly located among them, the people who live in the coastal towns are classified as Samaritans.*

I.14 A. *Now there is no problem understanding the prohibition of chairs of gentiles; it is because it would appear that people are doing business [on the Sabbath]. And it is also easy to understand why people don't go out wearing slippers, since they might fall off and end up carrying them four cubits in public domain. But how come brothers aren't supposed to bathe together?*

B. *It is in accord with that which has been taught on Tannaite authority:* With any person one may share a bath, except for one's father, father-in-law, mother's husband, and sister's husband. And R. Judah permits in the case of his father, because of the honor owing to his father, and the same is so of his mother's husband.

C. *But they [in Kabul] went and made a decree against two brothers' bathing together, because of the husband of the sister [lest that be allowed as well].*

I.15 A. *A Tannaite statement:*

B. A disciple should not bathe with his master, but if his master needs him, it is permitted.

The Bavli's utilization of the story preserves its integrity and introduces it as a citation from the received tradition. The story glosses at gloss, as indicated at I:13. It itself is then glossed at I:14, with a gloss of the gloss at I:15. The freestanding story in the Yerushalmi and the Bavli finds a comfortable place within the documentary program of Halakhic exegesis.

The upshot may be simply stated. To the Tosefta it is peripheral, because the Tosefta, like the Mishnah, takes as its task the exposition of the Halakhah by its topical category-formations. To the Yerushalmi and Bavli the same trilogy serves a primary function, because the Yerushalmi and the Bavli wish to transcend the topical limits of the Mishnah's and the Tosefta's Halakhic exposition and identify encompassing principles, applicable to a variety of cases or topics. The free-standing stories at hand form a negligible proportion of the Tosefta-chapter in which they occur and carry out a role that is scarcely even tangential. When cited later on, they serve the documentary program of the Yerushalmi and Bavli, fitting very nicely into the articulation of the generative principle that the stories illustrate.

To conclude, we must remind ourselves of the issue under discussion. It is not the literary history of the Tosefta, Yerushalmi, Bavli, or of free-standing compositions and composites autonomous of those documents. To be sure, we did make some fairly general observations on the likely history of the free-standing composite of stories. They represent a different theory of agglutination from that which governs in the Mishnah and the Tosefta, one that is remarkably comparable to the theory — emphasizing principles not topics and cases — that operates in the two Talmuds. The three stories have formal affinities, call upon the same principals (the patriarchal house), and make the same point. But they happily ignore the topics of the law that are covered.

What concerns us is the role of documents in the formation and arrangement of their contents. The documentary hypothesis maintains that that role is primary, though (except for the Mishnah) not exclusive. The successor-documents, beginning with the Tosefta, do contain compositions written in conformity with the documentary purpose and conventions, as well as compositions that ignore that purpose and those conventions. Now, as is clear, I maintain that free-standing stories in quantity form a negligible proportion, and in quality are tangential where they occur. Others see in the same type of writing a proportion and a task so critical to the documents as to obliterate all marks of documentary intervention in the composition and compilation of the contents of the respective collections (to use a more appropriate word than "document").

At stake in this chapter is the role of the free-standing story in the Mishnah and the Tosefta. What we have seen is that the Mishnah is comprised by writing that nearly wholly conforms to over-riding documentary rules and program. From a form-analytical viewpoint, it is a document so uniform that it apparently was given form by its final editors more than by any prayer body of authors or compilers.

The Tosefta encompasses non-documentary writing. The case before us shows two facts. First, in our sample non-documentary writing is exceptional and negligible in proportion. Second, that type of writing is assigned no task important to the document. We further observed a fact outside of the limits of our particular problem. It concerns the reception of this non-documentary writing of the Tosefta (and comparable compositions). That is, where later documents cite non-documentary writing from the Tosefta, the selection fully accords with those documents' plan and program. The Yerushalmi and the Bavli naturalize within their program, and with good and sufficient reason, what is external to the Tosefta that they cite. That means the compositor of the analytical exercise before us understood perfectly well how the non-documentary writing of Tosefta Moed Qatan transcended the limits of Moed Qatan and embodied a principle central to the exposition of Pesahim — precisely the work that the two Talmuds undertake for themselves and do so unerringly and well. But that interesting result is not pertinent to the issue that defines our work.

VI. THE AUTONOMOUS, DOCUMENTARY STANDING OF THE MISHNAH AND THE TOSEFTA

Those who insist upon the atomistic reading of the Rabbinic documents, denying their formal and topical-propositional cogency, confront a problem in the Mishnah and the Tosefta. The former, as we see, is highly formalized, start to finish. It contains very little non-documentary writing, and by definition, no extra-documentary writing. Matters are not so clear-cut for the Tosefta, but the upshot is no different.

The conclusion, based on our sample, is ineluctable. In proportion, autonomous traditions scarcely surface in the Mishnah and form a negligible part of the Tosefta. And no one has shown that within the program of the Mishnah and of the Tosefta, such free-standing writing as is present plays any significant part in accomplishing the documentary goals., A miniscule proportion of the Tosefta, and no significant proportion of the Mishnah at all, is comprised by free-standing compositions. And where they do occur, compositions of that classifications are scarcely tangential in context: they barely intersect in more than completely formal ways with the Tosefta-passage where they do occur. But everyone understands that in the Rabbinic canon the Mishnah is unique, and the Tosefta depends upon the Mishnah for coherence and overall program. What about an exegetical document of the Halakhic corpus, is it possible that a larger proportion there is comprised by free-standing compositions, and that said compositions play a critical part in registering the point that the composite wishes to make? To answer these questions, we turn to Sifra and examine a sample of its Halakhic-exegetical writing.

3.

PROPORTION AND POSITION: EVIDENCE OF SHARED, AUTONOMOUS TRADITIONS IN A SAMPLE OF SIFRA

I. THE DOCUMENTARY TRAITS OF SIFRA

Like the Mishnah and Scripture, Sifra is cited, but cites no other document. Our sample contains no instances of shared and autonomous traditions. In it I identify not one composition that violates the formal conventions of the document. And more to the point in this study, when for its part Sifra is cited by later compilations, the cited passage always exhibits the indicative documentary traits of Sifra. Conversely, it never displays those of the later document with which it intersects at a given passage. What that means is that, like the Mishnah, our sample of Sifra yields no instances of shared, autonomous traditions, circulating beyond documentary lines. None calls into question its integrity as a cogent statement.

The program of the document is unique among those of the canonical compilations. That is because the problem that generates the document has no counterpart elsewhere. This compilation of Midrash-exegeses on the book of Leviticus forms a massive and systematic statement concerning the definition of the Mishnah in relationship to Scripture. Sifra's statement is achieved formally by provision of proof texts, from Scripture, for statements of the Mishnah. This is much as is done in the two Talmuds. The Mishnah is explicitly cited, not simply utilized, e.g., through such language as, "on this basis they have said," which effects the required linkage.

But, still more profoundly, the statement is also effected through a patterned analysis of the interior structure of thought. That is effected by means of the critique of the Mishnah's practical logic and the rehabilitation of the probative logic of hierarchical classification, accomplished through the form of *Listenwissenschaft*. Sifra's authorship achieves the reunion of the two Torahs, written and oral, Scripture and Mishnah, into a single cogent statement within the framework, under the auspices, of the written Torah. This it does by penetrating into the deep composition of logic that underlay the creation of the world in its correct components, rightly classified, and in its right order, as portrayed by the Torah.

The exercise is done in two ways. Specifically, first, what is required is systematically demolishing the logic that sustains an autonomous Mishnah. That logic for the Mishnah appeals to the intrinsic traits of things to accomplish classification and hierarchization. Second, the case is made by demonstrating dependency, for the identification of the correct classification of things, not upon the traits of things viewed in the abstract, but upon the classification of things by Scripture in particular. The framers of Sifra recast the two parts of the Torah — oral and written, the Mishnah and Scripture — into a single coherent statement through unitary and cogent discourse. So in choosing, as to structure, a book of the Pentateuch, and, as to fixed syntactic pattern, the exegetical form involving paraphrase and amplification of a phrase of a base-text of Scripture, the authorship of Sifra made its entire statement *in nuce*. Then by composing a document that for very long stretches simply cannot have been put together without the Mishnah and at the same time subjecting the generative logical principles of the Mishnah to devastating critique, that same authorship took up its position. The destruction of the Mishnah as an autonomous and freestanding statement, based upon its own logic, is followed by the reconstruction of large tracts of the Mishnah as a statement wholly within, and in accord with, the logic and program of the written Torah in Leviticus. That is what defines Sifra.

So much for the program of the document, what about its forms? Three forms dictate the entire rhetorical repertoire of this document.

The first, the dialectical, is the demonstration that if we wish to classify things, we must follow the taxa dictated by Scripture rather than relying solely upon the traits of the things we wish to classify.

The second, the citation-form, invokes the citation of passages of the Mishnah or the Tosefta in the setting of Scripture.

The third is commentary form, in which a phrase of Scripture is followed by an amplificatory clause of some sort.

The forms of the document admirably express the polemical purpose of the authorship at hand. What they wish to prove is that a taxonomy resting on the traits of things without reference to Scripture's classifications cannot serve. They further wish to restate the oral Torah in the setting of the written Torah. And, finally, they propose to accomplish the whole by rewriting the written Torah. The dialectical form accomplishes the first purpose, the citation-form the second, and the commentary form the third.

First comes in the simple commentary form, which is characteristic of the so-called Tannaite Midrash-compilations, Sifra and the two Sifrés. In this form a verse, or an element of a verse, is cited, and then a very few words explain the meaning of that verse. Second come the complex forms, in which a simple exegesis is augmented in some important way, commonly by questions and answers, so that we have more than simply a verse and a brief exposition of its elements or of its meaning as a whole. The authorship of the Sifra time and again wishes to show that prior documents, the Mishnah or Tosefta, cited verbatim, require the support of exegesis of Scripture for important propositions, presented in the Mishnah and the Tosefta not on the foundation of exegetical proof at all. In the main, moreover, the authorship of Sifra tends not to attribute its materials to specific authorities, and most of the pericopes containing attributions are shared with Mishnah and Tosefta.

II. THE SAMPLE: SIFRA PARASHAT TAZRI'A 122-124

I take as my sample somewhat more than half of Sifra Parashat Tazri'a, which I reproduce in my form-analytical translation. I indent what I regard as tangential to the main work of the document, the purposeful exegesis of the verses of Scripture. In this case, that means, the systematic exegesis of Lev. 12:1-8. The dominant form of the document is citation and gloss of a verse. Compositions that adhere to that form then are at the left-hand margin. I indicate what is shared with other documents by LOWER CASE CAPS; what belongs to the Mishnah or the Tosefta is in **bold face type.** Readers are reminded that in the outline given in section iv, diverse type faces bear a different signification altogether.

For the indication of parallels, I consulted the apparatus of the edition of Sifra by Isaac Hirsch Weiss (Vienna, repr. N.Y., 1947). These focus on the two Talmuds.

SIFRA PARASHAT TAZRI'A

CHAPTER ONE HUNDRED AND TWENTY-TWO

PARASHAT TAZRI'A PARASHAH 1
CXXII:I

1. A. ["The Lord spoke to Moses, saying, Speak to the Israelite people thus: When a woman at childbirth bears a male, she shall be unclean seven days; she shall be unclean as at the time of her menstrual infirmity. On the eighth day the flesh of his foreskin shall be circumcised. She shall remain in a state of blood purification for thirty-three days. She shall not touch any consecrated thing, nor enter the sanctuary until her period of purification is completed. If she shall bear a female, she shall be unclean two weeks as during her menstruation, and she shall remain in a state of blood purification for sixty-six days. On the completion of her period of purification, for either son or daughter, she shall bring to the priest, at the entrance of the tent of meeting, a lamb in its first year for a burnt — offering, and a pigeon or a turtledove for a sin — offering. He shall offer it before the Lord and make expiation on her behalf; she shall then be clean from her flow of blood. Such are the rituals concerning her who bears a child, male or female. If however her means do not suffice for a sheep, she shall take two turtledoves or two pigeons, one for a burnt — offering and the other for a sin — offering. The priest shall make expiation on her behalf and she shall be clean" (Lev. 12:1 — 8):
   B. "...Israelite people":
   C. In this matter, the Israelite people are engaged, but idolaters are not engaged in this matter.
2. A. "...ISRAELITE PEOPLE":
   B. I KNOW ONLY THAT BORN-ISRAELITES ARE COVERED BY THE LAW.

C. HOW DO I KNOW THAT SUBJECT TO IT ARE ALSO WOMEN-PROSELYTES AND BOND-WOMEN, WHETHER FREED OR NOT?

D. SCRIPTURE SAYS, "...A WOMAN."

The passage occurs at b. Ker. 7b/B. Ker. 1:3-5 I:1 as follows:

I.1 A. *How on the basis of Scripture do we know the law on the slave-girl* [**And so a slave-girl who gives birth brings an offering, and it is eaten**]?

B. *It is in accord with that which our rabbis have taught on Tannaite authority:*

C. "SPEAK TO THE CHILDREN OF ISRAEL: IF A WOMAN CONCEIVES AND BEARS A MALE CHILD...SHE SHALL BRING..." (LEV. 12:2FF.) — ON THE BASIS OF THIS STATEMENT, I KNOW ONLY THAT THE REQUIREMENT TO BRING AN OFFERING WHICH IS EATEN APPLIES TO THE CHILDREN OF ISRAEL. HOW DO I KNOW THAT IT APPLIES ALSO TO A WOMAN CONVERT AND TO A SLAVE-GIRL?

D. Scripture states, "if a woman" — [thus, of any sort].

What we have is no more and no less than a verbatim citation of Sifra. It is in the context of demonstrating that the rule of the Mishnah rests on Scripture. So too b. Yeb. 74b presents the following:

Q. *Objected R. Shisha b. R. Idi, "But can you maintain that the verse at hand [Lev. 12:4] speaks of food in the status of priestly rations? Has it not been taught on Tannaite authority:*

R. "'SPEAK TO THE CHILDREN OF ISRAEL: IF A WOMAN CONCEIVES AND BEARS A MALE CHILD...' (LEV. 12:2FF.) — ON THE BASIS OF THIS STATEMENT, I KNOW ONLY THAT THE REQUIREMENT TO BRING AN OFFERING WHICH IS EATEN APPLIES TO THE CHILDREN

OF ISRAEL. HOW DO I KNOW THAT IT APPLIES ALSO TO A WOMAN CONVERT AND TO A SLAVE-GIRL? SCRIPTURE STATES, "IF A WOMAN" — [THUS, OF ANY SORT].'

S. *Now if it should enter your mind that at issue were food in the status of priestly rations, then do proselyte women or emancipated slave-women eat food in the status of priestly rations?!"*

Here is no instance in which a free-standing composition is cited in two documents, ignoring the preferences of them both. It is an instance of an explicit citation of Sifra by the statement attributed to Shisha b. R. Idi. It confirms the documentary lines of Sifra, rather than calling them into question. The remainder of Parashah One unit I is unique to Sifra.

3. A. "When a woman at childbirth bears a male, she shall be unclean seven days":
B. What is the point of this statement?
C. Since Scripture says, "You shall put the Israelites on guard against their uncleanness, lest they die through their uncleanness by defiling my tabernacle which is among them" (Lev. 15:31),
D. might I conclude that that is so whether the uncleanness takes place inside [through actually entering the building] or outside the tabernacle [through merely touching the building, for instance]?
E. Scripture says in connection with the woman who has given birth, "nor enter the sanctuary until her period of purification is completed."
4. A. Might one then claim that the woman after childbirth, who is unclean in a light measure, should impart uncleanness to the sanctuary if she goes into it, while as to other unclean persons, they do so whether inside or outside?
B. Scripture in context refers to the "Israelite people."
C. Lo, the Israelite people are in the same classification as the woman after childbirth.

D. Just as the woman after childbirth imparts uncleanness only from within, so all of them will impart uncleanness only from within.

5. A. I know only that that is the case in reference to one who is subjected to a most severe form of uncleanness, such as the woman after childbirth.

B. One who suffers from a less severe form of uncleanness, one who suffers from corpse — uncleanness, one who has had sexual relations and all who impart uncleanness to man — how do we know that the same rule applies?

C. Scripture says, "You shall put the Israelites on guard against their uncleanness, lest they die through their uncleanness by defiling my tabernacle which is among them" (Lev. 15:31),

D. thereby encompassing all of them.

6. A. "When a woman at childbirth bears a male":

B. This excludes the case of one who gives birth prior to the revelation of the Torah [since the formulation speaks of "when," understood to mean, in the future, but not prior to this time].

C. Might one suppose that I should also exclude the case of one who became pregnant prior to the revelation of the Torah but gave birth after the revelation of the Torah?

D. Scripture says, "If she shall bear a female...."

E. The entire matter depends only on the moment of actually giving birth.

7. A. "When a woman at childbirth bears a male":

B. This rule applies only to one who gives birth from the place at which fertilization takes place,

C. **excluding that case in which the child which goes forth from the side [M. Nid. 5:1D].**

D. R. Simeon says, "That which goes forth from the side, lo, it is like one that is born [from the womb].

E. "And they are liable on its account for a sacrifice.

F. "But the father is free [of the obligation to give to the priest] five *selas* for a [firstborn] son."

Apart from the citation of the Tosefta, so far as I know this entire passage is unique to Sifra.

CXXII:II
1. A. **"If a woman conceives and bears a male"** (Lev. 12:2):
B. What is the point of Scripture?
C. Because it is said, "And she shall be unclean for seven days, and on the eighth day he will be circumcised,"
D. I might infer that only the child who emerges alive imparts uncleanness of childbirth to his mother. How do I know that the child who is stillborn imparts uncleanness of childbirth to his mother?
E. Said R. Judah, "Lo, I reason as follows:
F. "If the one who is born alive, who does not impart uncleanness by reason of overshadowing a corpse ["in the Tent"] for seven days to his mother and to those that are with his mother, lo, such a one does impart uncleanness of childbirth to his mother, the stillborn child who does impart uncleanness by reason of overshadowing a corpse ["in the Tent"] for seven days to his mother and to those with his mother, is it not logical that he should impart uncleanness of childbirth to his mother?"
G. They said to R. Judah, "The logic that you adduce produces a stringent ruling at the outset and a lenient ruling at the end.
H. "Is it not logical that, if the living child does keep his mother clean [with reference to corpse — uncleanness in the Tent], should not the dead child preserve cleanness for his mother?"
I. Accordingly Scripture is required to state, A male — to encompass even the stillborn child.
2. A. I know only [that uncleanness applies to a child born] at the age of nine months.
B. How [do I know that a child born at] the age of eight, seven, six, five months [produces uncleanness]?

C. Scripture says, "And bears a male child" (Lev. 12:2) — anything to which she will give birth.

D. Or [perhaps] And she will give birth [means that] I know only that the child [produces the circumstance of uncleanness]?

E. HOW DO I KNOW THAT **SHE WHO ABORTS A SANDAL OR A PLACENTA**

N. **OR A SAC WHICH IS FORMED AND THAT WHICH GOES FORTH IN PIECES** [IS UNCLEAN]

O. SCRIPTURE SAYS, "WHEN A WOMAN CONCEIVES AND GIVES BIRTH — ANY SEED TO WHICH SHE GIVES BIRTH."

The intersection with the Mishnah produces a parallel at b. Nid. 23b. The same composition is cited nearly verbatim.

CXXII:III
1. A. Might I think that **she who aborts something like fish and locusts and insects and creeping things,** that she should be unclean?

B. SCRIPTURE SAYS, "MALE" —

C. JUST AS THIS IS DISTINCTIVE IN THAT IT BEARS THE LIKENESS OF MAN, SO THESE ARE EXCLUDED WHICH DO NOT BEAR THE LIKENESS OF MAN.

As above, the intersection with the Mishnah produces a parallel at b. Nid. 23b,

2. A. Might I think that she who aborts a creature with a head which is not formed, a creature with a body which is not formed, and that which has two backs and two spinal columns, that, since they have the likeness of man, she should be unclean on their account?

B. Scripture says, "And she will be unclean seven days. And on the eighth day he will be circumcised" (Lev. 12:2 — 3).

C. Just as this one is distinctive in that he is worthy of the creation of a soul, so these are excluded for they are not worthy of the creation of a soul [covenant of the eighth day].

D. "And she will be unclean" (Lev. 12:2).

E. She is unclean, but the child is not unclean.

F. And is [the opposite rule] not logical?

G. If the child has caused her to be unclean so that, lo, she is unclean, the child himself, who has caused her to be unclean — is it not logical that he should be unclean?

H. The goat which is sent forth will prove the matter, for it caused uncleanness, but lo, it is clean [while alive].

I. No, if you have said so in respect to the goat which is sent away, which is not subject to uncleanness, will you say so concerning the child, who is subject to uncleanness?

J. Since he is subject to uncleanness, let him be unclean.

K. Scripture says, "She" — she is unclean, but the child is not unclean.

The dialectical continuation, No. 2, has no counterpart in Bavli, which is rarely interested in examining, in the manner of Sifra ("is the opposite no logical") contrary positions to the one that its exegesis has produced.

CXXII:IV

1. A. "When a woman at childbirth bears a male, she shall be unclean seven days":

B. She should count the days from the birth of the final foetus.

C. Is that proposition not a matter of logic?

D. A woman contracts uncleanness from a corpse and she contracts uncleanness from the offspring.

E. Just as we find that, when she contracts uncleanness from a corpse, she counts the seven days from the moment only of the final point at which she contracted uncleanness [for the sprinkling on the third and seventh days],

F. so when the woman contracts uncleanness in childbirth, she should count only from the appearance of the last of a sequence of births.

G. Or take this route:

H. A woman contracts uncleanness from menstrual blood and she contracts uncleanness from an offspring.

I. Just as, when she contracts uncleanness from menstrual blood, she counts the seven days only from the moment of the first appearance of the unclean blood [on the first day of her period, so that, seven days later, she is clean, even though menstrual blood may occur on the immediately preceding day],

J. so when the woman contracts uncleanness in childbirth, she should count only from the appearance of the first in a sequence of births.

K. Let us then identify the appropriate analogy:

L. We should draw an analogy from uncleanness which derives from a source other than the woman herself for a form of uncleanness which likewise derives from a source other than the woman herself [the corpse, the offspring],

M. but let not the case of menstrual blood enter in, since that form of uncleanness derives from the woman's own body.

N. Or take this route:

O. We should drawn an analogy from a form of uncleanness that derives from the woman for another form of uncleanness that derives from the woman [the offspring, menstrual blood],

P. but let not the case of corpse — uncleanness enter in, which does not derive from the woman herself.

Q. Accordingly, it is necessary for Scripture to state, "When a woman at childbirth bears a male, she shall be unclean seven days":

R. She should count the days from the birth of the final foetus.

CXXII:IV is a perfect realization of the dialectical argument, which demonstrates that Scripture alone, and not hierarchical classification of traits of things, serves to produce a reliable result.

CXXII:V
1. A. "...seven days":
B. Might one think [that she should be unclean whenever blood occurs in respect to childbirth] whether the days are consecutive or separate?
C. Scripture says, "As the days of her menstrual period." Just as the days of her menstrual cycle are in sequence, so the days of her uncleanness by reason of childbirth are consecutive.
2. A. "Like the days of her menstrual period":
B. Scripture compares the days of her menstrual period to the days of her uncleanness by reason of childbirth.
C. Just as the days of her menstrual period are not subject to uncleanness by reason of *Zibah* and cannot be included in the counting of the seven days, so the days of her uncleanness by reason of childbirth are not subject to uncleanness by reason of *Zibah* and cannot be included in the counting of the seven [clean] days.
3. A. "Her sickness shall she be unclean" — to encompass the one who has intercourse with her.
B. "Her sickness shall she be unclean" — to encompass all the nights.
C. "Her sickness shall she be unclean" — to encompass the woman who gives birth while unclean as a *Zabah*, that she should not be deemed clean until she will sit out seven clean days.
4. A. "She will sit [Then she shall continue ("sit") for thirty—three days in the blood of her purifying":
— to encompass the one who is in hard labor during

the eleven days [of *Zibah*], that she should be clean in respect to *Zibah*.

B. Might one think that she should be clean of menstrual uncleanness?

C. Scripture says, "Her sickness — she shall impart uncleanness" — in the days of purifying, even though she sees [blood].

Here again, what is unique to Sifra is not cited in any other document.

Chapter One Hundred and Twenty-Three

Parashat Tazri'a Pereq 1

CXXIII:I
1. A. "AND ON THE EIGHTH DAY [THE FLESH OF HIS FORESKIN SHALL BE CIRCUMCISED]":
B. MIGHT ONE SUPPOSE THAT THIS MAY BE DONE EITHER BY DAY OR BY NIGHT?
C. SCRIPTURE SAYS, "...DAY,"
D. BY DAY AND NOT BY NIGHT.
E. I know only that the one who is circumcised on the eighth day after birth is to be circumcised by day. How do I know that, if the rite takes place on the ninth, tenth, or eleventh days after birth and all others that are to be circumcised should be circumcised only by day?
F. Scripture says, "and on the eighth day."

At B. Meg. 20a/B. 2:5 II.1 the Bavli goes over the matter before us. It proves that, among other rites, circumcision must be done in day light, not by night.

M. MEG. 2:5

A. One may not [1] read the Megillah, [2] nor circumcise, [3] nor immerse [in a miqveh], [4] nor sprinkle [cf. Num. 19:11-22], [5] nor, similarly, may one who waits a [single] day [for purification] corresponding to a [single] day [of impurity; cf. Lev. 15:25 ff] immerse herself until sunrise.

B. And any of them who did [the prescribed act] after the morning pillar [i.e., the beginning of daylight], it is acceptable.

I.1 A. *From where [do we derive that the reading of Esther must follow sunrise, 2:4A1]?*

B. As Scripture said, "...and these days are remembered and observed" (Est. 9:28) *[meaning] in the daytime, yes; at night, no.*

C. *One may say [this is] a response to R. Joshua ben Levi, because,* said R. Joshua ben Levi: A man is obligated to read the scroll [of Esther] at night and to study it in the daytime.

D. *When it was taught [in the Mishnah, it was dealing only with] the day.*

II.1 A. Nor circumcise, etc. [2:4A2].

B. As is written, "and on the eighth day [emphasizing the daytime], he shall circumcise" (Lev. 12:3).

This surely does not qualify as a free-standing composition, let alone a parallel; Sifra and Bavli go over the same ground. Sifra continues with a story and a reinforcement of the prooftext:

2. A. Said a certain disciple before R. Aqiba, "It is necessary to make the following observation:

B. "If Scripture had been formulated, 'she shall be unclean seven days. On the eighth day the flesh of his foreskin shall be circumcised,' one might have taken the view that the sum of seven and eight is fifteen [so the circumcision should be on the fifteenth day].

C. "Scripture accordingly says, 'and on the day....'"

D. Said to him R. Aqiba, "You dive into mighty waters and dredge up another shard in your hand!

E. "Is it not in any event stated, 'And throughout the generations every male among you shall be circumcised at the age of eight days' (Gen. 17:12)."

The continuation of the passage that follows reverts to the citation-gloss form, and it occurs elsewhere.

3. A. "AND ON THE EIGHTH DAY [THE FLESH OF HIS FORESKIN SHALL BE CIRCUMCISED]":

B. THIS TEACHES THAT THE ENTIRE DAY IS SUITABLE FOR CIRCUMCISION,

C. ALTHOUGH THOSE WHO ARE ZEALOUS PROMPTLY CARRY OUT RELIGIOUS DUTIES,

D. AS IT IS SAID, "AND ABRAHAM AROSE EARLY IN THE MORNING AND SADDLED HIS ASS" (GEN. 22:2).

B. Pes. 4a/1:1 I.14 cites the passage verbatim:

I.14 A. *Now that we have established it as a fact that all parties concur: the word at hand refers to the evening, then, since according to both R. Judah and R. Meir [below],* leaven is forbidden only from the sixth hour and later, *shouldn't the search be made in the sixth hour? And should you say,* people who are really prompt carrying out the religious duty before it is required to do so, *then why not make the search from the morning? For it is written,* "And in the eighth day the flesh of his foreskin shall be circumcised" (Lev. 12:3), and it has been taught on Tannaite authority:

B. THE ENTIRE DAY IS SUITABLE FOR THE RITE OF CIRCUMCISION, BUT PEOPLE WHO ARE REALLY PROMPT CARRY OUT THE RELIGIOUS DUTY BEFORE IT IS REQUIRED TO DO SO, AS IT IS SAID, "AND ABRAHAM GOT UP EARLY IN THE MORNING" (GEN. 22:3).

Once more, all we have is the citation of the syllogism of Sifra.

> **4.** A. "AND ON THE EIGHTH DAY [THE FLESH OF HIS FORESKIN SHALL BE CIRCUMCISED]":
> B. EVEN ON THE SABBATH.
> C. HOW THEN AM I TO INTERPRET THE STATEMENT, "THOSE THAT VIOLATE IT SHALL SURELY DIE" (EX. 31:14).
> D. THIS REFERS TO OTHER ACTS OF LABOR, EXCLUSIVE OF THOSE ACTUALLY INVOLVED IN THE ACT OF CIRCUMCISION.
> E. But might I interpret the statement, "Those that violate it shall surely die" (Ex. 31:14) to speak even of acts of labor actually involved in the act of circumcision?
> F. Then how should I carry out the statement, "And on the eighth day [the flesh of his foreskin shall be circumcised]"?
> G. It would mean, "unless it is the Sabbath."
> H. Accordingly, Scripture states, "And on the eighth day [the flesh of his foreskin shall be circumcised]":
> I. even on the Sabbath.

When the passage is cited, it is the citation and gloss component. The secondary development of the argument, E-I, is not replicated in the parallel. B. Shab. 132a/19:1.II.17 the exegetical part of the passage is cited verbatim:

> **II.17**A. "Circumcision and everything having to do with preparing it override the restrictions of the Sabbath," the words of R. Eliezer —
> B. *How does R. Eliezer know this fact? If it is from all of these others, then matters are as we have said. And furthermore, what distinguishes these other matters* **[132A]** *is that if the time for doing them passes, they are annulled [which is not the case of circumcision]. Rather, this is the scriptural basis for the position of R. Eliezer:*

C. SCRIPTURE SAYS, "AND IN THE EIGHTH DAY THE FLESH OF HIS FORESKIN SHALL BE CIRCUMCISED" (LEV. 12:3) — EVEN ON THE SABBATH.

D. *Well, then, let the All-Merciful make that statement with regard to circumcision, and let all of the other cases be derived by analogy from that case?*

E. *The reason that that is not feasible is that one may raise this objection to the analogy:* What distinguishes circumcision is that, on that account, thirteen covenants were made.

This is hardly an instance of a free-standing composition appearing in two documents (or more) and ignoring the formal preferences of both of them. Indeed, were we to rely only on the evidence of Sifra, we should not comprehend that to which the proponents of the autonomy of free-standing parallels have in mind. Only when we come to the later Midrash-compilations shall we come upon data that pertains to their thesis. But the thesis is expressed, e.g., in Goldberg-Schaefer-Becker's formulation, in the setting of the entirety of the Rabbinic canon (and beyond, with the Hekhalot!), not within the limitations of the documents that produce pertinent data.

5. A. "the flesh of his foreskin shall be circumcised":

B. even though there is a bright spot on the spot.

C. Then how shall I interpret the statement, "In cases of a skin affection, be most careful to do exactly as the Levitical priests instruct you" (Dt. 24:8)?

D. even with respect to circumcision [so do not circumcise if at the foreskin is a bright spot that may or may not indicate the presence of the skin affection].

E. Then how shall I interpret the statement, "the flesh of his foreskin shall be circumcised"?

F. When there is no bright spot.

G. Scripture says, "the flesh of his foreskin shall be circumcised":

H. even though there is a bright spot on the spot.

6. A. "...foreskin":

B. If it is assuredly the foreskin of a male child, then the rite overrides the restrictions of the Sabbath, but in a case of doubt, then the rite does not override the restrictions of the Sabbath.

C. "...foreskin":

D. **The circumcision of the foreskin of someone with clearly established male gender-traits overrides the restrictions of the Sabbath, but the circumcision of a baby bearing the sexual traits of both genders does not override the restrictions of the Sabbath.**

E. **R. Judah says, "The circumcision of an infant bearing the sexual traits of both genders does override the restrictions of the Sabbath, and the liability [for not doing so] is to extirpation" [M. Shab. 19:3G-H].**

The Mishnah's formal preferences are honored in the citation, by Sifra, of the Mishnah-passage. There is no pretense at linking the proof-text to the proposition of the law.

7. A. "...foreskin":

B. If it is assuredly the day [on which, eight days earlier, the child was born], then the rite overrides the restrictions of the Sabbath,

C. but [if it was born] at twilight [so that we do not know for certain that the Sabbath coincides with the eighth day after birth], then the rite does not override the restrictions of the Sabbath.

8. A. "...foreskin":

B. If it is assuredly a child born uncircumcised, then the rite of circumcision does override the restrictions of the Sabbath.

C. But the circumcision of a baby born circumcised does not override the restrictions of the Sabbath.

D. For the House of Shammai say, "It is necessary to draw from the infant a drop of blood as a mark of the covenant of circumcision nonetheless."

E. And the House of Hillel say, "It is not necessary."

F. Said R. Simeon b. Eleazar, "The House of Shammai and the House of Hillel did not dispute concerning the one who was born circumcised, that it is necessary to draw a drop of blood of the covenant of circumcision from him, for it is a foreskin which is pressed in.

G. "Concerning what did they dispute? Concerning a convert who converted already circumcised. For the House of Shammai say, 'It is necessary to draw from him a drop of blood of the covenant.' And the House of Hillel say, 'It is not necessary to draw from him a drop of blood of the covenant'" [T. Shab. 15:9K-O].

In the preceding, the Tosefta supplies Sifra with a composition that is primary to the Tosefta and secondary to Sifra.

The main point of the following passage, if not the exact detail, occurs in both Sifra and Bavli Keritot 10b, as shown here:

9. A. "SHE SHALL REMAIN IN A STATE OF BLOOD PURIFICATION FOR THIRTY-THREE DAYS":

B. MIGHT ONE SUPPOSE THAT THESE DAYS MAY BE EITHER CONSECUTIVE OR NOT CONSECUTIVE?

C. SCRIPTURE SAYS, "...DAY."

D. JUST AS A DAY IS WHOLLY ONE, SO THE PERIOD OF THIRTY-THREE DAYS MUST BE WHOLLY ONE AND CONSECUTIVE.

E. MIGHT ONE SUPPOSE THAT THIRTY DAYS MUST BE CONSECUTIVE, BUT AS TO THE OTHER

THREE, THEY MAY BE EITHER CONSECUTIVE OR NOT CONSECUTIVE?

F. SCRIPTURE SAYS, "...THIRTY DAYS AND THREE DAYS...":

G. JUST AS THE THIRTY DAYS MUST BE CONSECUTIVE, SO AS TO THE OTHER THREE, THEY MUST BE CONSECUTIVE AS WELL.

THE COMPARABLE PASSAGE IS AT B. KER. 10B/2:4A-C II.1, AS FOLLOWS:

V. *Furthermore, said R. Ashi, "Come and take note:* ["'BUT IF SHE BEARS A FEMALE CHILD, THEN SHE SHALL BE UNCLEAN TWO WEEKS, AS IN HER MENSTRUATION; AND SHE SHALL CONTINUE IN THE BLOOD OF HER PURIFYING FOR SIXTY]-SIX DAYS'(LEV. 12:5) — MIGHT ONE SUPPOSE THAT THIS IS EITHER CONTINUOUS OR DISRUPTED? SCRIPTURE SAYS, 'SIXTY.' JUST AS ALL SIXTY-DAYS MUST BE UNINTERRUPTED, SO THE SIX DAYS MUST ALL BE UNINTERRUPTED. *Now who is the authority behind this formulation? Should I say rabbis take the position that the days can be interrupted? And have not rabbis said that we do take account of the second birth? It must therefore be the position of R. Judah, and it must prove that R. Judah indeed maintains the view that he does only if it leads to a more strict rule, but not if it leads to a more lenient rule."*

Once more, all we have is an explicit citation, controlling for the comparable formulations, thirty-three and sixty-six. Presently we shall have a more exact match, sixty-six and sixty-six, with no variation in the upshot.

10. A. Scripture says, "...thirty days and three days...":

B. What is the sense of Scripture here?

C. One might have thought that in the case of a female, in which instance the number of days of uncleanness is great, the number of days of purifying will also be great.

D. In the case of a male, in which the number of days of uncleanness will be few, should not the days of purifying be still greater?

E. Scripture is explicit in saying, "...thirty days and three days...."

11. A. "She shall remain [in a state of blood purification for thirty-three days]":

B. this encompasses **the woman in protracted hard labor [for three days] during the eleven days between periods [during which a flow is deemed a flux in line with Lev. 15:25],**

C. **indicating that she is held to be clean as to flux [cf. M. Nid. 4:A, B].**

D. Might one suppose that she should be regarded as clean, also, as to menstrual uncleanness?

E. Scripture explicitly states, "she shall be unclean as at the time of her menstrual infirmity."

12. A. "...in a state of blood purification":

B. even though she produces blood.

13. A. "SHE SHALL NOT TOUCH ANY CONSECRATED THING":

B. MIGHT ONE SUPPOSE THAT THE PROHIBITION EXTENDS EVEN TO FOOD DESIGNATED AS TITHE?

C. SCRIPTURE SAYS, "NOR ENTER THE SANCTUARY,"

D. JUST AS IN THE CASE OF THE SANCTUARY, VIOLATION OF THE RULES OF UNCLEANNESS IS PENALIZED BY LOSING ONE'S LIFE, SO IN THE CASE OF HOLY THINGS UNDER DISCUSSION HERE, IT IS OF THE CLASSIFICATION IN WHICH VIOLATION OF THE RULES OF UNCLEANNESS IS PENALIZED BY LOSING ONE'S LIFE.

E. THAT THEN EXCLUDES THE MATTER OF FOOD THAT HAS BEEN DESIGNATED AS TITHE [TO WHICH SUCH A PENALTY DOES NOT APPLY].

At b. Yeb. 74b-75a/8:1-2E II.1R we find an allusion to the comparable matter of whether the woman after child birth may touch food designated as heave-offering (priestly rations):

> P. *Raba said, "Were the death penalty not involved, you could not say so* [and food in the status of priestly rations, bathing suffices, for tithe, waiting for sunset should be required (Slotki)], *for Scripture has said, 'And the priest shall make atonement for her and she shall be clean'* (Lev. 12:8), *meaning, up to that point she was unclean. Now if this spoke of Holy Things, then the verse 'and the flesh that touches any unclean thing shall not be eaten'* (Lev. 7:19) *should apply. So it must be inferred that [Lev. 12:4] speaks of food in the status of priestly rations."*
>
> Q. *Objected R. Shisha b. R. Idi, "But can you maintain that the verse at hand [Lev. 12:4] speaks of food in the status of priestly rations? Has it not been taught on Tannaite authority:* "'Speak to the children of Israel: if a woman conceives and bears a male child...she shall bring...'" (Lev. 12:2ff.) — on the basis of this statement, I know only that the requirement to bring an offering which is eaten applies to the children of Israel. How do I know that it applies also to a woman convert and to a slave-girl? Scripture states, "if a woman" — [thus, of any sort].' *Now if it should enter your mind that at issue were food in the status of priestly rations, then do proselyte women or emancipated slave-women eat food in the status of priestly rations?!"*
>
> R. *Said Raba, "But don't they?* **[75A]** *And has it not been stated in Scripture,* 'SHE SHALL TOUCH NO HOLY THINGS' — WHICH INCLUDES FOOD IN THE STATUS OF PRIESTLY RATIONS. *Rather, Scripture has dealt with a number of distinct topics* [each rule applying to a given class of persons (Slotki)].

This hardly qualifies for the present purpose. But whether comparable of not, the Bavli's rendition does not encompass the dialectical exercise that is integral to Sifra's polemic:

14. A. Then might one argue as follows:
    B. Just as in the case of the sanctuary, one who enters in a state of uncleanness is penalized by extirpation, so in the case of Holy Things, one who eats such food in a state of uncleanness will be penalized through extirpation, thus excluding food that has been designated as priestly rations?
    C. Scripture says, "She shall not touch any consecrated thing":
    D. thus encompassing food that has been designated as priestly rations.
15. A. Then might one argue as follows:
    B. just as in reference to Holy Things, what is subject to discussion is communication of uncleanness through actual contact, so in the case of the sanctuary, which is penalized is contamination through an act of actual contact.
    C. And how do I know that uncleanness affecting the sanctuary that has been brought in not through an act of actual contact [for example, if an unclean person enters the sanctuary in a wagon and does not actually touch the building] also is prohibited?
    D. Scripture says, "nor enter the sanctuary."
16. A. "...until her period of purification is completed":
    B. this encompasses the case of the birth of a female.

Chapter One Hundred and Twenty-Four

Parashat Tazri'a Pereq 2

CXXIV:I
1. A. "If she shall bear a female":
   B. I know only that the rule applies to a female. How do I know that it encompasses the one of doubtful sexual traits and the one who bears physical traits of both sexes?

C. Scripture says, "And if she bears a female, then she shall be unclean."
D. The matter depends solely upon the act of giving birth.
E. And she shall be unclean two weeks. Two weeks which are fourteen days.

What follows is a free-standing exposition that does not conform to the preferred forms of Sifra

CXXIV:II
1. A. HIS DISCIPLES ASKED R. JUDAH B. ROES, "MIGHT WE INTERPRET THE VERSE OF SCRIPTURE, 'SHE SHALL BE UNCLEAN TWO WEEKS' TO MEAN THAT SHE SHALL BE UNCLEAN FOR SEVENTY DAYS [SINCE THE WORDS 'TWO WEEKS' AND 'SEVENTY DAYS' ARE MADE UP OF THE SAME CONSONANTS]?
B. HE SAID TO THEM, "UNCLEANNESS AND CLEANNESS PERTAIN BOTH TO THE MALE AND TO THE FEMALE. JUST AS THE DAYS OF PURIFYING ARE TWICE IN THE CASE OF THE FEMALE WHAT THEY ARE IN THE MALE, SO THE DAYS OF UNCLEANNESS WILL BE TWICE IN THE CASE OF THE FEMALE WHAT THEY ARE IN THE MALE."
C. AFTER THE DISCIPLES HAD GONE THEIR WAY, HE WENT OUT AND CALLED THEM BACK AND SAID TO THEM, "I NEED NOT HAVE TAKEN YOUR QUESTION SERIOUSLY, BECAUSE THE MATRIX OF MEANING RESTS WITH THE VOWELS THAT WE ATTACH TO THE CONSONANTS [AND THESE CLEARLY INDICATE THE ANSWER, AS GIVEN IN THE TRANSLATION OF THE VERSE AT HAND]."

While the story, CXXIV:II.1, does not conform to the formal conventions of Sifra, No. 2, which follows, naturalizes the discussion into Sifra's norms. This is done by the moving argument, 2.A, challenged by 2.B, yielding the definitive exegesis at the end — all typical of Sifra's dialectical argument.

> 2. A. But this is the correct reply in this matter: Uncleanness and cleanness pertain both to the male and to the female. Just as the days of purifying are twice in the case of the female what they are in the male, so the days of uncleanness will be twice in the case of the female what they are in the male.
> B. But take this route:
> C. Since in the case of the male, the days of purifying are few, so the days of uncleanness will also be few.
> D. But in the case of the female, since the days of purifying are many, the days of uncleanness surely should be few.
> E. Scripture says, "she shall be unclean for two weeks, as during her menstruation.
> F. "And she shall be unclean two weeks":
> G. Two weeks which are fourteen days.

At B. San. 4b/1:1-6 II.4 E-GB, the passage is given a verbatim-citation, with minor variations in wording:

> II.4 A. *Said R. Isaac bar Joseph said R. Yohanan, "Rabbi, R. Judah b. Roes, the House of Shammai, R. Simeon, and R. Aqiba, all take the view that* we read Scripture in the way in which the supplied vowels direct it to be read."
> B. *As to Rabbi, evidence is as we have just now stated [that we interpret the word in accord with the supplied vowels, thus as a plural, rather than in accord with its consonantal form, which is in the singular].*
> C. *R. Judah b. Roes, as it has been taught on Tannaite authority:*
> D. *For it has been taught on Tannaite authority:*
> E. A DISCIPLE ASKED R. JUDAH B. ROES, "I READ [AT LEV. 12:5, 'IF SHE BEAR A FEMALE CHILD, SHE SHALL BE UNCLEAN FOR TWO WEEKS'] THE CONSONANTS AS 'TWO WEEKS.' IS IT POSSIBLE THAT A WOMAN WHO BEARS A FEMALE

CHILD SHOULD BE UNCLEAN FOR SEVENTY DAYS [READING THE CONSONANTS IN THAT WAY]?"

F. HE SAID TO THEM, "THE SCRIPTURE HAS IMPOSED UNCLEANNESS FOLLOWED BY A PERIOD OF CLEANNESS ON THE OCCASION OF BIRTH OF A MALE, AND, IN THE CASE OF THE FEMALE, IT IS FOR DOUBLE THE PERIOD SPECIFIED FOR A MALE. SO TOO WE WHEN THE SCRIPTURE IMPOSES A PERIOD OF UNCLEANNESS IN A MALE, FOR A FEMALE IT SHOULD BE DOUBLE THAT SAME PERIOD [AND HENCE, SINCE IT IS A WEEK OF UNCLEANNESS ON THE OCCASION OF THE BIRTH OF A MALE, IT SHOULD BE TWO WEEKS — NOT SEVENTY DAYS — FOR THE FEMALE]."

G. AFTER THEY HAD GONE FORTH, HE RAN AFTER THEM, BROUGHT THEM BACK, AND SAID TO THEM, "YOU DO NOT REQUIRE [THE ARGUMENT I JUST MADE], SINCE WE PRONOUNCE THE WORD AS 'TWO WEEKS', AND THE PRINCIPLE IS THAT WE FOLLOW THE VERSION OF SCRIPTURE IN THE WAY IN WHICH THE SUPPLIED VOWELS DIRECT THAT IT SHOULD BE READ."

The passage that occurs in Sifra is not woven into the Bavli's discussion, it is cited whole and complete, as from another compilation altogether. Omitted is CXXIV:II.2, which naturalizes the narrative-dialogue into the framework of Sifra.

What follows is already familiar, as noted just now.

3. A. "...SIXTY-SIX DAYS":
B. MIGHT ONE SUPPOSE THAT THESE DAYS MAY BE EITHER CONSECUTIVE OR NOT CONSECUTIVE?
C. SCRIPTURE SAYS, "...DAY."
D. JUST AS A DAY IS WHOLLY ONE, SO THE PERIOD OF SIXTY-SIX DAYS MUST BE WHOLLY ONE AND CONSECUTIVE.

E. Might one suppose that sixty days must be consecutive, but as to the other six, they may be either consecutive or not consecutive?

F. Scripture says, "...sixty days and six days...":

G. Just as the thirty days must be consecutive, so as to the other three, they must be consecutive as well.

4. A. Scripture says, "...sixty days and six days...":

B. What is the sense of Scripture here?

C. One might have thought that in the case of a male, in which instance the number of days of uncleanness is small, the number of days of purifying will also be small.

D. In the case of a female, in which the number of days of cleanness will be few, should not the days of purifying be still fewer?

E. Scripture is explicit in saying, "...sixty days and six days...."

5. A. "SHE SHALL CONTINUE [IN THE BLOOD OF HER PURIFYING FOR SIXTY-SIX DAYS]":

B. THIS ENCOMPASSES **THE ONE WHO GOES INTO HARD LABOR DURING THE EIGHTY DAYS OF PURIFYING FOR A FEMALE, THAT ALL THE BLOOD WHICH SHE SEES IS UNCLEAN, UNTIL THE CHILD WILL EMERGE.**

C. AND R. ELIEZER DECLARES IT UNCLEAN.

D. THEY SAID TO R. ELIEZER, "NOW IN A SITUATION IN WHICH THE LAW IS STRINGENT, IN THE CASE OF BLOOD WHICH APPEARS DURING A PERIOD OF RESPITE, BEFORE THE BIRTH, THE LAW RULES LENIENTLY IN THE MATTER OF BLOOD DURING RESPITE AFTER THE BIRTH, IN A SITUATION IN WHICH THE LAW RULED LENIENTLY [TO BEGIN WITH] — CONCERNING BLOOD WHICH IS PRODUCED DURING A PERIOD OF HARD LABOR BEFORE THE BIRTH, IS IT NOT LOGICAL THAT WE SHOULD RULE LENIENTLY IN CONNECTION WITH BLOOD PRODUCED THROUGH HARD LABOR AFTER THE BIRTH?"

E. He said to them, "It is sufficient if the inferred law [about giving birth during the sixty-six days] is as strict as that from which it is inferred [labor at any other time]. In what respect has the law ruled leniently for her? In respect to the uncleanness of her flux. But she is unclean in respect to the uncleanness of a menstruant."

F. They said to him, "Lo, we answer you in another wise. Now if in the case in which the law imposed a strict rule, in the case of respite before the birth, the law imposed a more lenient rule, in the case of hard labor, than in the case of respite, in a case in which the law gave a lenient rule to begin with, in the case of respite which is after the birth, is it not logical that we should impose a more lenient rule in the case of hard labor than in the case of respite?"

G. He said to them, "Even if you give such replies all day long, nonetheless: It is sufficient if the inferred law is as strict as that from which it is inferred.

H. "Just as [blood produced in] the first travail leaves the woman unclean with the uncleanness of menstruation, so the second hard labor leaves the woman unclean with the uncleanness of a menstruant."

At Bavli Nid. 38b/M. Nid. 4:6 I.1, the same materials recur:

M. Nid. 4:6

A. She who is in protracted labor during the eighty days [of cleanness] after the birth of a female —
B. any blood which she sees is clean,
C. until the child emerges.
D. And R. Eliezer declares [it] unclean.
E. They said to R. Eliezer, "Now in a situation in which the law is stringent, in the case of blood which appears during a period of respite, the law rules leniently in the matter of blood produced by hard labor,
F. "in a situation in which the law ruled leniently [to begin with], concerning blood which is produced during a period of respite, is it not logical that we should rule leniently in connection with blood produced through hard labor?"
G. He said to them, "It is sufficient if the inferred law is as strict as that from which it is inferred.
H. "In what respect has the law ruled leniently for her? In respect to the uncleanness of her flux. But she is unclean in respect to the uncleanness of a menstruant."
I.1 A. *Our rabbis have taught on Tannaite authority:*
B. "SHE SHALL CONTINUE IN THE BLOOD OF HER PURIFICATION" (LEV. 12:4) ENCOMPASSES A WOMAN WHO HAS HARD LABOR DURING THE EIGHTY DAYS FOLLOWING THE BIRTH OF A FEMALE, INDICATING THAT ANY SORT OF BLOOD THAT SHE PRODUCES IS CLEAN UNTIL THE BABY IS BORN."
C. AND R. ELIEZER DECLARES IT UNCLEAN.
D. THEY SAID TO R. ELIEZER, "NOW IN A CASE IN WHICH THE LAW HAS IMPOSED A STRICT RULING [DECLARING BLOOD TO BE UNCLEAN], NAMELY, DURING A RESPITE FROM PAIN PRIOR TO THE BIRTH OF THE CHILD, THE LAW HAS IMPOSED A LENIENT RULING, NAMELY, DURING A RESPITE FROM PAIN AFTER THE BIRTH OF THE CHILD [DURING THE SIXTY-SIX DAYS AFTER THE

BIRTH OF A FEMALE], IN A CASE IN WHICH THE LAW HAS IMPOSED A LENIENT RULING TO BEGIN WITH, NAMELY, UPON BLOOD THAT COMES DURING HARD LABOR THAT IS PRIOR TO THE BIRTH OF THE CHILD, IS IT NOT LOGICAL THAT WE SHOULD IMPOSE A LENIENT RULING UPON THE BLOOD THAT EMERGES DURING HARD LABOR AFTER THE BIRTH OF THE CHILD [THAT IS, DURING THOSE SIXTY-SIX DAYS]?"

E. HE SAID TO THEM, "**IT IS SUFFICIENT IF THE INFERRED LAW IS AS STRICT AS THAT FROM WHICH IT IS INFERRED.** IN WHAT ASPECT HAS THE LAW IMPOSED A LENIENT RULING ON HER? IT IS IN THE ASPECT OF THE UNCLEANNESS BY REASON OF FLUX. BUT SHE IS STILL SUBJECT TO UNCLEANNESS BY REASON OF MENSTRUATION."

F. THEY SAID TO HIM, "LO, WE SHALL REPLY TO YOU WITH ANOTHER STATEMENT. IF IN A CASE IN WHICH THE LAW HAS IMPOSED A STRICT RULING, IN REGARD TO THE BLOOD THAT FLOWS DURING A RESPECT THAT IS PRIOR TO THE BIRTH OF THE CHILD, THE LAW HAS IMPOSED A LENIENT RULING, NAMELY, ON THE BLOOD THAT FLOWS DURING HARD LABOR OF THAT SAME PERIOD, IN A CASE IN WHICH TO BEGIN WITH THE LAW HAS IMPOSED A LENIENT RULING, NAMELY, DURING A PERIOD OF RESPITE AFTER THE BIRTH OF THE CHILD, IS IT NOT LOGICAL THAT WE SHOULD IMPOSE A LENIENT RULING ON THE HARD LABOR THAT MAY ACCOMPANY THAT PERIOD?"

G. HE SAID TO THEM, "EVEN IF YOU WERE TO COMPOSE REPLIES TO ME THE ENTIRE DAY, **IT STILL IS SUFFICIENT IF THE INFERRED LAW IS AS STRICT AS THAT FROM WHICH IT IS INFERRED.** IN WHAT ASPECT HAS THE LAW IMPOSED A LENIENT RULING ON HER? IT IS IN THE ASPECT OF THE UNCLEANNESS BY REASON OF

FLUX. BUT SHE IS STILL SUBJECT TO UNCLEANNESS BY reason of menstruation."

H. *Said Raba, "In this argument, R. Eliezer could still have won over rabbis: 'have you not said the following:* "'Her blood" (Lev. 15:25) — her blood that is normally discharged, but not blood that is due to childbirth'? Here too, 'And she shall be cleaned from the fountain of her blood' (Lev. 12:7) — 'her blood' that is normally discharged, but not blood that is due to childbirth."

I. Might one say [as before], "Blood that flows during the menstrual period marks her as unclean by reason of menstruation, and that she flows during the Zibah-days is clean?"

J. Scripture states, "...she will sit...," meaning, continuously throughout all of these days.

The upshot is the same as before. The last thing we can claim is to address here a free-standing story. So much for our sample. Now to examine the outcome.

III. The Negligible Proportion of Free-standing Stories

The issue now is, of the items that occur in Sifra and in some other document, what proportion qualify as free-standing compositions of any sort? The criterion is, stories or composites that do not conform to the formal conventions of Sifra and that do occur in some document in addition to Sifra? I count in the American translation of the pertinent passages of Sifra approximately 4800 words. What proportion of these is comprised by free-standing stories? We cannot consider passages of Sifra cited by Yerushalmi or Bavli is "free-standing," since their documentary indicators are clearly exhibited. An example of what I do not encompass is at CXXII.I.2, a passage of Sifra that is cited verbatim at b. Ker. 7b. If we count only passages that do not exhibit the markers of Sifra or of any other document and that occur both in Sifra and elsewhere, we find the following: CXXIII:I.2 and CXXIV:II.1, approximately 280 words, 5.8%. That is, a negligible proportion of our sample is contributed by compositions that can be classified as free-standing and extra-documentary.

IV. THE PERIPHERAL ROLE OF FREE-STANDING STORIES

To what extent do other-than-documentary compositions figure in our sample of Sifra? The answer to that question affords perspective on the claim that documents exhibit indicative traits that differentiate one compilation from another, the materials that are primary to one document from those that are primary to another. I have alleged that Sifra is organized as a verse-by-verse commentary to the book of Leviticus. To show the extent to which Sifra follows a rigid formal pattern and no other, I outline the pertinent materials. The result is a graphic account of the shape and structure of the three chapters we have examined. I place at the margin the compositions that conform to what I allege to define the documentary form and program: citation of a verse and exegesis thereof. I indent what is secondary and derivative. The complex task of this analytical outline is carried out through the use of different visual signals, conveyed in diverse typefaces.

My task is to show precisely how Sifra holds together and carries out its purposes. As we have seen for our sample, that is through two types of writing: citation of a verse of Scripture and the statement of proposition based on that verse, and systematic methodical analysis of certain problems of abstract thought and argument. Everything else is clearly marked off as distinct from the documentary program.

Since the entire document is organized following the sequence of the verses of the book of Leviticus, that the sequential citation of verses defines the framework of the outline — but little else. Plain type serves.

Second comes the propositional program. The successive propositions are given in lower case capital letters.

Third comes the explicit specification of the method used for secondary expansion and testing of proposed propositions. I underline the opening proposition of the methodical-analytical exercises (e.g., "is the opposite not reasonable?), to show the cogent and recurrent demonstration of the inadequacy of the traits of objects in establishing the correct classification, therefore rule, governing them. Propositions deriving from Scripture are subjected to such an exercise via the question, "is it not a matter of logic?" Then why is proof from Scripture required. What follows will be the demonstration that Scripture alone establishes the valid taxonomy, therefore hierarchical classification and consequent rule.

Fourth, I use indentation to mark what varies the form, abandoning the citation and gloss and methodical-analytical language-patterns. That is, specifically, where I find reason to remove a composition or composite from the mainstream of the document's flow, I indent the entry; that signals the judgment that an entry is secondary and intruded or otherwise impedes the systematic and orderly progress of the whole. In that way, the outline highlights all three components of the document's construction: [1] the formal and [2] THE PROPOSITIONAL and [3] the methodological sequence. Where there is a topical or propositional motif that holds together a sequence of verses of Scripture, I insert the governing proposition or the organizing topic at the head of the units that formulate and demonstrate it.

What carries weight in the present exercise is the indented materials. There we find ourselves facing the non- or extra-documentary compositions of our sample. Visually, we immediately perceive the peripheral task that is assigned to them, their tangential position in the composite.

> CXXII:I.1 — 7 "...ISRAELITE PEOPLE": IN THIS MATTER, THE ISRAELITE PEOPLE ARE ENGAGED, BUT IDOLATORS ARE NOT ENGAGED IN THIS MATTER. "...ISRAELITE PEOPLE": I KNOW ONLY THAT BORN — ISRAELITES ARE COVERED BY THE LAW. HOW DO I KNOW THAT SUBJECT TO IT ARE ALSO WOMEN — PROSELYTES AND BONDWOMEN, WHETHER FREED OR NOT? "When a woman at childbirth bears a male, she shall be unclean seven days": What is the point of this statement? Since Scripture says, "You shall put the Israelites on guard against their uncleanness, lest they die through their uncleanness by defiling my tabernacle which is among them" (Lev. 15:31), might I conclude that that is so whether the uncleanness takes place inside [through actually entering the building] or outside the tabernacle [through merely touching the building, for instance]? Might one then claim that the woman after childbirth, who is unclean in a light measure, should impart uncleanness to the sanctuary if she goes into it, while as to other unclean persons, they do so whether inside or outside? I know only that that is the case in reference to one who is subjected to a most severe form of uncleanness, such as the woman after childbirth. "WHEN A WOMAN AT CHILDBIRTH BEARS A MALE": THIS EXCLUDES THE CASE OF ONE WHO GIVES BIRTH PRIOR TO THE REVELATION OF THE TORAH [SINCE THE FORMULATION SPEAKS OF "WHEN," UNDERSTOOD TO MEAN, IN THE FUTURE, BUT NOT PRIOR TO THIS TIME]. Might one suppose that I should also exclude the case of one who became pregnant prior to the revelation of the Torah but gave birth after the revelation of the Torah? "WHEN A WOMAN AT CHILDBIRTH BEARS A MALE": THIS RULE APPLIES ONLY TO ONE WHO GIVES BIRTH FROM THE PLACE AT WHICH FER-

TILIZATION TAKES PLACE, EXCLUDING THAT CASE IN WHICH THE CHILD WHICH GOES FORTH FROM THE SIDE [M. NID. 5:1D].

CXXII:II.1 — 2 "If a woman conceives and bears a male" (Lev. 12:2): What is the point of Scripture? Because it is said, "And she shall be unclean for seven days, and on the eighth day he will be circumcised," I might infer that only the child who emerges alive imparts uncleanness of childbirth to his mother. How do I know that the child who is stillborn imparts uncleanness of childbirth to his mother? I know only [that uncleanness applies to a child born] at the age of nine months. How [do I know that a child born at] the age of eight, seven, six, five months [produces uncleanness]?

CXXII:III.1 — 2 Might I think that she who aborts something like fish and locusts and insects and creeping things, that she should be unclean? Scripture says, "Male" — Just as this is distinctive in that it bears the likeness of man, so these are excluded which do not bear the likeness of man. Might I think that she who aborts a creature with a head which is not formed, a creature with a body which is not formed, and that which has two backs and two spinal columns, that, since they have the likeness of man, she should be unclean on their account? Scripture says, "And she will be unclean seven days. And on the eighth day he will be circumcised" (Lev. 12:2 — 3). Just as this one is distinctive in that he is worthy of the creation of a soul, so these are excluded for they are not worthy of the creation of a soul [QA: covenant of the eighth day]. "AND SHE WILL BE UNCLEAN" (LEV. 12:2). SHE IS UNCLEAN, BUT THE CHILD IS NOT UNCLEAN. And is [the opposite rule] not logical? If the child has caused her to be unclean so that, lo, she is unclean, the child himself, who has caused her to be unclean — is it not logical that he should be unclean? The goat which is sent forth will prove the matter, for it caused uncleanness, but lo, it is clean [while alive]. No, if you have said so in respect to the goat which is sent away, which is not subject to uncleanness, will you say so concerning the child, who is subject to uncleanness? Since he is subject to uncleanness, let him be unclean. Scripture says, "She" — she is unclean, but the child is not unclean.

CXXII:IV.1 "WHEN A WOMAN AT CHILDBIRTH BEARS A MALE, SHE SHALL BE UNCLEAN SEVEN DAYS": SHE SHOULD COUNT THE DAYS FROM THE BIRTH OF THE FINAL FOETUS. Is that proposition not a matter of logic? A woman contracts uncleanness from a corpse and she contracts uncleanness from the offspring. Just as we find that, when she contracts uncleanness from a corpse, she counts the seven days from the moment only of the final point at which she contracted uncleanness [for the sprinkling on the third and seventh days], so when the woman contracts uncleanness in childbirth, she should count only from the appearance of the last of a sequence of births. Or take this route: A woman contracts uncleanness from menstrual blood and she contracts uncleanness from an offspring. Just as, when she contracts uncleanness from menstrual blood, she counts the seven days only from the moment of the first appearance of the unclean blood [on the first day of her period, so that, seven days later, she is clean, even though menstrual blood may occur on the immediately preceding day], so when the woman contracts uncleanness in childbirth, she should count only from the appearance of the first in a sequence of births. Let us then identify the appropriate analogy: We should draw an analogy from uncleanness which derives from a source other than the woman herself for a form of uncleanness which likewise derives from a source other than the woman herself [the corpse, the offspring], but let not the case of menstrual blood enter in, since that form of uncleanness derives from the woman's own body. Or take this route: We should drawn an analogy from a form of uncleanness that derives from the woman for another form of uncleanness that derives from the woman [the offspring, menstrual blood], but let not the case of corpse — uncleanness enter in, which does not derive from the woman herself. Accordingly, it is necessary for Scripture to state, "When a woman at childbirth bears a male, she shall be unclean seven days": She should count the days from the birth of the final foetus.

CXXII:V.1 "...seven days": Might one think [that she should be unclean whenever blood occurs in respect to childbirth] whether the days are consecutive or separate? Scripture says, "As the days of her menstrual period." Just as the days of her menstrual cycle are in sequence, so the days of her uncleanness by reason of childbirth are consecutive. "LIKE THE DAYS OF HER MENSTRUAL PERIOD": SCRIPTURE COMPARES THE DAYS OF HER MENSTRUAL PERIOD TO THE DAYS OF HER UNCLEANNESS BY REASON OF CHILDBIRTH. JUST AS THE DAYS OF HER MENSTRUAL PERIOD ARE NOT SUBJECT TO UNCLEANNESS BY REASON OF *ZIBAH* AND CANNOT BE INCLUDED IN THE COUNTING OF THE SEVEN DAYS, SO THE DAYS OF HER UNCLEANNESS BY REASON OF CHILDBIRTH ARE NOT SUBJECT TO UNCLEANNESS BY REASON OF *ZIBAH* AND CANNOT BE INCLUDED IN THE COUNTING OF THE SEVEN [CLEAN] DAYS. "HER SICKNESS SHALL SHE BE UNCLEAN" — TO ENCOMPASS THE ONE WHO HAS INTERCOURSE WITH HER. "HER SICKNESS SHALL SHE BE UNCLEAN" — TO ENCOMPASS ALL THE NIGHTS. "HER SICKNESS SHALL SHE BE UNCLEAN" — TO ENCOMPASS THE WOMAN WHO GIVES BIRTH WHILE UNCLEAN AS A *ZABAH*, THAT SHE SHOULD NOT BE DEEMED CLEAN UNTIL SHE WILL SIT OUT SEVEN CLEAN DAYS. "SHE WILL SIT [THEN SHE SHALL CONTINUE ("SIT") FOR THIRTY-THREE DAYS IN THE BLOOD OF HER PURIFYING": — TO ENCOMPASS THE ONE WHO IS IN HARD LABOR DURING THE ELEVEN DAYS [OF *ZIBAH*], THAT SHE SHOULD BE CLEAN IN RESPECT TO *ZIBAH*. MIGHT ONE THINK THAT SHE SHOULD BE CLEAN OF MENSTRUAL UNCLEANNESS? SCRIPTURE SAYS, "HER SICKNESS — SHE SHALL IMPART UNCLEANNESS" — IN THE DAYS

OF PURIFYING, EVEN THOUGH SHE SEES [BLOOD].

CXXIII:I.1 "And on the eighth day [the flesh of his foreskin shall be circumcised]": might one suppose that this may be done either by day or by night? Scripture says, "...day," by day and not by night. I know only that the one who is circumcised on the eighth day after birth is to be circumcised by day. How do I know that, if the rite takes place on the ninth, tenth, or eleventh days after birth and all others that are to be circumcised should be circumcised only by day? Scripture says, "and on the eighth day."

CXXIII:I.2 Said a certain disciple before R. Aqiba, "It is necessary to make the following observation: If Scripture had been formulated, 'she shall be unclean seven days. On the eighth day the flesh of his foreskin shall be circumcised,' one might have taken the view that the sum of seven and eight is fifteen [so the circumcision should be on the fifteenth day]. Scripture accordingly says, 'and on the day....'" Said to him R. Aqiba, "You dive into mighty waters and dredge up another shard in your hand! Is it not in any event stated, 'And throughout the generations every male among you shall be circumcised at the age of eight days' (Gen. 17:12)."

CXXIII:I.4 — 16 "AND ON THE EIGHTH DAY [THE FLESH OF HIS FORESKIN SHALL BE CIRCUMCISED]": THIS TEACHES THAT THE ENTIRE DAY IS SUITABLE FOR CIRCUMCISION, ALTHOUGH THOSE WHO ARE ZEALOUS PROMPTLY CARRY OUT RELIGIOUS DUTIES, AS IT IS SAID, "AND ABRAHAM AROSE EARLY IN THE MORNING AND SADDLED HIS ASS" (GEN. 22:2). "AND ON THE EIGHTH DAY [THE FLESH OF HIS FORESKIN SHALL BE CIRCUMCISED]": EVEN ON THE SABBATH. How then am I to interpret the statement, "Those that violate it shall surely die" (Ex. 31:14). This refers to other acts of labor, exclusive of those actually involved in the act of circumcision. But might I interpret the statement, "Those that violate it shall surely die" (Ex. 31:14) to speak even of acts of labor actually involved in the act of circumcision? Then how should I carry out the statement, "And on the eighth day [the flesh of his foreskin shall be circumcised]"? It would mean, "unless it is the Sabbath." Accordingly, Scripture states, "And on the eighth day [the flesh of his foreskin shall be circumcised]": even on the Sabbath. "THE FLESH OF HIS FORESKIN SHALL BE CIRCUMCISED": EVEN THOUGH THERE IS A BRIGHT SPOT ON THE SPOT. Then how shall I interpret the statement, "In cases of a skin affection, be most careful to do exactly as the Levitical priests instruct you" (Dt. 24:8)? even with respect to circumcision [so do not circumcise if at the foreskin is a bright spot that may or may not indicate the presence of the skin affection]. Then how shall I interpret the statement, "the flesh of his foreskin shall be circumcised"? When there is no bright spot. Scripture says, "the flesh of his foreskin shall be circumcised": even though there is a bright spot on the spot. "...FORESKIN": IF IT IS ASSUREDLY THE FORESKIN OF A MALE CHILD, THEN THE RITE OVERRIDES THE RESTRICTIONS OF THE SABBATH, BUT IN A CASE OF DOUBT, THEN THE RITE DOES NOT OVERRIDE THE RESTRICTIONS OF THE SABBATH. "...FORESKIN": IF IT IS ASSUREDLY THE DAY [ON WHICH, EIGHT DAYS EARLIER, THE CHILD WAS BORN], THEN THE RITE OVERRIDES THE RESTRICTIONS OF THE SABBATH, BUT [IF IT WAS BORN] AT TWILIGHT [SO THAT WE DO NOT KNOW FOR CERTAIN THAT THE SABBATH COINCIDES WITH THE EIGHTH DAY AFTER BIRTH], THEN THE RITE DOES NOT OVERRIDE THE RESTRICTIONS OF THE SABBATH. "...FORESKIN": IF IT IS ASSUREDLY A CHILD BORN UNCIRCUMCISED, THEN THE RITE OF CIRCUMCISION DOES OVERRIDE THE RESTRICTIONS OF THE SABBATH. BUT THE CIRCUMCISION OF A BABY BORN CIRCUMCISED DOES NOT OVERRIDE THE RESTRICTIONS OF THE SABBATH. "She shall remain in a state of blood purification for thirty-three days": Might one suppose that these days may be either consecutive or not consecutive? Scripture says, "...day."

Just as a day is wholly one, so the period of thirty-three days must be wholly one and consecutive. Might one suppose that thirty days must be consecutive, but as to the other three, they may be either consecutive or not consecutive? Scripture says, "...thirty days and three days...": Just as the thirty days must be consecutive, so as to the other three, they must be consecutive as well. "SHE SHALL REMAIN [IN A STATE OF BLOOD PURIFICATION FOR THIRTY-THREE DAYS]": THIS ENCOMPASSES THE WOMAN IN PROTRACTED HARD LABOR [FOR THREE DAYS] DURING THE ELEVEN DAYS BETWEEN PERIODS [DURING WHICH A FLOW IS DEEMED A FLUX IN LINE WITH LEV. 15:25], INDICATING THAT SHE IS HELD TO BE CLEAN AS TO FLUX [CF. M. NID. 4:A, B]. Might one suppose that she should be regarded as clean, also, as to menstrual uncleanness? Scripture explicitly states, "she shall be unclean as at the time of her menstrual infirmity." "...IN A STATE OF BLOOD PURIFICATION": EVEN THOUGH SHE PRODUCES BLOOD. "She shall not touch any consecrated thing": Might one suppose that the prohibition extends even to food designated as tithe? Scripture says, "nor enter the sanctuary," just as in the case of the sanctuary, violation of the rules of uncleanness is penalized by losing one's life, so in the case of Holy Things under discussion here, it is of the classification in which violation of the rules of uncleanness is penalized by losing one's life. That then excludes the matter of food that has been designated as tithe [to which such a penalty does not apply]. Then might one argue as follows: Just as in the case of the sanctuary, one who enters in a state of uncleanness is penalized by extirpation, so in the case of Holy Things, one who eats such food in a state of uncleanness will be penalized through extirpation, thus excluding food that has been designated as priestly rations? Scripture says, "She shall not touch any consecrated thing": thus encompassing food that has been designated as priestly rations. Then might one argue as follows: just as in reference to Holy Things, what is subject to discussion is communication of uncleanness through actual contact, so in the case of the sanctuary, which is penalized is contamination through an act of actual contact. And how do I know that uncleanness affecting the sanctuary that has been brought in not through an act of actual contact [for example, if an unclean person enters the sanctuary in a wagon and does not actually touch the building] also is prohibited? Scripture says, "nor enter the sanctuary."

CXXIV:I.1 "If she shall bear a female": I know only that the rule applies to a female. How do I know that IT ENCOMPASSES THE ONE OF DOUBTFUL SEXUAL TRAITS AND THE ONE WHO BEARS PHYSICAL TRAITS OF BOTH SEXES?

CXXIV:II.1 — 2 His disciples asked R. Judah b. Roes, "Might we interpret the verse of Scripture, 'she shall be unclean two weeks' to mean that she shall be unclean for seventy days [since the words 'two weeks' and 'seventy days' are made up of the same consonants]? He said to them, "Uncleanness and cleanness pertain both to the male and to the female. Just as the days of purifying are twice in the case of the female what they are in the male, so the days of uncleanness will be twice in the case of the female what they are in the male."

CXXIV:II.3 — 4 "...sixty-six days": Might one suppose that these days may be either consecutive or not consecutive? Scripture says, "...day." Just as a day is wholly one, so the period of sixty-six days must be wholly one and consecutive. Might one suppose that sixty days must be consecutive, but as to the other six, they may be either consecutive or not consecutive? Scripture says, "...sixty days and six days...": Just as the thirty days must be consecutive, so as to the other three, they must be consecutive as well. Scripture says, "...sixty days and six days...": What is the sense of Scripture here? One might have thought that in the case of a male, in which instance the number of days of uncleanness is small, the number of days of purifying will also be small. In the case of a female, in which the number of days of cleanness will be few, should not the days of purifying be still fewer? Scripture is explicit in saying, "...sixty days and six days...."

CXXIV:II.5 "She shall continue [in the blood of her purifying for sixty-six days]": This encompasses the one who goes into hard labor during the eighty days of purifying for a female, that all the blood which she sees is unclean, until the child will emerge. And R. Eliezer declares it unclean.

First, we once more ask about proportions. The outline contains 2800 words. Of these, the two extrinsic compositions, CXXIII:I.2 and CXXIV:II.1 comprise about 220 words, or roughly 7%, that is, close to the same result as we achieved earlier. The extrinsic compositions form a negligible proportion of the sample. They certainly do not bear the weight of the document's main beams of exposition and argument.

Second, are the extra- or non-documentary components critical to the exposition or tacked on? The non-documentary component of the sample plays a peripheral role. It never is asked to register a point critical to the documentary polemic. If we removed the non-documentary components, we should follow the document's exposition, in context, without difficulty.

So far as in the context of Sifra we may speak at all of free-standing compositions, shared with other documents and not clearly borrowed by some other document from Sifra, a simple conclusion follows.

First, free-standing compositions are in proportion a negligible part of Sifra.

Second, they undertake a tangential task in the realization of the document.

This exercise calls into question the argument that "parallels," meaning, free-standing compositions and composites, form a corpus of evidence of substance and weight sufficient to upset the documentary reading of the canonical compilations. Indeed, after our encounter with the Mishnah, Tosefta, and Sifra, we must wonder why anyone who has worked through the canon, start to finish, and has noted the formal, topical, and logical boundaries of its components and their respective, unique definitions, should question the documentary reading. On what basis should an experienced master of the documents have imagined reading the compilations other than as purposive documents? But there are good grounds, and this is such a basis, as we shall now see. Genesis Rabbah awaits, and there, we may anticipate different results. For, on the very surface, it is hardly so uniform a piece of writing as the Mishnah or the Tosefta or Sifra.

4.

PROPORTION AND POSITION: EVIDENCE OF SHARED, AUTONOMOUS TRADITIONS IN A SAMPLE OF GENESIS RABBAH

I. THE DOCUMENTARY TRAITS OF GENESIS RABBAH

A highly propositional statement, Genesis Rabbah sets forth a coherent and original account of the book of Genesis. Generally thought to have reached closure at ca. 450 C.E., sometime after the Talmud of the Land of Israel had been redacted, Genesis Rabbah transforms the book of Genesis into an account of the laws of history and the rules of the salvation of Israel. In Genesis Rabbah the past becomes present, and the present takes place in the past. In this Midrash-compilation Scripture is turned from a genealogy and family history into the recapitulation, in the lives and deeds of the saints, of the history of the world. That yields a theology of Israel expressed in the narrative of mankind's history. The deeds of the founders become omens and signs for the final generations, origins are realized in the eschaton.

In Genesis Rabbah the entire narrative of Genesis is so formed as to point toward the sacred history of Israel, the Jewish people: its slavery and redemption; its coming Temple in Jerusalem; its exile and salvation at the end of time. The whole is formed into a paradigm of exile and return. In the rereading by the authorship of Genesis Rabbah, Genesis proclaims the prophetic message that the world's creation commenced a single, straight line of significant events, that is to say, selected history, leading in the end to the salvation of Israel and, through Israel, of all humanity that accepts God's dominion. The single most important proposition of Genesis Rabbah is that, in the story of the beginnings of creation, humanity, and Israel, we find the message of the meaning and end of the life of the Jewish people in the here and now of the fifth century. The deeds of the founders supply signals for the children about what is going to come in the future. So the biography of Abraham, Isaac, and Jacob also constitutes a protracted account of the history of Israel later on, but especially in the immediacy of the present tense. So much for the topic, the program of the document.

What about the indicative formal traits of the writing of Genesis Rabbah, which embody the documentary program?

The first of the three forms of the document is the recurrent mode of organization, namely, the base-verse/intersecting-verse construction. In the sort of passage under discussion, (1) a verse of the book of Genesis will be followed by (2) a verse from some other book of the Hebrew Scriptures. The latter (2) will then be subjected to extensive discussion. But in the end the exposition of the intersecting-verse will shed some light, in some way, upon (1) the base-verse, cited at the outset. The second paramount form, which always follows as second in sequence as well, is the exegesis of a verse, which is familiar: a verse of the book of Genesis will be subjected to sustained analysis and amplification, but not with reference to some other intersecting-verse but now, commonly with regard to numerous proof texts, or to no proof texts at all. Finally, the syllogism-form will cite a variety of verses, drawn from a broad range of books of the Hebrew Scriptures, ordinarily composed in a list of like grammatical and syntactical entries.

The power of the intersecting-verse/base-verse form — the juxtaposition of two verses, one derived from the biblical book at hand, the other from some other book of Scripture altogether — is simple. On the surface, the intersecting verse expands the frame of reference of the base verse, introducing data otherwise not present. But just beneath the surface lies the implicit premise: both the intersecting verse and the base verse make the same point. In their meeting each rises out of its narrow framework as a detail or an instance of a rule and instead testifies to the larger picture, the encompassing rule itself. The intersecting-verse/base-verse construction effectively generalizes the case at hand, turning an incident into a paradigm. It therefore yields a proposition that transcends both verses and finds proof in the cases of each, and that powerful way of composing something new forms the centerpiece of the present document and the two that follow.

The reason that the intersecting-verse/base-verse form serves so well derives from the program of the document. It is to demonstrate that there are reliable rules that govern Israel's history, specifically to discover and validate those fixed and governing rules within the details of stories of the origins of the family of Abraham, Isaac, and Jacob. That family is now constituted by Israel. A process of search for the governing laws of history and society requires not episodic incidents of we know not what, but general rules. Then an inductive process will demand that sages generate rules out of cases. The meeting of rhetoric, logic, and topic takes place here. Putting together the cases represented by two verses, one deep within the narrative of Genesis, the other far distant from that narrative, the exegetes found it possible to state a case. Then, along with the case, they point toward an implicit generalization yielded by the two or more distinct cases at hand. The rhetoric involves the recurrent arrangement of verses, the logic, the inquiry into the general rule that holds together two cases and makes of them a single statement of an overriding law, and the topic, the direction of the history of Israel, specifically, its ultimate salvation at the end of time.

So in the aggregate Genesis Rabbah conforms to important literary patterns. First come the forms. As I said, we are able to classify the bulk of its completed units of thought among the three forms or patterns, as specified. Second comes the sequence of the forms. The formal types of units of discourse are arranged in accord with a single set of preferences, with the intersecting-verse/base-verse always standing at the head of a composite, followed by the exegetical form. Within the formal structures may be discerned formally-miscellaneous material as well. Form I, for example, with its reference to an intersecting verse followed by its treatment of the base verse, not uncommonly carried in its wake materials of a formally quite miscellaneous character. The second still more commonly permits characterization only in the simplest way: first comes the citation of a verse of the book of Genesis, then comes some sort of comment on that verse. Within the requirements of so simple a pattern, a variety of arrangements and formulations found ample place. The form that sustains the construction of a list of facts to prove a given proposition is equally striking in its distinctive markers. With these formal indicators in hand, we turn to our sample.

II.   The Sample: Genesis Rabbah Parashah One

Since Genesis Rabbah presents a complex construction, with some components exhibiting formal traits intimate to the documentary programs, others sharing forms common among several documents, its miscellaneous character defines our problem. It is in two parts. First, as to the compositions and composites in rhetoric and topic to Genesis Rabbah, what proportion if any of these is shared with other compilations? Second, as to the components not particular in form and program to Genesis Rabbah, how large a proportion of these forms part of the common, circulating corpus of stories and sayings? These two questions form a negative and a positive test of the same proposition. The first is that the documents are fundamentally autonomous of one another. The second is that the parallel stories and sayings form a negligible part of any given document and that the non- or extra-documentary writing rarely impinges upon the fundamental structure of the document(s) that present it.

I have chosen as the sample the opening Parashah of our document. It touches upon questions of the broadest general interest, creation and its course, and is likely to intersect with a variety of other compilations. Not only so, but it also encompasses a variety of non-documentary writing, that is, compositions that are tangential in the composites in which they occur. The Parashah therefore offers a challenge to the notion that non-documentary writing is also extra-documentary, utilized in a number of compilations and particular to none of them. What we shall see is that most of the non-documentary components of the Parashah are unique to Genesis Rabbah and do not constitute elements of a large body of extra-documentary, peripatetic parallels. My form-analysis will show that Parashah One bears within itself a sizable component of compositions external to the primary documentary purpose of the Parashah. That is the exposition of Genesis 1:1. These non-documentary compositions are relevant in general but do not advance the particular propositional program in play. But, we shall soon see, the non-documentary writings are not also extra-documentary; they do not occur elsewhere.

Before us therefore is a challenging sample for testing the theory that documents signal what belongs and what does not. That marks a major step forward in our inquiry into non-documentary writing. What we see is worth emphasizing. It is this:

Parashah One contains more than a negligible proportion of compositions shared with other documents. But the character of the non-documentary, extra-documentary component of the Parashah yields a hypothesis on the pre- or non-documentary writing and its forms.

What is shared with other documents is a selection of exegeses of verses of Scripture with attached propositions proved by those verses. A fixed convention, external to the document at hand and clearly available to a variety of authorships, conveyed the knowledge that, to make a given point or register a determinate proposition, a particular verse of Scripture served. It is conceivable that the Rabbinic sages possessed a florilegium of such verses + the propositions that they prove. In any event, most, though not all, of the non- and extra-documentary writing of our sample falls into the classification of proof-texts and their propositions. And that corpus of writing forms more than a negligible proportion of the sample.

Let me explain how I have approached the sample, beginning with the question, how do I find the parallels between Genesis Rabbah and other compilations? For my cross-references, I have consulted the apparatus of J. Theodor and H. Albeck, *Midrash Bereshit Rabba. Critical Edition with Notes and Commentary* (Jerusalem, repr. 1965: Wahrmann Books), pp. 1-14. At issue is the canon of Rabbinic Judaism in its formative age; the character of the medieval compilations is not under discussion, only the definitive documents of the initial writings. So I limit the survey to documents of late antiquity, omitting the medieval Yalqutim, Pesiqta Rabbati, and the like. I could not always understand why Theodor and Albeck signaled a parallel, but I was able to find most of the pertinent ones, those in the late antique canon.

The purpose of sampling requires a clear definition. My main interest is in identifying the impact, upon the documentary quality — the integrity — of Genesis Rabbah, that is made by extra- and non-documentary writing. That is with special attention to the parallels that circulate among other documents. The distinction between extra- and non-documentary writing has already been signaled. Non-documentary writing does not conform to the formal conventions of the compilation in which it appears. Extra-documentary writing in addition occurs in more than a single document, in our case, in Genesis Rabbah and elsewhere. It is the latter classification of writing that is signaled. But only part of the non-documentary component of the compilation also is extra-documentary. There are sizable composites that stand on their own, as my outline shows at the end, and that appear only in Genesis Rabbah.

I extend the sample in another way. Where we do find compositions and even composites that occur in two or more documents, I want to show not only that that extra-documentary writing is negligible in proportion and trivial in purpose in Genesis Rabbah. I also want to indicate whether or not the same extra-documentary writing forms a significant part of the other document in which it occurs and whether it plays an important role in the documentary exposition. To do so, I present not only the "parallel passage" in Genesis Rabbah Parashah One. I also cite a sizable account of the setting elsewhere, a full account of the use of the same materials in the corresponding compilation, This is done so that we may gain perspective on the importance, in the several contexts in which they occur, not only in Genesis Rabbah, of peripatetic sayings and stories.

What we shall see is that the autonomous traditions occupy no more particular or important a position in the other documents where they occur than they do in Genesis Rabbah. More to the point, we shall begin to frame a hypothesis, based on a tiny sample to be sure, of the likely traits of the "parallel sayings," the kind of materials that are likely to be found in more than one document of the late antique canon, the kind that are not likely to be found in more than a single document. The results, in that matter, will mostly speak for themselves, but my comments in sequence will point to some likely paths for further inquiry.

As before, I signal the presence of a shared pericope in our base-document, Genesis Rabbah, by printing it in LOWER CASE CAPS.

In the documents other than Genesis Rabbah I signal the "parallel passages" — those that contain the same pericope — through <u>underlining</u>, then identifying the shared pericope in the same lower case caps as in Genesis Rabbah, THUS THE PARALLEL REAPPEARS, NOW UNDERLINED.

The passages of Genesis Rabbah are flush at the right hand margin. The "parallel passages" are indented at the right hand margin. I could not touch the left hand margin, because so much of my analysis of the components of the Parashah and their relationships to the plan of the Parashah is contained in the visual signals of indentation from the left hand margin. What is primary is flush with the left hand margin. What is secondary, derivative, interpolated, or otherwise not part of the fundamental statement of the document, is indented and is otherwise marked as extrinsic. Accordingly, I reproduce flush at the left hand margin what I take to be the compositions of Genesis Rabbah that are primary to that document. These carry out the documentary plan and realize its purpose, by the criteria of topic/proposition and rhetoric/form that I have already set forth. Then I progressively indent compositions that I deem to be subordinate or otherwise secondary, for reasons that readers will readily discern. In line with my analysis of the massive miscellanies of the Bavli, I have identified counterpart composites here. I found a few massive miscellanies in the Parashah, and these are marked off, given sub-heads, and indented at both the left- and the right-hand margins. In that way they are clearly marked as non-documentary, that is, not part of the documentary repertoire that the compilers and writers of Genesis Rabbah have assembled.

As I explained, my sample of the intersecting documents is generous. I cite more than the parallel as it occurs in, e.g., Yerushalmi or Bavli. Instead, I provide a lavish selection of the documents containing parallels. This is so that readers will immediately recognize that the parallels form a paltry proportion of not only Genesis Rabbah but the counterpart documents. In many cases the extra-documentary compositions constitute at best mere shards. What we see in this somewhat tedious exercise is how the Goldberg-Schaefer-Becker school has vastly overstated the problem of parallels. The critics of the documentary hypothesis persist in composing series of one — examples of we know not what or of how much more than themselves.[16]

---

[16] In Volume Three of this study, *Extra- and Non-Documentary Writing in the Canon of Formative Judaism*. III. *Peripatetic Parallels*, I show how vastly the Goldberg-Schaefer-Becker school has overstated the issue of diverse wordings or versions of the same story. To deny the integrity of the canonical documents of Rabbinic Judaism and to dismantle the whole into shards and remnants of incoherent writings, the German school has misrepresented the proportions of the documents that are comprised by extra-documentary writing and has enormously exaggerated the extent of

Before beginning, let me now provide a brief prospectus. This permits me to show the relationships of the parts of Genesis Rabbah. I follow the order of the components of Parashah One as set forth by Theodor-Albeck. They reorder some of the components, and that accounts for the sequence of the entries.

Parashah One to the entirety of the composite. Parashah One begins with a large-scale construction in the intersecting-verse/base-verse mode, I:I.1-I.III.1. The final entry draws in its wake a large-scale topical appendix, composed in the manner of the appendices of the Bavli, in which the general theme of the concluding proem, mysteries of creation, is amplified. None of the components of the composite is exegetical in intent or even in form, and the whole looks parachuted down, though with very sound reason. I:X.1-5 then introduce the exegetical compositions, shaped into a fine and coherent composite, on a problem connected to the base-verse of the chapter, Gen. 1:1. After another complex composite working on the general theme, but not the specific proposition, we are given yet another exegetical composite, I:XII.1. The next miscellany, I:XIV.1ff., is takes shape around its own theme and is introduced because of its general relevance to the theme, heaven and earth, of the verse at hand. Here again, there is no pretense that we engage in exegesis. If, then, we ignore the topical composites, we find a simple sequence: intersecting-verse/base-verse construction, then exegetical compositions. None of the latter requires a complex form, and in the main, the exegetical-form provides a cover for a quite propositional intent (why the creation begins with a B, how creation attests God's kingship, how creation shows God's fine craftsmanship). A clause-by-clause reading has not

---

variation of wordings of stories reproduced in more than a single document. This I show over and over again.

yet taken place. The outline given in section iv portrays these conclusions in visual form.

PARASHAH ONE. GENESIS 1:1

I:I.

1. A. "In the beginning God created" (Gen. 1:1):

B. R. Oshaia commenced [discourse by citing the following verse:] "'Then I was beside him like a little child, and I was daily his delight [rejoicing before him always, rejoicing in his inhabited world, and delighting in the sons of men]' (Prov. 8:30-31).

C. "The word for 'child' uses consonants that may also stand for 'teacher,' 'covered over,' and 'hidden away.'

D. "Some hold that the word also means 'great.'

E. "The word means 'teacher,' in line with the following: 'As a teacher carries the suckling child' (Num. 11:12).

F. "The word means 'covered over,' as in the following: 'Those who were covered over in scarlet' (Lam. 4:5).

G. "The word means 'hidden,' as in the verse, 'And he hid Hadassah' (Est. 2:7).

H. "The word means 'great,' in line with the verse, 'Are you better than No-Ammon?' (Nah. 3:8). This we translate, 'Are you better than Alexandria the Great, which is located between rivers.'"

2. A. Another matter:

B. The word means "workman."

C. [In the cited verse] the Torah speaks, "I was the work-plan of the Holy One, blessed be he."

D. In the accepted practice of the world, when a mortal king builds a palace, he does not build it out of his own head, but he follows a work-plan.

E. And [the one who supplies] the work-plan does not build out of his own head, but he has designs and diagrams, so as to know how to situate the rooms and the doorways.

F. Thus the Holy One, blessed be he, consulted the Torah when he created the world.

G. So the Torah stated, "By means of 'the beginning' [that is to say, the Torah] did God create..." (Gen. 1:1).

H. And the word for "beginning" refers only to the Torah, as Scripture says, "The Lord made me as the beginning of his way" (Prov. 8:22).

Genesis Rabbah Parashah One Continued

I:V.

1. A. R. HUNA IN THE NAME OF BAR QAPPARA COMMENCED [DISCOURSE BY CITING THE FOLLOWING VERSE]: "'LET THE LYING LIPS BE MADE DUMB [WHICH ARROGANTLY SPEAK MATTERS KEPT SECRET AGAINST THE RIGHTEOUS]' (PS. 31:19).

B. "[TRANSLATING THE HEBREW WORD FOR DUMB INTO ARAMAIC ONE MAY USE WORDS MEANING] 'BOUND,' 'MADE DUMB,' OR ' SILENCED.'

C. "'LET [THE LYING LIPS] BE BOUND,' AS IN THE FOLLOWING VERSE: 'FOR BEHOLD, WE WERE BINDING SHEAVES' (GEN. 37:7).

D. "'LET THE LYING LIPS BE MADE DUMB,' AS IN THE USAGE IN THIS VERSE: 'OR WHO MADE A MAN DUMB.' (EX. 4:11).

E. "'LET THEM BE SILENCED' BEARS THE OBVIOUS MEANING OF THE WORD."

F. "WHICH ARROGANTLY SPEAK MATTERS KEPT SECRET AGAINST THE RIGHTEOUS" (PS. 31:19):

G. "...WHICH SPEAK AGAINST THE RIGHTEOUS," THE LIFE OF THE AGES, MATTERS THAT HE KEPT SECRET FROM HIS CREATURES [FREED-

MAN: THE MYSTERIES OF CREATION].

H. "WITH PRIDE" (PS. 31:19):

I. THAT IS SO AS TO TAKE PRIDE, SAYING, "I SHALL EXPOUND THE WORK OF CREATION."

J. "AND CONTEMPT" (PS. 31:19): SUCH A ONE TREATS WITH CONTEMPT THE HONOR OWING TO ME.

K. For R. Yosé b. R. Hanina said, "Whoever gains honor through the humiliation of his fellow gains no share in the world to come.

L. "For one does so through the honor owing to the Holy One, blessed be he, how much the more so!"

M. And what is written after the cited verse [Ps. 31:19]?

N. How abundant is your goodness, which you have stored away for those who revere you" (Ps. 31:20).

O. Rab said, "Let one [who reveals the mysteries of creation] not have any share in your abundant goodness.'

P. "Under ordinary circumstances, if a mortal king builds a palace in a place where there had been sewers, garbage, and junk, will not whoever may come and say, 'This palace is built on a place where there were sewers, garbage and junk,' give offense? So too, will not whoever comes and says, 'This world was created out of chaos, emptiness, and darkness' give offense?"

Q. R. Huna in the name of Bar Qappara: "Were the matter not explicitly written in Scripture, it would not be possible to state it at all: 'God created heaven and earth' (Gen. 1:1) — from what? From the following: 'And the earth was chaos' (Gen. 1:2).

I:V.1 forms, an exegetical composition devoted to Ps. 31:19, which is systematically expounded at B-J. The point is to show that it is an act of pride and contempt to reveal what God has kept secret. Now let us see how the same passage is

204 *Paltry Parallels*

preserved in other documents. I give the entire context in which our shared composite occurs at Yerushalmi Hag. 2:1 III:10, which is III:3-9 and III:11ff., to show how a common theme serves as a collecting point for thematically intersecting materials. These then form a topical composite. In the present instance, the topic is, trying to find out the secrets of nature, which are beyond man's comprehension. The composite introduces the fate of principal sages who inquired after forbidden truth, with special reference to Ben Zoma and Aher (the Other), Elisha b. Abbuyah. In each case the theme shades over into a biographical composite. Then, at III.10, our parallel-passage occurs, nearly verbatim: an exegesis of Ps. 31:19 and related verses that underscore the condemnation of the arrogance of those who quest beyond their natural limits of intellect. That marks a new composite, the Elisha-block having run its course, and III:12 takes up the same general theme. III:11 is a secondary development of the theme of III:10 of self-aggrandizement. The upshot, we now see, is that the parallel-passage forms a minor part in a large composite on a general theme, and its point of intersection is the proposition sustained by its proof-text as interpreted in what appears to be a standard manner. Put simply: a proof-text and its exegesis constitute the circulating composition.

Yerushalmi Hagigah 2:1

[III:3 A] Another time, R. Joshua was walking on a road and Ben Zoma came up opposite him. Joshua greeted him, but he did not reply to him. He said to him, "Whence and where, Ben Zoma?"

[B] Ben Zoma said to him, "I have been speculating on the Work of [77b] Creation. Between the upper and the lower waters there is nothing but a hand's breadth. It is said here, 'hovering,' and it is said there: 'As an eagle stirs up its nest [and] hovers over its young' (Dt. 32:11). Just as the 'hovering' which is spoken of there [implies] almost touching but not quite, so the 'hovering' spoken of here is 'almost touching but not quite.'"

[C] R. Joshua said to his disciples, "See, Ben Zoma is outside."

[D] It was only a few days before Ben Zoma died.

[III:4   A] R. Judah bar Pazzi in the name of R. Yosé b. R. Judah: "Three put forward their teaching [on this subject] before their master, R. Joshua before Rabban Yohanan ben Zakkai, Rabbi Aqiba before R. Joshua, Hananiah ben Hakhinai before R. Aqiba. After that time their knowledge becomes unclear [i.e., the oral tradition of the Merkabah is no longer reliable]."

[III:5   A] Four entered the Garden [or Paradise]. One cast a look and died. One cast a look and was stricken [or went mad]. One cast a look and cut among the shoots. One entered safely and departed safely.

[B] Ben Azzai cast a look and was stricken. Of him Scripture says: "If you have found honey, eat only enough for you" (Prov. 25:16).

[C] Ben Zoma cast a look and died. Of him Scripture says: "Precious in the sight of the Lord is the death of his saints" (Ps. 116:15).

[D] Aher cast a look and cut among the shoots.

[III:6   A] *Who is Aher?* Elisha ben Abbuyah, who slew the young scholars of the Torah.

[B] *They say: He used to kill every disciple he saw mastering the Torah. Moreover, he used to enter the schoolhouse, and when he saw the pupils in the presence of the teacher he would say, "What are these doing here? This one should be a mason; this one should be a carpenter; this one should be a fisherman; this one should be a tailor."*

[C] *When they heard this they would leave [the teacher] and go [and become workmen].*

[D] Of him Scripture says: "Let not your mouth lead you into sin" (Qohelet 5:5).

[E] For he ruined his own [good] deeds. *Also at the time of the persecution they [the Romans] made [the Jews] carry burdens [on the Sabbath], and the Jews arranged it so that two people should share one load, because of the rule that two people doing one piece of work [are not liable in regard to a Sabbath violation].*

[G] *Elisha said, "Make them carry the loads by themselves."*

[H] *They went and made them carry them by themselves, but they arranged to unload in a karmelit [an area that cannot be classified either as private ground or as public ground], so that they might not bring them out from private to public ground [which is forbidden].*

[I] *Elisha said, "Make them carry bottles" [which would get broken if left lying].*

[J] R. Aqiba entered safely, and departed safely. Of him Scripture says: "Draw me after you, let us run" (Song of Songs 1:4).

[III:7 A] *Rabbi Meir was sitting teaching in the schoolhouse of Tiberias. Elisha, his master, passed by, riding on a horse on the Sabbath day. They came and said to him, "Look, your master is outside." He stopped his teaching and went out to him.*

[B] *He said to him, "What were you expounding today?"*

[C] [Meir] said to him, "And the Lord blessed the latter days of Job more than his beginning" (Job 42:12).

[D] Elisha said to him, "With what [verse] did you begin to expound it?"

[E] He said to him, "And the Lord gave Job twice as much as he had before" (Job 42:10), for he doubled for him all his wealth.

[F] *Elisha said, "Alas for the things that are lost and not found [masters of Torah]. Aqiba, your master, did not explain it thus, but,* 'And the Lord blessed the latter days of Job from [i.e., because of] his beginning' on account of the merit of the commandments and good deeds that he possessed in his former state."

[G] *[Elisha] said to him, "And what else have you been expounding?"*

[H] He said to him, "Better is the end of a thing than its beginning" (Qohelet 7:8).

[I] He said to him, "How did you begin to expound it?"

[J] He said to him, "[By comparing it] with a man who begot children in his youth and they died, then in his old age he started again. The end of the matter was better than its beginning. [Also by comparing it] with a man who did business in his youth and lost money, while in his old age he made a profit. The end of the matter was better than its beginning. [Also by comparing it] with a man who learned Torah in his youth and forgot it, while in his old age he learned and remembered it [lit., kept it alive] . The end of the matter was better than its beginning."

[K] *[Elisha] said, "Alas for the things that are lost and not found! Aqiba, your master, did not explain it thus, but,* 'The end of a thing is better than its beginning' so long as it is good from its beginning.

[L] "And so it happened to me. My father, Abbuyah, was one of the important people in Jerusalem. When the day of my circumcision came, he invited all the important people of Jerusalem and sat them down in one room, with R. Eliezer and R. Joshua in another room.

[M] *"When they had eaten and drunk they began stamping their feet and dancing.*

[N] "R. *Eliezer said to R. Joshua, "While they are occupying themselves in their way we will occupy ourselves in our way.'* So they sat down and engaged in the study of the Torah, from the Pentateuch to the Prophets, and from the Prophets to the Writings. And fire fell from heaven and surrounded them.

[O] "Abbuyah said to them, 'My masters, have you come to burn my house down around me?'

[P] "They said, 'God forbid! But we were sitting searching around in the words of the Torah from the Pentateuch to the Prophets, and from the Prophets to the Writings, and the words were as alive as when they were given from Mt. Sinai. And the fire shone around us as it shone from Mt. Sinai.'

[Q] "And the essential attribute of their being handed over at Sinai? They were given only by fire:

'And the mountain burned with fire to the heart of heaven' (Dt. 4:11).

[R] "Abbuyah, my father, said to them, 'My masters, if this is the power of the Torah, if this son of mine lives I will dedicate this son of mine to Torah.' Because his [original] intention was not pure [lit., for the sake of heaven], therefore it was not realized in the case of this man [Elisha, speaking of himself in the third person]."

[S] He said to him, "And what else have you been expounding?"

[T] He said to him, "Gold and glass cannot equal it" (Job 28:17).

[U] He said to him, "How did you begin to expound it?"

[V] He said to him, "The words of Torah are hard to acquire like vessels of gold but easy to lose like vessels of glass. Just as vessels of gold and glass, when they are broken, can be repaired and become as they [originally] were, so a scholar who forgets his learning can go and learn it [again] as at the beginning."

[W] He said to him, "[You have gone] far enough, Meir. Here is the Sabbath limit."

[X] *He said to him, "How do you know it?"*

[Y] *He said to him, "From the steps [lit., hooves] of my horse which I am counting; he has gone two thousand cubits."*

[Z] *He said to him, "You have all this wisdom, yet you do not repent!"*

[AA] *"I cannot," he said.*

[BB] "Why not?" R. Meir said to him.

[CC] Elisha said, "Once I was passing before the Holy of Holies riding upon my horse on the Day of Atonement which happened to fall upon a Sabbath, and I heard an echo coming out of the Holy of Holies saying, 'Repent, children, except for Elisha ben Abbuyah, for he knew my power yet rebelled against me!'" [allusion to Jer. 3:22].

[DD] *Why did all this happen to him?*

[EE] Once Elisha was sitting and studying in the

plain of Gennesaret, and he saw a man climb to the top of a palm tree, take a mother bird with her young, and descend safely. The following day he saw another man climbing to the top of the palm tree; he took the young birds but released the mother. When he descended a snake bit him and he died.

[FF] Elisha thought, "It is written, '[If you chance to come upon a bird's nest, in any tree or on the ground, with young ones or eggs, you shall not take the mother with the young;] you shall let the mother go, but the young shall you take to yourself; that it may go well with you, and that you may live long' (Dt. 22:6f.). Where is the welfare of this man, and where his length of days?"

[GG] He did not know that R. Jacob had explained it before him: "That it may go well with you" in the World to Come which is wholly good, "And that you may live long," in the time which is wholly long.

[FHH] Some say [he defected] because he saw the tongue of Rabbi Judah the Baker, dripping blood, in the mouth of a dog. He said, "This is the Torah, and this its reward! This is the tongue that was bringing forth the words of the Torah as befits them. This is the tongue that labored in the Torah all its days. This is the Torah, and this its reward! It seems as though there is no reward [for righteousness] and no resurrection of the dead."

[II] But some say that when his mother was pregnant with him, she passed by some heathen temples and smelled their particular kind of incense. And that odor pierced her body like the poison of a snake.

[III:8 A] Sometime later Elisha fell sick. *They came and told R. Meir, "Behold, your master is ill." He went, intending to visit him, and he found him ill.* [77c] *He said to him, "Will you not repent?"*

[B] *He said, "If sinners repent, are they accepted?"*

[C] [Meir] replied, "Is it not written thus: 'You cause a man to repent up to the point when he becomes dust' (Ps. 90:3)? Up to the time when life is crushed are repentant sinners received."

[D] At that moment, Elisha wept, then he departed [this life] and died. And R. Meir rejoiced in his heart, thinking, "My master died in repentance."

[E] *When they buried him,* fire came down from heaven and consumed his grave. *They came and told R. Meir, "Behold, your master's grave has been set on fire."*

[F] *He went, intending to visit it, and found it burning.*

[G] *What did he do? He took his long prayer cloak and spread it over the corpse saying,* "'Pass the night,' (Ruth 3:13). Stay in this world which is like the night. 'And it shall be in the morning' (Ruth 3:13). This is the world to come which is all morning. 'If he will redeem you, well and good; let him redeem you' (Ruth 3:13) — this is the Holy One, blessed be he, of whom it is written: 'The Lord is good to all, and his compassion is over all that he has made' (Ps. 145:9). 'And if it does not please him to redeem you, then, as the Lord lives, I will redeem you'" (Ruth 3:13).

[H] *Then the fire was extinguished.*

[I] *They said to R. Meir, "If they ask you in that world [to come, after death], 'Whom do you intend to visit [first], your father or your master' [what will you do]?"*

[J] *He said to them, "I will visit my master first, and after that, my father."*

[K] *They said to him, "Will they hearken to your plea [for Elisha]?"*

[L] *He said to them, "Have we not been taught thus:* **They may save the casing of the scroll together with the scroll [and] the casing of the phylacteries together with the phylacteries [M. Shab. 16:1]?** Elisha Aher will be saved through the merit of his [study of the] Torah."

[III:9 A] Some time later, Elisha's daughters went to receive alms from Rabbi. Rabbi decreed saying, "'Let there be none to extend kindness to him, nor any to pity his fatherless children'" (Ps. 109:12).

[B] They said to him, "Rabbi, do not look upon his deeds but on his Torah."

[C] At that moment Rabbi wept and decreed that they should be provided for. He said, "If these are [the children] raised by this man who labored in the Torah for the wrong motives, how much more would be achieved by one who labors in it for the right motives [lit., for the sake of heaven]!"

[III:10 A] R. Eleazar said in the name of Ben Sirah, "'Why attempt to find out what is hidden from you? Why search out what is deeper than Sheol? Reflect [only] on what is permitted to you. Hidden things are no concern of yours'" (Qoh. 3:20-21).

[B] Rab said, "'LET THE LYING LIPS BE DUMB' (PS. 31:19). LET THEM BE CONFOUNDED, CRUSHED, SILENCED. LET THEM BE CONFOUNDED — AS YOU SAY: 'AND THE LORD SAID TO HIM, "WHO HAS MADE MAN'S MOUTH? WHO MAKES HIM DUMB, OR DEAF, OR SEEING, OR BLIND?"' (EX. 4:11). LET THEM BE CRUSHED, AS YOU SAY: 'BEHOLD WE WERE BINDING SHEAVES' (GEN. 37:7). LET THEM BE SILENCED, ACCORDING TO THE LITERAL MEANING: 'WHICH SPEAK ARROGANTLY AGAINST THE RIGHTEOUS' (PS. 31:19), WHO SPEAK CONCERNING THE RIGHTEOUS ONE OF THE WORLD WORDS THAT HE HAS WITHHELD FROM HIS CREATURES.

[C] "'IN PRIDE AND CONTEMPT' (PS. 31:19) — THIS REFERS TO THE ONE WHO BOASTS, SAYING, 'I WILL EXPOUND THE WORK OF CREATION,' THINKING THAT HE IS LIKE ONE WHO EXALTS [HIS CREATOR], WHILE IN REALITY HE IS ONLY LIKE ONE WHO DESPISES HIM."

[III:11 A] R. Yosé ben Hanina said, "He who exalts himself at the cost of his fellow's humiliation has no share in the World to Come. How much more he who exalts himself against the Life of the Worlds! *What is written after it?* 'How abundant is your goodness, which you have laid up for those who fear you' (Ps. 31:20). Let him have no [share] in your abundant goodness."

[III:12 A] R. Levi said, "'It is the glory of God to

conceal a thing' (Prov. 25:2). It is the glory of God to conceal a thing before the world was created. 'It is the glory of kings to search a thing out' (Prov. 25:2) — after the world was created."

[B] R. Levi said, "'Do you know this from of old?' [i.e., before creation,] but you [can have knowledge] 'since man was placed on the earth'" (Job 20:4).

[III:13 A] R. Jonah said in the name of R. Abba, "It is written, 'For ask now about the former days which were before you' (Dt. 4:32). One might conclude that [one may inquire what happened] before the Work of Creation. [But] Scripture says: 'Since the day when God created man upon the earth' (Dt. 4:32).

[B] "May one suppose that this means from the sixth day [of Creation] onward?

[C] "Scripture says, 'First.' After Scripture includes [by referring to "former days"] it excludes [by referring to "the day"]. So we learn [that one may inquire] from the sixth day. Just as the sixth day is specially designated, being one of the six days of creation — so you may include [in your exposition] only that which like the sixth day [is specially designated, i.e., the Six Days of Creation]

[D] "May one [seek] to know what is above the heaven or below the abyss?

[E] "Scripture says, 'And from one end of the heaven to the other' (Dt. 4:32). If you are investigating [what happened] before the world was created, keep it to yourself [lit., your heart contemplates]. If you go on [to investigate what happened] after the world was created, then your voice may go from one end of the world to the other."

[F] *Bar Qappara taught* [that one may investigate] from the [First] Day [of Creation onward].

[G] *R. Judah bar Pazzi agrees with Bar Qappara.*

[H] *R. Hiyya agrees with R. [Ab]ba.*

The only thing that has shifted is the attribution. The exegetical disquisition is carried forward without major changes. I have already accounted for the inclusion of the "parallel," which consists of a verse and its exegesis, taken over and intersecting in the agglutination of a thematic composite.

Genesis Rabbah Parashah One Continued
I.VI.

1. A. R. Judah bar Simon commenced discourse [by citing the following verse:] "'And he reveals deep and secret things' (Dan.2:22).

   B. "The word for deep things refers to Gehenna, as it is written, 'But he does not know that the shades are there, that in the depths of the nether world are her guests' (Prov. 9:18).

   C. "And the word for 'secret things' speaks of the Garden of Eden, as it is written, 'And for a refuge and for a hiding place' (Is. 4:6). [This hiding place, using the same word, is taken to mean the Garden of Eden]."

2. A. Another matter:

   B. "And he reveals deep and secret things" (Dan. 2:22):

   C. This refers to deeds performed by the wicked [which God brings out into the open], as it is said, "Woe to the ones who try to hide their plans from the Lord" (Is. 29:15).

   D. "He knows what is in the darkness" (Dan. 2:22):

   E. This refers to deeds performed by the wicked, as it is written, "And their works are in the darkness" (Is. 4:6).

   F. "But the light dwells with him" (Dan. 2:22):

   G. This refers to deeds performed by the righteous, as it is said, "Light is sown for the righteous" (Ps. 97:11).

3. A. Said R. Abba of Sarangayya, "'Light dwells with him' (Dan. 2:22) refers to the messiah-king."

4. A. SAID R. JUDAH BAR SIMON, "TO BEGIN WITH, WHEN THE WORLD WAS BEING CREATED, 'HE REVEALS DEEP AND SECRET THINGS,' FOR IT IS WRITTEN, 'IN THE BEGINNING GOD CREATED THE HEAVEN (GEN. 1:1).' BUT THE MATTER WAS NOT SPELLED OUT.

B. "WHERE THEN WAS IT SPELLED OUT?

C. "ELSEWHERE: 'WHO STRETCHES OUT THE HEAVEN AS A CURTAIN' (IS. 40:22).

D. "'....AND THE EARTH' (GEN. 1:1). BUT THIS MATTER, TOO, WAS NOT THEN SPELLED OUT.

E. "WHERE THEN WAS IT SPELLED OUT?

F. "ELSEWHERE: 'FOR HE SAYS TO THE SNOW, "FALL ON THE EARTH"' (JOB 37:6).

G. "AND GOD SAID, LET THERE BE LIGHT' (GEN. 1:3).

H. "AND THIS TOO WAS NOT SPELLED OUT.

I. "WHERE THEN WAS IT SPELLED OUT?

J. "ELSEWHERE: 'WHO COVERS YOURSELF WITH LIGHT AS WITH A GARMENT' (PS. 104:2)."

The shared material consists of a proposition, that the course of creation was not revealed at the outset, but only later on, by Job, Isaiah, and Psalms.

Yerushalmi Hagigah 2:1
[II:1 A] Nor the Work of Creation to two. R. [Ab]ba in the name of R. Judah: "This *[halakhah]* comes from R. Aqiba."

[B] But they expound [the Work of Creation before two], as R. Ishmael holds.

[C] *One deduces that the law is according to R. Ishmael from the FOLLOWING:*

[D] R. *JUDAH BAR PAZZI SAT TEACHING,* "IN THE BEGINNING THE WORLD CONSISTED OF

WATER UPON WATER."

[E] R. JUDAH BAR PAZZI EXPOUNDED, "IN THE BEGINNING THE WORLD CONSISTED OF WATER [HEAPED] ON WATER." That indicates that the law accords with the view of R. Ishmael.

[F] *WHAT IS THE PROOF?* "AND THE SPIRIT/WIND OF GOD MOVED OVER THE FACE OF THE WATERS" (GEN. 1:2).

[G] THEN HE MADE THE SNOW — "HE CASTS FORTH HIS ICE LIKE MORSELS" (PS. 147:17).

[H] THEN HE MADE THE EARTH — "FOR TO THE SNOW HE SAYS, 'BECOME EARTH'" (JOB 37:6).

[I] AND THE EARTH STANDS ON THE WATERS: "TO HIM WHO SPREAD OUT THE EARTH ON THE WATERS" (PS. 136:6).

[J] AND THE WATERS STAND ON THE MOUNTAINS: "THE WATERS STOOD OVER THE MOUNTAINS" (PS. 104: 6).

[K] And the mountains stand on the wind: "For behold, he forms the mountains and creates the wind" (Amos 4:13).

[L] And the air depends on the storm-wind: "The storm-wind fulfills his command" (Ps. 148:8).

[M] The Holy One, blessed be he, made the storm-wind like a sort of amulet suspended from his arm, as it is said, "And underneath are the arms of the world" (Dt. 33:27).

The parallel contains a more elaborate statement of the same matter.

Genesis Rabbah Parashah One Continued

I.VII.

1. A. R. Isaac commenced [discourse by citing the following verse]: "'The beginning of your word is truth [and all your righteous ordinance endures forever]' (Ps.

119:16).″

B. Said R. Isaac [about the cited verse], "From the beginning of the creation of the world, 'The beginning of your word was truth.'

C. "'In the beginning God created' (Gen. 1:1).

D. "'And the Lord God is truth '(Jer. 10:9).

E. "Therefore: 'And all your righteous ordinance endures forever' (Ps. 119:16).

F. "For as to every single decree which you lay down for your creatures, they accept that degree as righteous and receive it in good faith, so that no creature may differ, saying ' , 'Two powers gave the Torah, two powers created the world.'

G."[Why not?]' Because here it is not written, 'And gods spoke,' but rather, 'And God spoke' (Ex. 20:1).

H. "'In the beginning [gods] created is not written, but rather, 'in the beginning [God] created' [in the singular]."

As I explained at the outset, the order of the components of the Parashah follows that preferred by Theodor-Albeck, which accounts for the enumeration of the parts.

Genesis Rabbah Parashah One Continued

I.II.

1. A. R. Joshua of Sikhnin in the name of R. Levi commenced [discourse by citing the following verse]: "'He has declared to his people the power of his works, in giving them the heritage of the nations' (Ps. 111:6).

B. "What is the reason that the Holy One, blessed be he, revealed to Israel what was created on the first day and what on the second?

C. "It was on account of the nations of the world. It was so that they should not ridicule the Israelites, saying to them, 'Are you not a nation of robbers [having stolen the land from the Canaanites]?'

D. "It allows the Israelites to answer them, 'And as to you, is there no spoil in your hands? For surely: "The Caphtorim, who came forth out of Caphtor, destroyed them and dwelled in their place" (Dt. 2:23)!

E. "'The world and everything in it belongs to the Holy One, blessed be he. When he wanted, he gave it to you, and when he wanted, he took it from you and gave it to us.'

F. "That is in line with what is written, '....in giving them the heritage of the nations, he has declared to his people the power of his works' (Ps. 111:6).. [So as to give them the land, he established his right to do so by informing them that he had created it.]

G. "He told them about the beginning: 'In the beginning God created...' (Gen. 1:1)."

Genesis Rabbah Parashah One Continued
I.III.

1. A. R. Tanhuma commenced discourse, "For you are great and do wonderful things, you alone are God "(Ps. 86:10).

B. Said R. Tanhum b. R. Hiyya, "As to a skin, if it has a hole as small as the eye of a needle, all of the air will escape for from it.

C. "But as to a human being, a person is made with many apertures and holes, but the spirit does not go forth through them.

D. "Who has done it in such a way? 'You alone are God' (Ps. 86:10)."

2. A. When were the angels created?

B. R. Yohanan said, "On the second day of creation [Monday] were they created.

C. "That is in line with this verse of Scripture: 'Who lays the beams of your upper chambers in the waters' (Ps. 104:3), after which it is written, 'Who makes the spirits of your angels' (Ps. 104:4). [The waters were divided into upper and lower parts, and on that same day the angels were created.]"

D. R. Hanina said, "They were created on the fifth day of creation [Thursday]. For it is written, 'Let fowl fly above the earth' (Gen. 1:20), and it is written, 'And with two did the angel fly' (Is. 6:21). [Freedman, p. 5, n. 3: Thus angels too fall within the category of beings that fly and were created on the same day as all flying creatures.]"

E. R. Luliani b. R. Tabari in the name of R. Isaac: "Both from the viewpoint of R. Hanina and from that of R. Yohanan, there is agreement that nothing at all was created on the first day.

F. "That is so that you will not reach the false conclusion that Michael was there, stretching out the heaven at the south, with Gabriel at the north, and the Holy One, blessed be he, measuring from the middle.

G. "Rather: 'I the Lord do everything by myself, stretching out the heaven on my own and spreading forth the earth by myself' (Is. 44:24).

H. "'By myself' is written [in Scripture, as if to mean, 'who is with me?'] [That is, God asks, 'Who was my partner in creating the world?'

I. "In ordinary affairs when a mortal king is honored by a province the nobles of the province are honored with him. Why? Because they bear the burden with him.

J. "But that is not how it is with the Holy One, blessed be he.

K. "But he on his own created his world, so he on his own is glorified in his world."

3. A. Said R. Tanhuma, "'For you are great and do wonderful things' (Ps. 86:10).

B. "Why so? Because: 'You alone are God' (Ps. 86:10).

C. "You by yourself created the world.

D. "'In the beginning God created' (Gen. 1:1)."

Now we have a massive miscellany, a topical composite that is parachuted down because of the intersection of the theme and proposition of Genesis Rabbah with the theme of the composite.

Genesis Rabbah Parashah One Continued
A TOPICAL COMPOSITE ON THE THEME, WHAT WAS IN BEING BEFORE CREATION

I:IV.

1. A. ["In the beginning God created" (Gen. 1:1):] Six things came before the creation of the world, some created, some at least considered as candidates for creation.

B. THE TORAH AND THE THRONE OF GLORY WERE CREATED [BEFORE THE CREATION OF THE WORLD].

C. THE TORAH, AS IT IS WRITTEN, "THE LORD MADE ME AS THE BEGINNING OF HIS WAY, PRIOR TO HIS WORKS OF OLD" (PROV. 8:22).

D. THE THRONE OF GLORY, AS IT IS WRITTEN, "YOUR THRONE IS ESTABLISHED OF OLD" (PS. 93:2).

E. The patriarchs were considered as candidates for creation, as it is written, "I saw your fathers as the first-ripe in the fig tree at her first season" (Hos. 9:10).

F. Israel was considered [as a candidate for creation], as it is written, "Remember your congregation, which you got aforetime" (Ps. 74:2).

G. THE TEMPLE WAS CONSIDERED AS A CANDIDATE FOR CREATION], AS IT IS WRITTEN, "YOU, THRONE OF GLORY, ON HIGH FROM THE BEGINNING, THE

PLACE OF OUR SANCTUARY" (JER. 17:12).

H. The name of the Messiah was kept in mind, as it is written, "His name exists before the sun" (Ps. 72:17).

I. R. Ahbah bar Zeira said, "Also [the power of] repentance.

J. "That is in line with the following verse of Scripture: 'Before the mountains were brought forth' (Ps. 90:2). From that hour: 'You turn man to contrition and say, Repent, you children of men' (Ps. 90:3)."

K. Nonetheless, I do not know which of these came first, that is, whether the Torah was prior to the throne of glory, or the throne of glory to the Torah.

L. SAID R. ABBA BAR KAHANA, "THE TORAH CAME FIRST, PRIOR TO THE THRONE OF GLORY.

M. "FOR IT IS SAID, 'THE LORD MADE ME AS THE BEGINNING OF HIS WAY, BEFORE HIS WORKS OF OLD' (PROV. 8:22).

N. "IT CAME PRIOR TO THAT CONCERNING WHICH IT IS WRITTEN, 'FOR YOUR THRONE IS ESTABLISHED OF OLD' (PS. 93:2)."

The topical composite, I:IV.1, includes the claim that the Torah and the throne of glory were created before the creation of the world, with standard proof-texts to sustain that proposition, Prov. 8:22 and Ps. 93:2. We shall now see how more elaborate composites on the same general theme, what takes precedence, take over the same verses and expositions thereof. The sample yields a hypothesis that where we do find non- and extra-documentary writing, it will surface not in the primary blocks of the base-document (here: Genesis Rabbah) but in the subsidiary and subordinated ones, the topical appendices. That is the case not only here but in the concluding units, Genesis Rabbah I:XIV, all of which are miscellaneous and of merely topical interest, and all of which are shared with other documents.

SIFRÉ DEUTERONOMY XXXVII:I.2
XXXVII:I

1. A. "And if you do obey these rules and observe them carefully, the Lord you God will maintain faithfully for you the covenant that he made on oath with your fathers. He will favor you and bless you and multiply you" (Dt. 7:12).

B. "For the land that you are about to enter and possess is not like the land of Egypt from which you have come. There the grain you sowed had to be watered by your own labors, like a vegetable garden; but the land you are about to cross into and possess, a land of hills and valleys, soaks up its water from the rains of heaven. It is a land which the Lord your God looks after, on which the Lord your God always keeps his eye, from year's beginning to year's end" (Dt. 11:10-12):

C. This passage was stated as reassurance for the Israelites when they were going out of Egypt.

D. For they were saying, "Perhaps we may enter a land not as lovely as this one."

E. Said to them the Omnipresent, "For the land that you are about to enter and possess is not like the land of Egypt from which you have come."

F. That indicates that the Land of Israel is lovelier than it.

2. A. Is it in praise of the Land of Israel of the Land of Egypt that Scripture speaks?

B. Scripture says, "Now Hebron was built seven years before Zoan in Egypt" (Num. 13:22).

C. Now what sort of town was Zoan? It was a royal city, for so Scripture says, "For his princes are at Zoan" (Is. 30:4).

D. Now what sort of town was Hebron? It was a backwater in the Land of Israel.

E. For Scripture says, "And Sarah died in Kiriath-Arba – the same is Hebron...And Abraham rose

rose up, saying, 'Give me a possession of a burying place with you'" (Gen. 23:2-4).

F. Now this yields an argument *a fortiori:*

G. If Hebron, a mere backwater in the Land of Israel, lo, it is deemed praiseworthy over the best place in the Land of Egypt, the most praiseworthy of all lands, all the more so is the Land of Israel most praiseworthy [among all lands]!

H. Now if you might propose to argue that the one who built this one is not the one who built that [so Zoan and Hebron really are not comparable, and no such argument *a fortiori* can be composed,]

I. Scripture states, "And the sons of Ham: Cush, Mizraim, and Put and Canaan" (Gen. 10:6).

J. The sense is that Ham is the one who built both this and that [Ethiopia/Cush, Mizraim/Egypt, Put and Canaan].

K. It is not possible that he first built the dreary place, then the lovely one.

L. But first he built the lovely place, then the dreary one [and it follows that the dreary place was in Egypt, the lovely one in Canaan, so Zoan is the lesser, Hebron the greater].

M. So since Hebron was the lovelier place, it was built first.

3. A. AND SO YOU FIND IS THE WAY OF THE OMNIPRESENT, THE ONE WHO IS THE MORE BELOVED TAKES PRECEDENCE OVER THE OTHER.

B. TORAH, THE MOST BELOVED [OF ALL THINGS], WHICH TAKES PRECEDENCE OVER EVERYTHING ELSE, WAS CREATED FIRST OF ALL,

C. FOR IT IS SAID, "THE LORD MADE ME AS THE BEGINNING OF HIS WAY, THE FIRST OF HIS WORKS OF OLD" (PROV. 8:22).

D. AND IT IS FURTHER SAID, "I WAS SET UP FROM EVERLASTING, FROM THE BEGINNING OR EVER THE EARTH WAS" (PROV. 8:23).

E. THE HOUSE OF THE SANCTUARY, THE MOST BELOVED, WHICH TAKES PRECEDENCE OVER EVERYTHING ELSE, WAS CREATED FIRST OF ALL,

F. FOR IT IS SAID, "THE THRONE OF GLORY ON HIGH FROM THE BEGINNING, YOUR PLACE OF OUR SANCTUARY" (JER. 17:12).

G. The Land of Israel, the most beloved, which takes precedence over everything else, was created first of all,

H. for it is said, "While as yet he had not made the earth nor the fields nor the beginning of the dust of the world" (Prov. 8:26).

4. A. R. Simeon b. Yohai says, "The word for 'world' refers to the Land of Israel, as it is said, 'Playing with the world, his land' (Prov. 8:31).

B. "Why [is the Land of Israel] called by the word for 'world'?

C. "Because it bears the flavor of all things [using the letters for the word for 'world'], for as to all other lands, what one country has, another country lacks, and what one country has, another country lacks, but as to the Land of Israel, it lacks nothing.

D. "For so it is said: 'You shall not lack anything in it' (Dt. 8:9)."

The same proof-text, Prov. 8:22, figures in a comparable list, but it plays no critical role in the agglutination of that list. The point that is made shifts slightly, but the repertoire of fixed verses and their propositions remains intact.

BAVLI PESAHIM 54A/4:4C-E 1.5

I.5 A. *But was light created at the end of the Sabbath? And lo, it has been taught on Tannaite authority:* Ten things were created on the eve of the Sabbath at twilight, and these are they: the well [Num. 21:16-18], the manna, the rainbow, writing and writing instruments, the tablets of the ten commandments, the burial cave of Moses, the cave in which Moses and Elijah stood, the opening of the ass's mouth, and the opening of the earth's mouth to swallow up the wicked. R. Nehemiah said in his father's name, "Also fire and the mule." R. Josiah said in his father's name, "Also the ram and the shamir-worm." R. Judah said, "Tongs, too." *He would say,*

"Tongs are made with tongs, so who made the first tongs? It was a creation in Heaven." They said to him, "But it's possible to make it in a mould and shape it simultaneously? So it was made by man." [Note the formulation in tractate Abot: Ten things were created on the eve of the Sabbath [Friday] at twilight, and these are they: (1) the mouth of the earth (Num. 16:32); (2) the mouth of the well (Num. 21:16-18); (3) the mouth of the ass (Num. 22:28); (4) the rainbow (Gen. 9:13); (5) the manna (Ex. 16:15); (6) the rod (Ex. 4:17); (7) the Shamir; (8) letters; (9) writing; and (10) the tables of stone [of the ten commandments, (Ex. 32:15f.)]. And some say, "Also the destroyers, the grave of Moses, and the tamarisk of Abraham, our father." And some say, "Also: the tongs made with tongs [with which the first tongs were made]" [M. Abot 5:6].

B. *No problem! The one speaks of fire that serves us, the other, the fire of Gehenna. The fire that serves human beings was created at the end of the Sabbath, the fire of Gehenna on the eve of the Sabbath.*

C. *But was the fire of Gehenna created on the eve of the Sabbath? And lo, it has been taught on Tannaite authority:*

D. Seven things were created before the world was made, and these are they: Torah, repentance, the Garden of Eden, Gehenna, the throne of glory, the house of the sanctuary, and the name of the messiah

E. TORAH: "THE LORD POSSESSED ME IN THE BEGINNING OF HIS WAY, BEFORE HIS WORKS OF OLD" (PROV. 8:22).

F. Repentance: "Before the mountains were brought forth, or even you had formed the earth and the world...you turn man to destruction and say, Repent, you sons of men" (Ps. 90:2).

G. The Garden of Eden: "And the Lord God planted a garden in Eden from aforetime" (Gen. 2:8).

H. Gehenna: "For Tophet is ordained of old" (Is. 30:33).

I. The throne of glory: "Your throne is established from of old" (Ps. 93:2).

J. THE HOUSE OF THE SANCTUARY: "A GLORIOUS HIGH THRONE FROM THE BEGINNING

IS THE PLACE OF OUR SANCTUARY" (JER. 17:12).

K. And the name of the Messiah: "His name shall endure forever and has existed before the sun" (Ps. 72:17).

L. *Say: Only its hole was created before the world was created, but its fire was created on the eve of the Sabbath.*

M. *So was its fire created on the eve of the Sabbath? And hasn't it been taught on Tannaite authority:* R. Yosé says, "The fire that the Holy One, blessed be He, created on the second day of the week [Monday of creation] can never be put out: 'And they shall go forth and look upon the carcasses of the men who have rebelled against me, for their worm shall not die, neither shall their fire be quenched' (Is. 66:24)"? And said R. Benaah b. R. Ulla, "Why was 'it was good' not said concerning the creation of the second day of the week? Because the fire of Gehenna was created that day." And said R. Eleazar, "Even though 'it was good' was not said in regard to that day's creations, nonetheless, God went and treated it as part of the generalization that he set forth on the sixth day, as it is said, 'And God saw everything that he had made, and behold, it was very good' (Gen. 1:31)."

N. *Rather, the hole was made before the world was created, and its fire was made on the second day of the week; but as to the fire that serves humanity, on the eve of the Sabbath he decided to create it, but it was not created until the end of the Sabbath. For it has been taught on Tannaite authority:* R. Yosé says, "There were two things that entered God's mind to create on the eve of the Sabbath, but were not created until the end of the Sabbath, and at the end of the Sabbath the Holy One, blessed be He, gave to the first man knowledge in the model of knowledge on high, so he brought two stones and rubbed them together, and fire came forth from them, and he brought two beasts and mated them, and the mule came forth."

O. Rabban Simeon b. Gamaliel says, "The mule came into being in the days of Anah: 'This is the Anah who found the mules in the wilderness' (Gen. 36:24)."

I.6 A. Those who expound Scripture in the manner

of the homer would say, "The mule was unfit as a hybrid, therefore he brought unfit beasts into the world: 'These are the sons of Seir the Horite...and Zibeon and Anah' (Gen. 36:20), and it is written, 'And these are the children of Zibeon: Aiah and Anah' (Gen. 36:24) [so he was a brother but not he is a son]. So this teaches that Zibeon had sexual relations with his mother and produced Anah."

B. *So maybe there were two Anahs?*

C. Said Raba, "I'm going to say something that 'King Shapur' said — and who is that? It is Samuel," and there are those who say, said R. Pappa, "I'm going to say something that 'King Shapur' said — and who is that? It is Raba, 'Said Scripture, "That is Anah" means, that is the one and only Anah.'"

FORMAL COMPOSITE SUPPLEMENTING THE FOREGOING

I.7 A. *Our rabbis have taught on Tannaite authority:*

B. Ten things were created on the eve of the Sabbath at twilight, and these are they: the well (Num. 21:16-18), the manna, the rainbow, writing and writing instruments, the tablets of the ten commandments, the burial cave of Moses, the cave in which Moses and Elijah stood, the opening of the ass's mouth, and the opening of the earth's mouth to swallow up the wicked.

C. And there are those who say, "Also the staff of Aaron, its almonds and its blossoms" (Num. 17:23). And there are those who say, "Also demons."

D. And there are those who say, "Also **[54B]** the garment of Adam."

I.8 A. *Our rabbis have taught on Tannaite authority:*

B. Seven things are hidden from human beings, and these are they: the day of one's death, the day of consolation, the full extent of divine judgment; and someone doesn't know what his fellow is thinking; and someone doesn't know how he will make a living; and when the kingdom of the house of David will return; and when the condemnable kingdom [Rome] will come to an end.

I.9 A. *Our rabbis have taught on Tannaite authority:*
   B. Three things entered God's mind for creation, and if they hadn't come into his mind, it is logical that he should have thought of them: that a corpse should stink, that a deceased person should be forgotten from the heart, and that produce should rot [so as to prevent hoarding].
   C. And some say, also, that coins should circulate.

Here I have given an enormous abstract, to show how minor a position, how fixed and conventional a role, are assigned to our proof-texts and their conventional propositions, respectively. The two proof-texts, Prov. 8:20 and Jer. 17:12, continue to figure in composites that require the themes they sustain. Prov. 8:20 and Jer. 17:20 with their stereotype comments scarcely qualify as extra-documentary writing in any weighty sense!

The fact before us once again invites the hypothesis, already announced, that pre- or non-documentary writing included free-standing citations of verses with fixed, attached propositions, thus, a corpus or florilegium of standard propositions and their scriptural foundations.[17] The next entry

---

[17] If I were engaged in the study of the pre-documentary writing, not only the non- and extra-documentary writing, I would inquire after the agglutination of sets of verses and their fixed propositions. These would represent documentary building blocks for the various Midrash-compilations, just as the Mishnah with its corresponding Tosefta contributes building blocks for Talmudic composition and compilation. "The antecedents of…," e.g., Sifra or the two Sifrés seem to me accessible in this way. But, as usual, Sifra would present an anomaly, since, as we have seen in our sample, the documentary writing that conforms to the documentary patterns and propositions of Sifra forms nearly the whole of the final product, Sifra as we know it. It does seem to me that the Rabbinic sages know what verse links to, demonstrates the validity, of what proposition, and whenever they wish to introduce said proposition, it will be with the

goes over now-familiar ground.

B. NEDARIM 39B/4:4A-C I.3

I.3 A. Raba interpreted a verse of Scripture, "What is the meaning of what is written, 'But if the Lord make a new thing and the earth open her mouth' (Num. 16:30)?

B. "Said Moses before the Holy One, blessed be He, 'If Gehenna has been created, well and good, and if not, let the Lord now create it.'"

C. *Is this so? But has it not been taught on Tannaite authority:* Seven things were created before the world was made, and these are they: Torah, repentance, the Garden of Eden, Gehenna, the throne of glory, the house of the sanctuary, and the name of the messiah

D. TORAH: "THE LORD POSSESSED ME IN THE BEGINNING OF HIS WAY, BEFORE HIS WORKS OF OLD" (PROV. 8:22).

E. Repentance: "Before the mountains were brought forth, or ever you had formed the earth and the world...you turn man to destruction and say, Repent, you sons of men" (Ps. 90:23).

F. The Garden of Eden: "And the Lord God planted a garden in Eden from aforetime" (Gen. 2:8).

G. Gehenna: "For Tophet is ordained of old" (Is. 30:33).

H. The throne of glory: "Your throne is established from of old" (Ps. 93:2).

I. THE HOUSE OF THE SANCTUARY: "A GLORIOUS HIGH THRONE FROM THE BEGINNING IS THE PLACE OF OUR SANCTUARY" (JER. 17:12).

J. And the name of the Messiah: "His name shall endure for ever and has existed before the sun" (Ps. 72:17).

K. *Rather, this is what he said: "If a mouth has already*

---

prescribed verse alongside. Not only so, but the fixed repertoire of verses linked to propositions affects the telling of stories as well, as my comparison of the versions of the story of Hillel and the poor man shows, in volume III of this research report.

been created for Gehenna, well and good, but if not, then let the Lord make one."

L. But isn't it written, 'There shall be no new thing under the sun" (Qoh. 1:9)?

M. Rather, this is what he said: "If the mouth of Gehenna is not near here, then bring it near."

Once more, Prov. 8:22 figures in a sizable complex, playing the same role as elsewhere. Where a given program calls for it, the evidence that the Torah takes priority in the order of things is adduced. We now continue our survey of Genesis Rabbah Parashah One. As the outline given below will show, the topical composite plays no role in the exposition of the principal program of Parashah One, but illustrates a general theme.

Genesis Rabbah Parashah One Continued
The Topical Composite Resumes:
What Was in Being before Creation

I:IV.

2. A. R. Huna, R. Jeremiah in the name of R. Samuel b. R. Isaac: "Intention concerning the creation of Israel came before all else.

B. "The matter may be compared to the case of a king who married a noble lady but had no son with her. One time the king turned up in the market place, saying, 'Buy this ink, inkwell, and pen on account of my son.'

C. "People said, 'He has no son. Why does he need ink, inkwell, and pen?'

D. "But then people went and said, 'The king is an astrologer, so he sees into the future and he therefore is expecting to produce a son!'

E. "Along these same lines, if the Holy One, blessed be he, had not foreseen that, after twenty-six generations, the Israelites would be destined to accept the Torah, he would never have written in it, 'Command the children of Israel.' [This proves that God foresaw Israel and created the world on that account.]"

3. A. SAID. R. BENAIAH, "THE WORLD AND EVERYTHING IN IT WERE CREATED ONLY ON ACCOUNT OF THE MERIT OF THE TORAH.

B. "'THE LORD FOR THE SAKE OF WISDOM [TORAH] FOUNDED THE EARTH' (PROV. 3:19)."

C. R. BEREKHIAH SAID, "IT WAS FOR THE MERIT OF MOSES.

D. "'AND HE SAW THE BEGINNING FOR HIMSELF, FOR THERE A PORTION OF A RULER [MOSES] WAS RESERVED' (DT. 33:21)."

4. A. R. Huna in the name of Rab repeated [the following]: "For the merit of three things was the world created, for the merit of dough-offerings, tithes, and first fruits.

B. "For it is said, 'On account of [the merit of] what is first, God created...' (Gen. 1:1).

C. "And the word 'first' refers only to dough-offering, for it is written, 'Of the first of your dough' (Num. 15:20).

D. "The same word refers to tithes, as it is written, 'The first fruits of your grain' (Dt. 18:4).

E. "And the word 'first ' refers to first fruits, for it is written, 'The choicest of your land's first fruit' (Ex. 23:19)."

Genesis Rabbah Parashah One Continued
The Topical Composite Carries Forward:
What Was in Being before Creation

I:VIII.

1. A. R. Menahem and R. Joshua b. Levi in the name of R. Levi: "One who builds requires six things: water, dust, wood, stones, canes, and iron. And should you say that [since God] is rich, he will not need canes [which are used only in hovels], lo, he requires a cane for measuring, for it is written, 'And a measuring reed in his hand' (Ez. 40:3).

B. "The Torah came before those six things [as indicated by Prov. 8:22]." [Freedman: The idea is that six expressions of precedence are employed in reference to the Torah]: 'the first,' 'of old,' 'from everlasting,' 'from the beginning,' and 'or ever,' which stands for two such usages as at Prov. 8:22: 'The Lord made me...the first of his works of old, I was set up from everlasting, from the beginning or ever the earth was' (Freedman, p. 8, n. 3).]

Genesis Rabbah Parashah One Continued The Topical Composite Carries Forward: What Was in Being before Creation

I:IX.

1. A. A philosopher asked Rabban Gamaliel, saying to him, "Your God was indeed a great artist, but he had good materials to help him."

B. He said to him, "What are they?"

C. He said to him, "Unformed [space], void, darkness, water, wind, and the deep."

D. He said to him, "May the spirit of that man [you] burst! All of them are explicitly described as having been created by him [and not as pre-existent].

E. "Unformed space and void: 'I make peace and create evil' (Is. 45:7).

F. "Darkness: 'I form light and create darkness' (Is. 45:7).

G. "Water: 'Praise him, you heavens of heavens, and you waters that are above the heavens' (Ps. 148:4). Why? 'For he commanded and they were created' (Ps. 148:5).

H. "Wind: 'for lo, he who forms the mountains creates the wind' (Amos 4:13).

I. "The depths: 'When there were no depths, I was brought forth' (Prov. 8:24)."

The point of intersection is the issue of merit: on account of what, or whose, merit was the world created? At Gen. R. I:IV.3, we have a dispute between Benaiah and Berekhiah, the former maintaining the world was created on account of the merit of the Torah, Berekhiah holding it was the merit of Moses. The key proof-texts then are Prov. 3:19 and Dt. 33:21. We shall now see how the same proof-texts circulate.

LEVITICUS RABBAH XXXVI:IV.1

XXXVI:IV
1. A. "But now thus says the Lord, he who created you is Jacob, and he who formed you is Israel" (Is. 43:1).

B. R. Phineas in the name of R. Reuben said, "[Said] the Holy One, blessed be he, to his world, 'O my world, my world! Shall I tell you who created you? Shall I tell you who formed you? Jacob is the one who created you, Israel is the one who formed you,' as it is written, 'He who created you is Jacob, and he who formed you is Israel'" (Is. 43:1).

C. R. Joshua of Sikhnin in the name of R. Levi said, "Behemoth was created only on account of the merit of Jacob, as it is written, 'Behold now behemoth, which I made with you'" (Job 40:15).

D. R. Joshua b. Nehemiah in the name of R. Haninah bar Isaac: "The heaven and the earth were created only on account of the merit of Jacob.

E. "What is the proof text? 'For he established a testimony on account of Jacob' (Ps. 78:5) and 'testimony' can mean
only heaven and earth, as it is written, 'I call heaven and earth to testify against you this day'" (Dt. 4:26).

F. R. Berekhiah said, "The heaven and earth were created only on account of the merit of Jacob, whose name is Israel.

G. "What is the proof text? 'On account of the beginning did God create heaven and earth' [Gen. 1:1]. And 'beginning' refers only to Israel, as it is written, 'Israel is holy to the Lord, the beginning of his harvest'" (Jer. 2:3).

H. SAID R. BENAIAH, "THE HEAVEN AND EARTH WERE CREATED ONLY ON ACCOUNT OF THE MERIT OF MOSES.

I. "FOR IT IS WRITTEN, 'AND HE CHOSE A BEGINNING PART [NAMELY MOSES] FOR HIMSELF'" (DT. 33:21).

J. Said R. Abbahu, "Everything was created only on account of the merit of Jacob.

K. "That is in line with the following verse of Scripture: 'Not like these is the portion of Jacob, for he [that is, Jacob] is the one who formed everything'" (Jer. 10:16).

2. A. R. Berekhiah and R. Levi in the name of Samuel bar Nahman: "Abraham was saved from the furnace of fire only because of the merit of Jacob.

B. "The matter may be compared. To what is it like? It is like the case of someone who was judged before the ruler, and the judgment came forth from the ruler that he was to be put to death through burning.

C. "The ruler perceived through his astrological science that [the condemned man] was going to beget a daughter, who was going to be married to a king. He said, 'This one is worthy to be saved through the merit of the daughter that he is going to beget, who is going to be married to a king.'

D. "So in the case of Abraham, judgment against him came forth from Nimrod that he was to be put to death through burning. But the Holy One, blessed be he, foresaw that Jacob was going to come forth from him. So he said, 'That one is worthy of being saved on account of the merit of Jacob.'

E. "That is in line with the following verse of Scripture: 'Thus said the Lord to the House of Jacob, who redeemed Abraham'" (Is. 29:22).

F. And rabbis say, "Abraham himself was created only on account of the merit of Jacob.

G. "That is in line with the following verse of Scripture: 'For I have known him, that he may charge his children and his household after him to keep the way of the Lord by doing righteousness and justice' (Gen. 18:19).

H. "Now righteousness and justice are only with Jacob, for it is written, 'You have made justice and righteousness in Jacob'" (Ps. 99:4).

XXXVI:V

1. A. Why (at Lev. 26:42) are the patriarchs listed in reverse order [Jacob, Isaac, Abraham]?

B. It is as if to say, if the deeds of Jacob are insufficient, there are the deeds of Isaac, and if the deeds of Isaac are insufficient, there are the deeds of Abraham.

C. Each one of them is sufficient for [his merit] to sustain [the world].

2. A. And why is the matter of remembrance stated with respect to Abraham and Jacob but not with respect to Isaac?

B. R. Berekhiah and rabbis:

C. R. Berekhiah said, "It was because he was a child born of sorrow."

D. And rabbis say, "They regard the ashes of Isaac as if they were piled up on the altar."

3. A. And why is the word "even" used with respect to Abraham and Isaac but not with respect to Jacob?

B. It was because the fruit of the bed of Jacob, our father, was whole [and unblemished], while from the bed of Abraham came forth dross, Ishmael and the sons of Keturah, and from the bed of Isaac came forth dross, Esau and all of his nobles.

C. But in the case of Jacob, his bed was unblemished, for all the sons that were born of him were righteous men.

4. A. I know that that is the case of the patriarchs. How do I know that [God remembers the merit of the matriarchs]?

B. Scripture uses the accusative particle ('T) three times, and these refer only to the matriarchs,

C. for it is said, "There they buried Abraham and [accusative particle] Sarah his wife" (Gen. 49:31).

5. A. And when why, when the Scripture (at Lev. 26:42) makes mention of the patriarchs, does it make mention of the merit of the land with them?

B. Said R. Simeon b. Laqish, "[The matter may be compared] to a king whose three sons and one handmaiden raised them all. When, therefore, the king would ask about how his sons were, he would also say, 'Tell me about the welfare of the one who raises them.'

C. "So the Holy One, blessed be he, makes mention of the merit of the fathers and alongside he makes mention of the merit of the land: 'Then I will remember my covenant with Jacob, [and I will remember my covenant with Isaac and my covenant with Abraham,] and I will remember the land'" (Lev. 26:42).

Dt. 33:21 serves for the same proposition at Leviticus Rabbah XXXVI:IV.1H-I, the name of the sponsoring authority shifting from Berekhiah to Benaiah. We see that the "parallel" plays no considerable role in the composite that encompasses it. We now revert to Genesis Rabbah Parashah One.

Genesis Rabbah Parashah One Continued

I:X.

1. A. ["In the beginning God created" (Gen. 1:1):] R. Jonah in the name of R. Levi: "Why was the world created with [a word beginning with the letter] B?

B. "Just as [in Hebrew] the letter B is closed [at the back and sides but] open in front, so you have no right to expound concerning what is above or below, before or afterward."

C. BAR QAPPARA SAID, "'FOR ASK NOW OF THE DAYS PAST WHICH WERE BEFORE YOU, SINCE THE DAY THAT GOD CREATED MAN UPON THE EARTH' (DT. 4:32).

D. "Concerning the day *after* which days were created, you may expound, but you may not make an exposition concerning what lies before then.'

E. "'And from one end of the heaven to the other' (Dt. 4:32).

F. "[Concerning that space] you may conduct an investigation, but you may not conduct an investigation concerning what lies beyond those points."

G. R. Judah b. Pazzi gave his exposition concerning the story of creation in accord with this rule of Bar Qappara.

The exegesis of Dt. 4:32 yields the familiar point that there are matters about which one is forbidden to inquire, specifically, the world before creation, the world beyond creation. We shall now see that the same verse serves the same purp0ose in the same context of Bavli Hagigah 11b/2:1 III.1.

Bavli Hagigah 11b/2:1 III.1

III.1A. The works of creation [Gen. 1-3] before two:

B. *How on the basis of Scripture do we know this fact?*

C. *It is as our rabbis have taught on Tannaite authority:*

D. "For ask you now of the days past" (Dt. 4:32) — one may ask, two may not.

E. Might one suppose that a person may raise questions about what is prior to the creation of the world?

F. Scripture states, "Since the day that God created man upon the earth" (Dt. 4:32).

G. MIGHT ONE SUPPOSE THAT A PERSON MAY NOT RAISE QUESTIONS ABOUT THE SIX DAYS OF CREATION?

H. SCRIPTURE STATES, "THE DAYS PAST THAT WERE BEFORE YOU" (DT. 4:32).

I. MIGHT ONE SUPPOSE ONE MAY RAISE QUESTIONS ABOUT WHAT IS ABOVE AND WHAT IS BELOW, WHAT IS BEFORE AND WHAT IS AFTER?

J. SCRIPTURE STATES, "AND FROM ONE END OF HEAVEN TO THE OTHER" (DT. 4:32) — THUS: "AND FROM ONE END OF HEAVEN TO THE OTHER" YOU MAY RAISE QUESTIONS, BUT YOU MAY NOT RAISE QUESTIONS ABOUT WHAT IS ABOVE AND WHAT IS BELOW, WHAT IS BEFORE AND WHAT IS AFTER.

K. **[12A]** *NOW THAT THAT FACT IS DERIVES FROM THE LANGUAGE,* "AND FROM ONE END OF HEAVEN TO THE OTHER" (DT. 4:32), *THEN WHAT NEED DO I HAVE FOR THE LANGUAGE,* "SINCE THE DAY THAT GOD CREATED MAN UPON THE EARTH" (DT. 4:32)?

L. *IT IS IN ACCORD WITH WHAT R. ELEAZAR SAID, FOR* SAID R. ELEAZAR, "THE FIRST ADAM WAS FROM EARTH TO THE FIRMAMENT: 'SINCE THE DAY THAT GOD CREATED MAN UPON THE EARTH' (DT. 4:32). BUT WHEN HE WENT SOUR, THE HOLY ONE, BLESSED BE HE, PUT HIS HAND ON HIM AND CUT HIM DOWN TO SIZE: 'YOU HAVE FASHIONED ME AFTER AND BEFORE AND LAID YOUR HAND UPON ME' (PS. 89:5)."

THE SAME PROPOSITION, LINKED TO THE SAME VERSE, IS RESTATED IN A MUCH MORE ELABORATE WAY, BUT WITH THE SAME RESULT. NOW WE REVERT TO OUR PARASHAH.

2. A. Why with a B?

B. To tell you that there are two ages [this age and the age to come, for the letter B bears the numerical value of two].

3. A. Another matter: Why was the world created [with a word beginning with the letter] B?

B. Because that is the letter that begins the word for blessing.

C. And why not with an A?

D. Because that is the first letter of the Hebrew word for curse.

4. A. Another matter: Why not with an A?

B. So as not to give an opening to the *minim* to claim, "How can the world endure, when it has been created with a word meaning curse!"

C. Rather, said the Holy One, blessed be he, "Lo, I shall write it with a letter standing for the word 'blessing,' and may the world endure!"

5. A. Another matter: Why with a B?

B. Because the letter B has two points, one pointing upward, the other backward, so that [if] people say to it, "Who created you?" it will point upward.

C. It is as if to say, "This one who is above has created me."

D. "And what is his name?" And it points for them with its point backward: "The Lord is his name," [pointing to the first letter in the alphabet, backward from the second, which is the A, standing for the One].

6. A. R. Eleazar bar Abinah in the name of R. Aha: "For twenty-six generations the letter A made complaint before the Holy One, blessed be he, saying to him, 'Lord of the world! I am the first among all the letters of the alphabet, yet you did not create your world by starting with me!'

B. "Said the Holy One, blessed be he, to the A, 'The world and everything in it has been created only through the merit of the Torah. Tomorrow I am going to come and give my Torah at Sinai, and I shall begin only with you: "I [beginning with the A] am the Lord your God" (Ex. 20:1).'"

7. A. Bar Hutah said, "Why is it called '*alef*'? Because that is the word for a thousand: 'The word which he commanded for a thousand [*elef*] generations' (Ps. 105:8)."

I:XI.

1. A. R. Simon in the name of R. Joshua b. Levi: "[The fact that the letters] M, N, S, P, and K [when appearing at the end of the word have a form different from that used when they appear at the beginning or the middle of a word] is a law revealed to Moses at Sinai."

B. R. Jeremiah in the name of R. Hiyya bar Abba: "It is that which seers ordained."

2. A. ONCE ON AN OVERCAST DAY, ON WHICH SAGES DID NOT COME INTO THE ASSEMBLY HOUSE, THERE WERE CHILDREN THERE. THEY SAID, "LET'S TAKE UP [THE TOPIC OF THE FINAL FORM OF THE LETTERS AS THESE HAVE BEEN ORDAINED BY] THE SEERS."

B. THEY SAID, "WHAT IS THE REASON THAT THERE ARE TWO FORMS FOR THE WRITING OF THE LETTERS M, N, S, P, AND K?

C. "FROM WORD TO WORD [THE WORD AT HAND BEGINS WITH M], FROM FAITHFUL TO FAITHFUL [THE WORD BEGINS WITH N], FROM RIGHTEOUS ONE TO RIGHTEOUS ONE [WITH AN S], FROM MOUTH TO MOUTH [WITH A P], FROM HAND TO HAND [WITH A K].

D. "FROM THE HAND OF THE HOLY ONE, BLESSED BE HE, TO THE HAND OF MOSES."

E. SAGES TOOK NOTE OF WHO THESE CHILDREN WERE, AND GREAT SAGES IN ISRAEL EMERGED FROM THAT GROUP.

F. THERE ARE THOSE WHO HOLD THAT THESE WERE R. ELIEZER, R. JOSHUA, AND R. AQIBA.

G. They recited in their regard the following verse: "Even a child is known by his doings" (Prov. 20:11).

THE STORY ON THE ALPHABET-SPECULATION OF THE CHILDREN CIRCULATES, IN PRETTY MUCH FIXED FORM, IN OTHER DOCUMENTS, AS WE SHALL NOW SEE. THIS STORY SERVES MOST COMPOSITES DEVOTED TO THE THEME OF THE MORAL PROPERTIES OF LETTERS OF THE HEBREW ALPHABET.

Yerushalmi Megillah 1:9 II.10

[II:10 A] In the case of the double letters of the alphabet, one writes the first ones at the beginning and middle of a word, and the second [final forms] at the end.

[B] If one did otherwise, the scroll is invalid.

[C] In the name of R. Matteniah b. Heresh they have said, "Those letters — M, N, S, P, K [that appear in two forms] — were revealed as a law to Moses at Sinai."

[D] What are the meaning of these letters?

[E] R. Jeremiah in the name of R. Samuel, R. Isaac, "'What the seers have prepared for you.'"

[F] *Who are these seers?*

[G] THERE IS THE FOLLOWING STORY: ON A CLOUDY DAY, ON WHICH SAGES DID NOT COME TO THE MEETINGHOUSE, THE CHILDREN CAME IN AND SAID, "LET US HOLD A SESSION, SO THAT THE STUDY TIME WILL NOT BE LOST."

[H] THEY SAID, "WHAT IS THAT WHICH IS WRITTEN: [TWO KINDS OF] M, N, S, P, K? IT MEANS, "FROM SAYING [OF THE LORD] TO SAYING, FROM FAITHFUL TO THE FAITHFUL, FROM THE RIGHTEOUS ONE TO THE RIGHTEOUS, FROM THE MOUTH TO THE MOUTH, FROM THE PALM OF THE HAND OF THE HOLY ONE, BLESSED BE HE, TO THE PALM OF THE HAND OF MOSES."

[I] THE SAGES MADE NOTE OF THEM, AND ALL OF THEM GREW UP TO BE GREAT.

[J] *THEY SAY THAT R. ELIEZER AND R JOSHUA WERE AMONG THEM.*

[K] R. Jeremiah in the name of R. Hiyya b. Ba and R. Simon both say, "As to the Torah as it was written in former generations, the *He* as they wrote it and the *Mem* as they wrote it were not closed. Lo, the *Samekh* as they wrote it was closed."

[L] R. Simon and R. Samuel bar Nahman both say, "The men of Jerusalem would write 'Jerusalem' as 'to Jerusalem' and [sages] did not scruple in this regard."

[M] *"Along these same lines,* 'north' was written 'to the north,' and 'south' was written 'to the south.'"

I SEE NO IMPORTANT WAYS IN WHICH THE STORY CHANGES. I GIVE THE FOLLOWING BECAUSE IT INTERSECTS THEMATICALLY, BUT THE COMPOSITE DOES NOT CALL UPON THE STORY OF THE CHILDREN, ELIEZER AND JOSHUA, NOR DOES THEIR PROPOSITION RECUR HERE.

BAVLI SHABBAT 104A/12:3 II.6
TOPICAL APPENDIX ON
THE MEANINGS OF LETTERS OF THE
ALPHABET

II.6 A. *Rabbis said to R. Joshua b. Levi, "Just now children have come to the study house and said things the like of which even in the days of Joshua b. Nun were never said. Thus:* alef bet means, learn wisdom; gimmel dalet means, show kindness to the poor. *How come the foot of the gimmel reaches out to the dalet?* Because it is appropriate for the benevolent to pursue the poor. *Why is the roof of the dalet reaching out to the gimmel?* Because the poor must make himself available to him. *How come the face of the dalet is turned away from the gimmel?* Because the donor must give the help in secret, so as not to shame him. He, vav — that is the name of the Holy One, blessed be He. Zayyin, het, tet, yod, kaf, lamed — and if you do this, the Holy One, blessed be He, will sustain you, give you a heritage, bind a crown on you in the world to come. As to the open mem and the closed mem — the open mem refers to a word that is stated in the open, the closed one, to one that is kept secret. The bent nun and the straight nun — the faithful, if humble, will be straightened out. Samekh, ayyin — support the poor. Another reading of the same: samekh, ayyin stand for: make a mnemonic in the Torah and so acquire it. The bent pe and the straight pe: an open mouth, a closed mouth. The bent saddi and the straight saddi: the righteous one is bent in this world, the righteous one is straightened up in the next world."

B. *But that's the same message as* the faithful, if humble, will be straightened out!?

C. "Scripture thus adds humility to his humility, so teaching us that the Torah was given with a bowed head.

D. "Quf — holy; Resh — evil — *why is the face of the Quf turned away from the resh?* Said the Holy One, blessed be He, 'I can't bear to look upon the evil.'

E. *"And how come the crown of the quf is turned toward the resh?* Said the Holy One, blessed be He, 'If he repents, I shall tie on him a crown like mine.'

F. *"And how come the foot of the quf is suspended and not tied to any other stroke? It is to show, if he repents, he can enter and be brought in through this opening."*

G. That supports what R. Simeon b. Laqish, for said R. Simeon b. Laqish, "What is the meaning of the verse of Scripture, 'As to the scorners, he scorns them, but as to the humble he gives grace' (Prov. 3:34)? If someone comes wanting to be purified, he is helped to do so; if he comes wanting to be made unclean, they open the way for him."

H. Shin stands for sheqer, lie, and tav stands for emet, truth. *How come the letters for the word for lie, SH, Q, R, stand close together, while those of the word for truth, alef, mem, tav, stand far apart? Because falsehood is consecutive, truth, rare. And how come the word for lie, in Hebrew letters, stands on one foot, while the word for truth stands on a founda-*

tion of brooks? Because truth stands, falsehood can't.

II.7 A. [If we match the letters, so that] the alef stands for a tav, and the bet for a shin, we get: he who rejects me — shall I desire him?

B. Exchanging the bet for the shin: he who doesn't delight in me — shall my name rest on him?

C. Gimel/resh: he has defiled his body, shall I have mercy on him? dalet/quf: he has closed my doors, shall I not cut off his horns — thus far is the hermeneutic for the wicked.

D. But as for the hermeneutic for the righteous:

E. Alef/tav, bet/shin: if you are ashamed to sin, then dwell in Heaven.

F. He/saddi, Vav/Peh: there will be a barrier between you and wrath.

G. Saddi Het Samekh Tet Nun: nor will you tremble before Satan.

H. K/L: the prince of Gehenna said to the Holy One, blessed be He, "Lord of the world, to the sea let all be consigned." But the Holy One, blessed be He, replied, "Alef het samekh, bet tet gimmel peh [combining the first, eighth, and fifteenth letters, so, too, the second, ninth, and sixteenth, etc. (Freedman)]: meaning, "I spare them, because they spurned sensual pleasures; they are contrite; they are true; they are righteous; you have no portion in them.

I. Gehenna cried out before him, "Lord of the world, my lord, satisfy me with the seed of Seth."

J. He replied, "You have naught in them. Where shall I lead them? To the garden of myrtles."

K. Gehenna cried out before the Holy One, blessed be He, "Lord of the world, I am faint with hunger."

L. To that he said, "These are the seed of Isaac; wait, I have entire platoons of gentiles whom I shall give you."

The thematic possibilities of the Eliezer/Joshua story are not exploited in this sizable account of the same matter. Here the omission of the fixed story is striking, but I do not know what to make of it.

Genesis Rabbah Parashah One Continued

I:XII.

1. A. ["In the beginning God created..." (Gen. 1:1):] R. Yudan in the name of Aqilas: "*This* one it is appropriate to call God. [Why so?]

B. "Under ordinary circumstances a mortal king is praised in province even before he has built public baths for the population or given them private ones. [God by contrast created the world before he had received the praise of humanity, so it was not for the sake of human adulation that he created the world.]"

2. A. Simeon b. Azzai says, "'And your modesty has made me great' (2 Sam. 22:36). A mortal person mentions his name and afterward his title, for example, 'Mr. So-and-so, the prefect,' 'Mr. Such-and-such, and whatever title he gets.' But the Holy One, blessed be he, is not that way.

B. "Rather, only after he had created what was needed in his world did he make mention of his name, thus, 'In the beginning, created...,' and only afterward: ' God.'"

I:XIII.

1. A. R. SIMEON B. YOHAI TAUGHT, "HOW [ON THE BASIS OF SCRIPTURE] DO WE KNOW THAT ONE SHOULD NOT SAY, 'FOR THE LORD, A BURNT OFFERING,' 'FOR THE LORD, A MEAL-OFFERING,' 'FOR THE LORD, A PEACE-OFFERING.'

B. "RATHER ONE SHOULD SAY, 'A BURNT-OFFERING FOR THE LORD,' 'A MEAL-OFFERING FOR THE LORD,' 'A PEACE-OFFERING FOR THE LORD'?

C. "SCRIPTURE SAYS, "AN OFFERING FOR THE LORD' (LEV. 1:2).

D. "AND LO, THIS PRODUCES AN ARGUMENT *A FORTIORI* :

E. "IF IN THE CASE OF ONE WHO IS PLANNING TO DECLARE SOMETHING SANCTIFIED, THE TORAH HAS SAID THAT ONE SHOULD MAKE USE OF THE NAME OF HEAVEN ONLY IN CONNECTION WITH AN OFFERING [THAT HAS ALREADY BEEN SANCTIFIED BY BEING DESIGNATED],

F. "THOSE WHO BLASPHEME, CURSE, AND WORSHIP IDOLS, ALL THE MORE SO THAT THEY SHOULD BE BLOTTED OUT OF THE WORLD."

THE FREE-STANDING COMPOSITION ATTRIBUTED TO SIMEON B. YOHAI IS TACKED ON BECAUSE IT INTERSECTS IN PRINCIPLE: GOD'S NAME IS GIVEN AN APPROPRIATE POSITION IN A SENTENCE. BUT I:XIII.1 DOES NOT CARRY FORWARD I:XII.2, ITSELF A SUBORDINATE INTERPOLATION. NOW WE SHALL SEE HOW THE SAME FREE-STANDING EXEGESIS OF LEV. 1:2 CIRCULATES ELSEWHERE.

Sifra III:IV.1-3

III:IV

1. A. ["Speak to the Israelite people and say to them, 'When] any of you presents [an offering of cattle to the Lord, he shall choose his offering from the herd or from the flock:]"

B. Might one suppose that it is by decree [that such an offering is presented]?

C. Scripture says, "When...presents...," which is only optional [and not obligatory].

2. A. "an offering of cattle to the Lord:"

B. "[Since the order of the words is, 'offering,' then, 'to the Lord,' the sense is that one should first undertake the act of sanctification of the beast for the sacrifice, and then offer it up," the words of R. Judah.

3. A. SAID R. SIMEON, "HOW ON THE BASIS OF SCRIPTURE DO WE KNOW THAT A PERSON

SHOULD NOT SAY, 'FOR THE LORD, A BURNT-OFFERING,' 'FOR THE LORD, A MEAL-OFFERING,' 'FOR THE LORD, PEACE-OFFERINGS,' BUT RATHER HE SHOULD SAY, 'A BURNT-OFFERING FOR THE LORD,' 'A MEAL-OFFERING FOR THE LORD, 'PEACE-OFFERINGS FOR THE LORD'?

B. "SCRIPTURE SAYS, 'AN OFFERING [OF A GIVEN CLASSIFICATION] FOR THE LORD.' [THE WORD-ORDER THEN IS TO BE FOLLOWING, SUCH AND SUCH A CLASSIFICATION OF OFFERING APPLIES TO THE BEAST AT HAND, THEN, 'FOR THE LORD.']

C. "AND LO, THIS YIELDS AN ARGUMENT *A FORTIORI:*

D. "IF IN THE CASE OF ONE WHO IS GOING TO UNDERTAKE AN ACT OF SANCTIFICATION OF A BEAST, THE TORAH HAS SAID, 'THE NAME OF HEAVEN SHOULD NOT BE TREATED AS PROFANE IN CONNECTION WITH THE OFFERING,' [BUT RATHER, THE OFFERING HAS TO BE NAMED FIRST, ONLY THEN THE NAME OF HEAVEN IS INVOKED, AS AT B],

E. "HOW MUCH THE MORE SO [ARE TO BE CONDEMNED] THOSE WHO MAKE MENTION OF THE NAME OF HEAVEN FOR ANY NULL-PURPOSE WHATSOEVER!"

III:V

1. A. R. Yosé says, "Any passage in which 'an offering' is stated along with the divine name, lo, it is so as not to give unbelievers occasion to cavil.

HERE IS THE PRIMARY HOME OF THE FREE-STANDING COMPOSITION, WHICH NOW GOES OVER THE GROUND OF THE EXEGESIS OF LEV. 1:2 ATTRIBUTED TO JUDAH.

Sifré to Deuteronomy CCCVI:XXIX.1-3

CCCVI:XXIX

1. A. "For the name of the Lord I proclaim; give glory to our God":

B. We find that Moses made mention of the name of the Lord only after twenty-one words.

C. From whom did he learn to do it that way? From the ministering angels.

D. For the ministering angels make mention of the name of the Lord only after saying the three "holies," as it is said, "And this one calls to that, saying, 'Holy, holy, holy is the Lord of hosts'" (Is. 6:3).

E. Said Moses, "It is sufficient that I should be seven times as modest as the ministering angels."

2. A. Now this produces an argument a fortiori:

B. If Moses, the wisest of the wise and the greatest of the great, the father of the prophets, made mention of the name of the Lord only after twenty-one words,

C. one who makes mention of the Omnipresent for naught – how much the more so!

3. A. R. SIMEON B. YOHAI SAYS, "HOW ON THE BASIS OF SCRIPTURE DO WE KNOW THAT [WHEN CONSECRATING AN ANIMAL OR SOME OTHER SUBSTANCE FOR A SACRIFICE] A PERSON SHOULD NOT PHRASE MATTERS AS, 'FOR THE LORD, A BURNT-OFFERING,' 'FOR THE LORD, A MEAL-OFFERING,' 'FOR THE LORD, PEACE-OFFERINGS,' BUT RATHER, 'A BURNT-OFFERING FOR THE LORD,' 'A MEAL-OFFERING FOR THE LORD,' 'PEACE-OFFERINGS FOR THE LORD'?

B. "SCRIPTURE SAYS, 'AN OFFERING FOR THE LORD' (LEV. 1:2).

C. "NOW THIS PRODUCES AN ARGUMENT A FORTIORI:

D. "NOW IF IN THE CASE OF THESE, WHICH ARE CONSECRATED FOR HEAVEN, THE HOLY ONE, BLESSED BE HE, SAID, 'LET NOT MY NAME BE PROFANED ON THEIR ACCOUNT UNTIL THEY HAVE ACTUALLY BEEN CONSECRATED [AT WHICH POINT MY NAME MAY BE USED,' ONE WHO MAKES MENTION OF THE HOLY ONE, BLESSED BE HE, FOR NAUGHT OR THAT OF THE OMNIPRESENT IN A DISGRACEFUL WAY – HOW MUCH THE MORE SO!"

Once more, Simeon's exegesis of Lev. 1:2 is tacked on for thematic reasons.

Bavli Nedarim 10a/1:2 I.2G
MISHNAH-TRACTATE NEDARIM 1:2

A. He who says to his fellow, "Qonam," "Qonah," "Qonas" – lo, these are euphemisms for the Qorban [a vow to bring a sacrifice, and are valid].

B. [He who says to his fellow,] "Hereq," "Herekh," "Heref," lo, these are euphemisms for a herem [ban].

C. [He who says to his fellow,] "Naziq," "Naziah," "Paziah" – lo, these are euphemisms for Nazirite vows.

D. [He who says,] "Shebutah," "Shequqah,"

E. [or if he] vowed [with the word] "Mohi,"

F. lo, these are euphemisms for "shebuah" [oath].

BAVLI COMMENTARY ON MISHNAH-TRACTATE NEDARIM 1:2

I.1 A. *It has been stated:*

B. As to euphemisms –

C. R. Yohanan said, "These represent foreign words."

D. R. Simeon b. Laqish said, "This is language that sages have invented for use in taking vows. And so Scripture says, 'in the month which he had devised in his heart' (1 Kgs. 12:33)."

I.2 A. *How come rabbis made up euphemisms for vows [such as Qonam]?*

B. *It is to avoid using the Hebrew word for offering, which is Qorban.*

C. *So why avoid saying Qorban anyhow?*

D. *Someone might then say,* "An offering to the Lord."

E. *So why avoid saying* "An offering to the Lord"*?*

F. *He might end up saying,* "for the Lord" *without saying* "an offering," *in which case,* he would end up gratuitously expressing the Name of Heaven.

G. THAT IS IN LINE WITH WHAT WE HAVE LEARNED ON TANNAITE AUTHORITY:

H. SAID R. SIMEON, [10B] "HOW ON THE BASIS OF SCRIPTURE DO WE KNOW THAT A PERSON SHOULD NOT SAY, 'FOR THE LORD, A BURNT-OFFERING,' 'FOR THE LORD, A MEAL-OFFERING,' 'FOR THE LORD, PEACE-OFFERINGS,' BUT RATHER HE SHOULD SAY, 'A BURNT-OFFERING FOR THE LORD,' 'A MEAL-OFFERING FOR THE LORD, 'PEACE-OFFERINGS FOR THE LORD'?

I. 'SCRIPTURE SAYS, 'AN OFFERING [OF A GIVEN CLASSIFICATION] FOR THE LORD.' [THE WORD ORDER THEN IS TO BE FOLLOWING, SUCH AND SUCH A CLASSIFICATION OF OFFERING APPLIES TO THE BEAST AT HAND, THEN, 'FOR THE LORD.']

J. "AND LO, THIS YIELDS AN ARGUMENT A FORTIORI: IF IN THE CASE OF ONE WHO IS GOING TO UNDERTAKE AN ACT OF SANCTIFICATION OF A BEAST, THE TORAH HAS SAID, 'THE NAME OF HEAVEN SHOULD NOT BE TREATED AS PROFANE IN CONNECTION WITH THE OFFERING,' [BUT RATHER, THE OFFERING HAS TO BE NAMED FIRST, ONLY THEN THE NAME OF HEAVEN IS INVOKED], HOW MUCH THE MORE SO [ARE TO BE CONDEMNED] THOSE WHO MAKE MENTION OF THE NAME OF HEAVEN FOR ANY NULL PURPOSE WHATSOEVER!" [SIFRA VAYYIQRA DIBURA DENEDABAH PARASHAH 2 III:IV.1].

THE FREE-STANDING EXEGESIS OF LEV. 1:2 IS CITED YET AGAIN, ONCE MORE WITHOUT AN INTIMATE RELATIONSHIP TO THE CONTEXT BUT SERVING AS BACKUP FOR WHAT IS SAID IN AN INTEGRATED WAY. THE BASIC PROPOSITION SURELY IS PARTICULAR TO SIFRA AND SHOULD NOT BE REGARDED AS EXTRA-DOCUMENTARY AT ALL. BUT IN MY ASSESSMENT OF THE PROPORTIONS OF EXTRA-DOCUMENTARY WRIT-

ING IN GENESIS RABBAH PARASHAH ONE, I INCLUDE THIS ITEM IN MY CALCULATION.

Genesis Rabbah Parashah One Continued

2. A. ["...the heaven and the earth" (Gen. 1:1):] Rabbis said, "When a mortal builds a building, if the building goes as planned, he may continue to broaden the structure as it rises, but if not, he has to make it broad at the bottom but narrow at the top.

B. "But that is not how things are for the Holy One, blessed be he. But: '...*the* heaven' meaning that very form of heaven as it had come to mind, first, and then: '...and *the* earth...,' as it had originally been planned."

3. A. R. Huna in the name of R. Eliezer, son of R. Yosé the Galilean: "Even those concerning which Scripture states, 'For behold, I create a new heaven' (Is. 65:17) were in fact created from the six days of creation.

B. "This is in line with the following verse: 'For as the new heaven remains before me' (Is. 66:22), not 'new,' but '*the new*.'" [Freedman, p. 12, n. 5: The definite article implies the specific new heavens, those created aforetime.]

Genesis Rabbah Parashah One Continued
A Miscellany

To understand what is to follow, a brief preface is in order. Genesis Rabbah Parashah One concludes with a three part miscellany. The three components of the composite are free-standing, intersecting in theme but not in proposition, and they carry none of the burden of the Parashah as it unfolds. Each of the compositions has its parallels in other compilations. And each point at which the parallel utilization of the composition occurs, the item stands essentially

Proportion and Position: Evidence in a Sample of Genesis Rabbah 251

autonomous of its setting, just as is the case here. To show what is to come, I present a brief precis of the matter, taken from the outline of the Parashah presented later in this chapter. The outline systematically indents materials that are secondary or interpolated, and the indentation indicated here shows that the miscellaneous entries play no important role in the Parashah's execution of its program. That fact will be clearer when we consider the complete outline of the Parashah, which follows:

> I:XIV.1. ["...THE HEAVEN AND THE EARTH" (GEN. 1:L):] R. ISHMAEL ASKED R. AQIBA, SAYING TO HIM, "BECAUSE YOU SERVED NAHUM OF GIMZO AS DISCIPLE FOR TWENTY-TWO YEARS, [LEARNING FROM HIM THE EXEGETICAL PRINCIPLES THAT] THE WORDS 'EXCEPT' AND 'ONLY' ARE TO BE INTERPRETED AS EXCLUSIONARY, AND THE ACCUSATIVE PARTICLE *'ETH'* AND 'ALSO' SERVE AS INCLUSIONARY WORDS [INDICATING THAT MORE IS COVERED BY THE STATEMENT AT HAND THAN THAT WHICH IS EXPLICITLY MENTIONED IN IT], AS TO THE ACCUSATIVE PARTICLE IN THE VERSE BEFORE US [GEN. 1:1], WHAT IS THE EXEGESIS THAT THAT USAGE APPLIES?"
>
> > I:XV.L. ["...THE HEAVEN AND THE EARTH" (GEN. 1:L):] THE HOUSE OF SHAMMAI SAY, "THE HEAVEN WAS CREATED FIRST." THE HOUSE OF HILLEL SAY, "THE EARTH WAS CREATED FIRST."
> >
> > > 2. [T. KER. 4:14: R. SIMEON SAYS,] "IN EVERY PLACE SCRIPTURE GIVES PRECEDENCE TO ABRAHAM OVER ISAAC, AND TO ISAAC OVER JACOB. BUT IN ONE PASSAGE SCRIPTURE SAYS, 'AND I REMEMBERED MY COVENANT WITH JACOB [...ISAAC AND ABRAHAM...]' (LEV. 26:42). THIS TEACHES THAT THE THREE OF THEM ARE EQUIVALENT TO ONE ANOTHER. IN EVERY PAS-

SAGE SCRIPTURE ACCORDS PRECEDENCE TO MOSES OVER AARON, BUT IN ONE PLACE SCRIPTURE STATES, 'THAT IS AARON AND MOSES' (EX. 6:26). THIS TEACHES THAT THE TWO OF THEM ARE EQUIVALENT TO ONE ANOTHER.

THIS ABBREVIATED VERSION SUFFICES TO MAKE THE POINT THAT THE TWO PRINCIPAL ITEMS ARE FREE-STANDING, I:XIV.1 AND I:XV.1, AND THE PASSAGE OF THE TOSEFTA IS TACKED ON FOR THEMATIC REASONS; IT DOES NOT EXPAND ON THE POINT OF I:XV.1 BUT ILLUSTRATES ITS PRINCIPLE OF HIERARCHICAL CLASSIFICATION. SO WHAT WE SEE IS, COMPOSITIONS THAT SERVE MORE THAN ONE DOCUMENT DO IGNORE DOCUMENTARY LINES, BUT THEY ALSO MAKE NO WEIGHTY CONTRIBUTION TO THE DOCUMENTS THAT INTRODUCE THEM; THEY FALL INTO THE CATEGORY OF TOPICAL APPENDICES. NOW LET US TURN BACK TO EXAMINE IN FULL EACH ITEM IN TURN.

Genesis Rabbah Parashah One Continued

I:XIV.

1. A. ["...THE HEAVEN AND THE EARTH" (GEN. 1:1):] R. ISHMAEL ASKED R. AQIBA, SAYING TO HIM, "BECAUSE YOU SERVED NAHUM OF GIMZO AS DISCIPLE FOR TWENTY-TWO YEARS, [LEARNING FROM HIM THE EXEGETICAL PRINCIPLES THAT] THE WORDS 'EXCEPT' AND 'ONLY' ARE TO BE INTERPRETED AS EXCLUSIONARY, AND THE ACCUSATIVE PARTICLE 'ETH' AND 'ALSO' SERVE AS INCLUSIONARY WORDS [INDICATING THAT MORE IS COVERED BY THE STATEMENT AT HAND THAN THAT WHICH IS EXPLICITLY MENTIONED IN IT], AS TO

THE ACCUSATIVE PARTICLE IN THE VERSE BEFORE US [GEN. 1:1], WHAT IS THE EXEGESIS THAT THAT USAGE APPLIES?"

B. [ISHMAEL] SAID TO [AQIBA], "IF IT WERE STATED, 'IN THE BEGINNING CREATED GOD [WITHOUT THE ACCUSATIVE PARTICLE], HEAVEN, AND EARTH, ' WE MIGHT HAVE TAKEN THE VIEW THAT HEAVEN AND EARTH ARE DIVINE. [WITHOUT THE ACCUSATIVE PARTICLE, WE MIGHT HAVE UNDERSTOOD THE WORDS 'HEAVEN' AND 'EARTH' TO BE SUBJECTS OF THE VERB 'CREATE,' ALONG WITH GOD. THUS WE MIGHT HAVE THOUGHT THAT THE WORLD WAS MADE BY THREE: GOD, HEAVEN, AND EARTH. SO THE ACCUSATIVE PARTICLE IS NOT INCLUSIONARY BUT HAS ITS OWN PURPOSE.]"

C. [AQIBA] SAID TO [ISHMAEL], "'FOR IT IS NO EMPTY THING FROM YOU,' (DT. 32:46) MEANS THAT IF THE TORAH SEEMS EMPTY, IT IS FROM YOU [AND YOUR OWN FAULT], SPECIFICALLY BECAUSE YOU DO NOT KNOW HOW TO EXPOUND SCRIPTURE.

D. "RATHER, THE ACCUSATIVE PARTICLE PRIOR TO THE WORD 'HEAVEN' SERVES TO INCLUDE THE SUN, MOON, STARS, AND PLANETS, AND THE ACCUSATIVE PARTICLE PRIOR TO THE WORD 'EARTH' SERVES TO ENCOMPASS TREES, GRASS, AND THE GARDEN OF EDEN."

THE EXEGETICAL PROBLEM OF THE ACCUSATIVE PARTICLE, FRAMED BY ISHMAEL AND SOLVED BY HIM, IS THEN RECONSIDERED BY AQIBA AND SOLVED IN A BETTER WAY. THE WHOLE IS TACKED ON TO THE

parashah but is not positioned where the phrase of Gen. 1:1 is taken up. We shall now see that it circulates elsewhere, and, more important, it is everywhere autonomous of its setting.

Sifré Deuteronomy Pisqa Forty-Eight

XLVIII:I
1. A. "If then you faithfully keep all this instruction [that I command you, loving the Lord your God, walking in all his ways, and holding fast to him, the Lord will dislodge before you all these nations; you will dispossess nations greater and more numerous than you. Every spot on which your foot treads shall be yours; your territory shall extend from the wilderness to the Lebanon, and from the River, the Euphrates, to the Western Sea. No man shall stand up to you: the Lord your God will put the dread and the fear of you over the whole land in which you set foot, as he promised you]" (Dt. 11:22-25):
    B. Why is this said?
    C. Since it is said, "And it shall come to pass, if you will certainly listen to my commandments" (Dt. 11:13), might I draw the inference that if someone has heard teachings of the Torah and rested on his laurels and not repeated [and so reviewed] them, [that suffices]?
    D. Scripture says, "If then you faithfully keep...,"
    E. which indicates that just as one has to take care of his coin, that it not get lost, so he has to take care of his learning, that it not get lost.
2. A. And so Scripture says, "If you seek her as silver" (Prov. 2:45) –
    B. just as silver is hard to come by, so teachings of the Torah are hard to come by.
    C. Might one then say, just as silver is hard to lose, so teachings of Torah are hard to lose?

D. Scripture says, "Gold and glass cannot equal it" (Prov. 2:4).

   E. [Teachings of the Torah] are as hard to come by as gold and as easy to lose as glass.

F. "…neither shall the exchange thereof be vessels of fine gold" (Job 28:17).

3. A. R. Ishmael says, "'Only watch out and keep your soul diligently' (Dt. 4:9) –

   B. "The matter may be compared to a mortal king who caught a bird and handed it over to his servant, saying to him, 'Keep for this bird for my son. If you lose it, do not think that you lost a bird worth a penny, but it is tantamount to your life that you will have lost.'

   C. "SO SCRIPTURE SAYS, "FOR IT IS NO VAIN THING FOR YOU, BECAUSE OF IT IS YOUR VERY LIFE' (DT. 32:47).

   D. "SOMETHING THAT YOU SAY IS VAIN IN FACT IS YOUR VERY LIFE."

4. A. R. Simeon b. Yohai says, "The matter may be compared to the case of two brothers who inherited money from their father.

   B. "One of them converted it into ready cash and consumed it, and the other converted it into ready cash and put it aside.

   C. "As to the one of them who converted it into ready cash and consumed it, he turned out to have nothing in hand.

   D. "But the one who converted it into ready cash and put it aside got rich after a while.

   E. "So disciples of sages learn two or three things in a day, two or three chapters in a week, two or three lections in a month. Such a one turns out to get rich after a while.

   F. "That is in line with the following verse of Scripture: "He who gathers little by little shall increase' (Prov. 13:11).

   G. "But the one who says, 'Today I shall learn [what I need], tomorrow I shall learn [what I need], today I shall review [what I need], tomorrow I shall review [what I need], turns out to have nothing in hand.'

256 *Paltry Parallels*

And concerning him Scripture says, 'A wise son gathers in summer, but a son who does shamefully sleeps in harvest' (Prov. 10:5).

H. "And further: 'The sluggard will not plow when winter comes, therefore he shall beg in harvest and have nothing' (Prov. 20:4).

I. "And further: 'He who observes the wind shall not sow' (Qoh. 11:4).

J. "'I went by the field of the slothful man and by the vineyard of the man void of understanding, and lo, it was all grown over with thistles; the face of it was covered with nettles, and the stone wall was broken down' (Prov. 24:30-31)."

The snippet involving Dt. 32:47 makes its appearance, used for the same purpose as in Genesis Rabbah but out of the setting of Gen. 1:1 altogether.

<u>Yerushalmi Peah. 1:1</u>

[U] AND THIS ACCORDS WITH THAT WHICH R. MANA SAID, "FOR THIS [I.E., THE TORAH AND ITS LAWS] IS NOT A TRIFLING THING FOR YOU: [IT IS YOUR VERY LIFE; THROUGH IT YOU SHALL LONG ENDURE ON THE LAND THAT YOU ARE TO POSSESS UPON CROSSING THE JORDAN]' (DT. 32:47).

[V] "AND IF [THE TORAH'S LAWS ARE BUT A] TRIFLING THING, THAT IS YOUR [OWN FAULT]! WHY [SHOULD THAT BE THE CASE]? BECAUSE YOU DO NOT DEVOTEDLY LABOR IN [THE TORAH].

[W] " 'IT IS YOUR VERY LIFE' (DT. 32:47) — UNDER WHAT CIRCUMSTANCES IS IT YOUR LIFE? WHEN YOU LABOR DEVOTEDLY IN IT, [AND THEREBY UPHOLD THE LAWS DECREED BY AN EARLIER COURT, BUT FORGOTTEN IN THE INTERIM]."

[X] [What follows is a series of four exegeses (X, Y, Z, and AA-EE) proving the point established at T, namely, that turning one's attention to the matter at hand leads to fulfilling the law as stated to Moses on Sinai.] R. Tanhuma in the name of R. Huna: " 'Now Bezalel, son of Uri, son of Hur, of the tribe of Judah, had made all that the Lord had commanded Moses' (Ex. 38:22). [Note the phrasing of this verse]: ['Bezalel had made... all that] Moses [commanded] him' is not written here, but rather, '... all that the Lord had commanded Moses.' [This is meant to indicate that] with regard to even those items [that God had described to Moses, but] that [Bezalel] had never heard his master [describe, [Bezalel] independently arrived at [Moses'] thoughts, [and made the items] just as spoken to Moses on Sinai."

[Y] R. Yohanan in the name of R. Beniah: " 'Just as the Lord had commanded his servant Moses, so Moses had charged Joshua, and so Joshua did; he left nothing undone of all that the Lord had commanded Moses' (Josh. 11:15). [Again, note the phrasing of this verse]: ['Joshua did...all that Moses commanded him'] is not written here, but rather, '...all that the Lord had commanded Moses.' [This is meant to indicate that] with regard to even those items [that Joshua] had never heard from his master, [Joshua] independently arrived at [Moses'] thoughts, [and did those things] just as spoken to Moses on Sinai."

[Z] R. Yohanan in the name of R. Beniah, R. Huna in the name of Rabbi: " 'Proper rulings (i.e., torah) were in his mouth...' (Malachi 2:6a) — [this refers to Levi's performing] those matters that he explicitly heard from his master [God]. '... And nothing perverse was on his lips' (Malachi 2:6b) — [this is meant to indicate that Levi performed] even those matters he never heard from his master."

Once again, the exegesis of Dt. 32:47 stands on its own, outside of the treatment of Gen. 1:1. Here is clearly a suitable elaboration of the matter.

Bavli Hagigah 12a/2:1 I.14
12. A. What is the meaning of the word for heaven?

B. Said R. Yosé bar Hanina, "[Reading the Hebrew letters of the word, we find:] 'there is water.'"

13. A. In a Tannaite statement it is set forth: [The letters for the word heaven yield] fire and water, teaching that the Holy One, blessed be he, brought them and combined them with one another and from them made the firmament.

14. A. R. ISHMAEL ASKED R. AQIBA WHEN THEY WERE MAKING A TRIP TOGETHER, SAYING, "NOW YOU, WHO SERVED AS DISCIPLE OF NAHUM OF GIMZU FOR TWENTY TWO YEARS — THE MASTER WHO WOULD INTERPRET EVERY ACCUSATIVE PARTICLE IN THE TORAH — HOW DID HE INTERPRET THE LANGUAGE, 'ACCUSATIVE PARTICLE + HEAVEN' AND 'ACCUSATIVE PARTICLE + EARTH'?"

B. He said to him, "If Scripture said, omitting the accusative particle, 'heaven and earth,' I might have said, 'heaven' and 'earth' are names of the Holy One, blessed be he. But not that the accusative particle is inserted prior to heaven and earth, it can only mean heaven and earth literally."

C. **[12B]** "AND WHY [DO WE FIND THE] 'ACCUSATIVE PARTICLE + EARTH'?"

D. "TO GIVE PRIORITY TO HEAVEN OVER EARTH."

15. A. "Now the earth was unformed and void" (Gen. 1:2):

B. Note that the verse places heaven first? So why then does it narrate the process of making the earth first of all?

C. A Tannaite statement of the household of R. Ishmael:

D. "The matter may be compared to the case of a mortal king, who said to his staff, 'I want you at my door at the crack of dawn.' He got up early and found women and men. Whom does he praise? The one who doesn't usually get up early but got up early that day."

Here Dt. 32:47 plays no role, the focus is on the matter of the accusative particle. But the point has shifted. The accusative particle bears the meaning, not to encompass the moon and the stars, but rather, to give priority to heaven over earth. So the message has shifted altogether.

BAVLI PESAHIM 22B/2:1 V.4

V.1 A. **And one should not kindle an oven or a double stove with it:**

B. *That's obvious!*

C. *No, it was necessary to teach the rule in accord with R. Judah, who has said,* **"The only valid form of removal of leaven is through burning.** *It might have entered your mind to suppose, since R. Judah has said, properly performing the commandment concerning it requires burning it, then, along with burning it, he may as well derive benefit from it. So we are informed that that is not the case.*

2. A. Said Hezekiah, "How on the basis of Scripture do we know that, on Passover, it is forbidden to derive benefit from leaven? As it is said, 'There shall be no leavened bread be eaten' (Ex. 13:3) — in it there will be no aspect in which eating may be permitted."

B. *The operative consideration, therefore, is that it is written,* "There shall be no leavened bread be eaten" (Ex. 13:3), *but if it had not been written,* "There shall be no leavened bread be eaten" (Ex. 13:3), *I might have supposed that while there is an implication that eating it is prohibited, there is no implication that deriving benefit from it is prohibited. Then he differs from R. Abbahu, for* said R. Abbahu, "In any passage in which it is stated, 'it shall not be eaten,' or 'you shall not eat,' or 'you [pl.] shall not eat,' all the same are the prohibitions against eating and against deriving benefit, unless Scripture expressly spells out the contrary, as is the case with carrion. *For it has been taught on Tannaite authority:* "'You shall not eat of anything that dies of itself; to the stranger that is within your gates you may give it that he may eat it; or you may sell it to a gentile" (Dt. 14:21) ["stranger" is one who has renounced idolatry but does not yet observe the food taboos]. I know only that one may give it to a stranger or sell it to a gentile. How on the basis of Scripture do I know that it may be sold to a gentile? Scripture says, "You may give it...or sell it." How do we know that you may give it to a gentile? Because Scripture says, "You may give it that he may eat it or you may sell it to a gentile." So it follows that both giving and selling pertain to both a stranger and a gentile,' the words of R. Meir. R. Judah says, 'Matters are just as they are written out: to a foreigner the food is transferred as a gift, and to a gentile, through sale.'"

3. A. *What is the scriptural basis for R. Judah's view?*

B. *If you think that matters are as R. Meir has stated them, then the All-Merciful ought to have written, 'you shall give it and he may eat, and sell it....' Why does Scripture say, 'or sell it'? It is to indicate that matters are just as they are written out."*

C. *And R. Meir?*

D. *The formulation we have indicates that it is a priority to give it away to a stranger rather than sell it to a gentile.*

E. *And R. Judah?*

F. *Since in the case of a stranger, you are commanded to keep him alive, and concerning a Canaanite you are not commanded to keep him alive, it is hardly necessary to have a verse of Scripture to tell us to give priority to the stranger.*

4. A. *Not there is no problem from the perspective of R. Meir, who has said,* So it follows that both giving and selling pertain to both a stranger and a gentile, *since a verse of Scripture is required to permit deriving benefit [through sale to a gentile] of carrion, then* everything else forbidden in the Torah would be covered by a prohibition as to both eating and deriving benefit. *But from the perspective of R. Judah, who has said,* Matters are just as they are written out, *then how does he know concerning* everything else forbidden in the Torah would be covered by a prohibition as to both eating and deriving benefit?

B. *He derives that proposition from the verse,* "You shall not eat any meat that is torn of beasts in the field, [22A] you shall cast it to the dogs" (Ex. 22:30) — "it" you cast to the dogs, but you don't cast to the dogs anything else that is forbidden in the Torah [but you may derive benefit from it, e.g., by selling it to a gentile].

C. *And R. Meir?*

D. "it" you cast to the dogs, but you don't cast to the dogs unconsecrated meat from animals slaughtered in the Temple courtyard.

E. *And the other party?*

F. Not deriving benefit from unconsecrated meat from animals slaughtered in the Temple courtyard *is a negative commandment that derives from the Torah itself.*

G. *Objected R. Isaac Nappaha, "Lo, there is the matter of the sciatic nerve! Even though the All-Merciful has said,* 'Therefore the children of Israel do not eat the sinew of the thigh vein' Gen. 32:33), *yet we have learned in the Mishnah:* **A man sends to a gentile a thigh in which the sinew of the hip [is located], because its place [presence] is known [M. Hul. 7:2A]."**

H. *R. Abbahu takes the view that* when carrion was permitted, permissibility extended to it, its forbidden fat, and its thigh sinew [and that's why one may derive benefit from these, by selling them to gentiles].

I. *That poses no problem to him who has said* the sinews impart flavor [if boiled with meat, so thè meat would be forbidden as well]. *But from the perspective of him who has said* that the sinews don't impart a flavor, *what is to be said?* [Freedman: on that view the sinews are as meat and therefore when carrion was permitted the permission included the sinews.]

J. *Of whom have you heard who takes the view that* the sinews don't impart a flavor? *It is R. Simeon, for it has been taught on Tannaite authority:* He who eats of the thigh sinew of an unclean animal — R. Judah declares him liable on two counts, and R. Simeon declares him exempt [on account of eating meat of an unclean animal, since there is no taste in the sinew, and he is not liable on the sinew, because he would be liable on that count only if the meat of the beast were permitted, but not when the meat also is forbidden (Freedman)].

K. *But R. Simeon too declares it is forbidden for benefit, for it has been taught on Tannaite authority:* "The sinew of the thigh is permitted as to benefit," the words of R. Judah. And R. Simeon prohibits it.

L. *But then there is the matter of blood, of which the*

All-Merciful has said, "No soul of you shall eat blood" (Lev. 17:12), *and yet we have learned in the Mishnah:* [He tossed the blood on the top of the altar seven times. Then did he pour out the residue of the blood onto the western base of the outer altar. And that [the residue of the blood sprinkled on] the outer altar he poured out on the southern base.] The two streams of blood then mingled together in the [flow of the] surrounding channel and flowed down into the Qidron brook. They are sold to gardeners for fertilizer. And the law of sacrilege applies to them [until the sale] [M. Yoma 5:6].

M. *The case of blood is exceptional, since it is treated as comparable to water, as it is written,* "You shall not eat it, you shall pour it out upon the earth as water" (Dt. 12:24) — just as water is permitted, so blood is permitted.

N. But say: like water that is poured out as a libation on the alter?

O. Said R. Abbahu, "'like water' means, like water in general."

P. *Yeah, sure, and is it written,* "like water in general"?

Q. Rather, said R. Ashi, "Like water that is poured out, but not like water that is presented as a libation."

R. *Well, then, why not say,* "like water that is poured out before an idol"?

S. There too it's still called a libation: "They drank the wine of their drink offering" (Dt. 32:38).

T. **[22B]** *And from the perspective of Hezekiah, for what practical purpose is blood treated as comparable to water?* [Freedman: since he holds that only the passive form, "shall not be eaten," implies a prohibition of all benefit, but not the active, "you shall not eat," benefit from blood is permitted in any case, for the prohibition is not expressed in the passive; then what is the purpose of treating blood as equivalent to water?]

U. *It is in accord with R. Hiyya bar Abba, for* said R. Hiyya bar Abba said R. Yohanan, "How on the basis of Scripture do we know that blood of Holy Things does not make anything susceptible to uncleanness? As it is said, 'You shall pour it on the earth as water' (Dt. 12:24) — blood that is poured out like water imparts susceptibility to uncleanness, blood that is not poured out does not impart susceptibility to uncleanness."

V. *But what about the limb of a living animal, for, although it is written,* "You shall not eat the life with the meat" (Dt. 12:23), *yet it has been taught on Tannaite authority:* said R. Nathan, "How on the basis of Scripture do we know that one should not extend a cup of wine to a Nazirite [who is forbidden to drink wine] or a limb cut from a living beast to a child of Noah [who may not eat such meat, and that means, anybody]? Scripture states, "you shall not put a stumbling block before the blind" (Lev. 19:14)" — *lo, it is permitted to give it to dogs?*

W. *The limb from the living animal is exceptional, for it is compared to blood, as it is written,* "Only be steadfast in not eating the blood, for the blood is the life" (Dt. 12:23).

X. *And from the perspective of Hezekiah, for what practical purpose is blood treated as comparable to water?*

Y. *He may say to you:* blood is comparable to the limb from the living animal and not vice versa, thus: just as a limb from a living animal is forbidden [only as to eating], so blood from a living animal is forbidden, and what blood is that? It is the blood of arteries from which life flows out.

Z. *But what about the ox that is to be stoned, for though the All-Merciful has said,* "its meat shall not be eaten" (Ex. 21:28) [so benefit in general is forbidden, not only eating], *yet it has been taught on Tannaite authority:*

AA. Since Scripture is explicit, "The ox will certainly be stoned" (Ex. 21:28), do I not know that the carcass is carrion, and it is forbidden to eat carrion? So why in the world does Scripture find it necessary to state explicitly, "And its meat shall not be eaten" (Ex. 21:28)?

BB. Scripture thereby informs you that if after the court decree has been issued, the beast was properly slaughtered [rather than stoned], it is forbidden to eat it.

CC. I know only that the prohibition extends to eating it; how do I know that it is prohibited also to derive benefit from the carcass [e.g., by selling it as dog food]?

DD. Scripture states, "But the owner of the ox shall be clean" (Ex. 21:28).

EE. *How does that prove the point?*

FF. Simeon b. Zoma says, "It is like someone saying to another, 'So-and-so has gone forth clear of all his property and can get no benefit from anything.'"

GG. *So the operative consideration is that Scripture has said,* "But the owner of the ox shall be clean" (Ex. 21:28). *But if we had deduced the rule from the language,"* And its meat shall not be eaten" (Ex. 21:28) , *that would have implied that it is prohibited to eat it but not to derive benefit from it!*

HH. *In point of fact, the language,* "And its meat shall not be eaten" (Ex. 21:28) *bears the meaning that it is forbidden for eating and also for benefit, and the statement,* "But the owner of the ox shall be clean" (Ex. 21:28). *serves the purpose of dealing with its hide [that too is forbidden]. And it was necessary to cover all this ground in so many words. For it might have entered your mind to suppose that since it is written,* "And its meat shall not be eaten" (Ex. 21:28), *the meaning is, that covers the meat but not the hide. So we are informed that it covers the hide as well.*

II. *But from the perspective of those Tannaite authority who read the verse in a different context altogether, namely, to cover half ransom and damages for minors [indicating that half ransom would be payable even when the damage is done by an ox, not by a person], how we know that use of the hide is forbidden?*

JJ. *They derive it from the use of the accusative particle prior to the noun,* "its meat," *meaning to encompass under the prohibition what is secondary to the meat, which is the hide.*

KK. *And the other party?*

LL. *He does not derive lessons from the appearance of the accusative particle. That is in accord with what has been taught on Tannaite authority:*

MM.   SIMEON THE IMSONITE — SOME

SAY, NEHEMIAH THE IMSONITE — WOULD DERIVE A LESSON FROM THE USE OF EVERY ACCUSATIVE PARTICLE THAT IS IN THE TORAH. WHEN HE REACHED THE VERSE THAT PLACES THE ACCUSATIVE PARTICLE BEFORE THE WORD "LORD," NAMELY, "THE LORD YOUR GOD YOU SHALL FEAR" (DT. 10:20), HE REFRAINED FROM DOING SO [SINCE HE DID NOT WISH TO SUGGEST THERE WAS MORE THAN ONE GOD]. HE DISCIPLES SAID TO HIM, "MY LORD, WHAT THEN WILL BE THE FATE OF ALL THE OTHER ACCUSATIVE PARTICLES FROM WHICH YOU HAVE DRAWN LESSONS [IF YOU PICK AND CHOOSE AMONG THEM]?"

NN. HE SAID TO THEM, "JUST AS I HAVE RECEIVED A REWARD FOR THE LESSONS THAT I HAVE DERIVED, SO I SHALL RECEIVE A WORD FOR REFRAINING FROM DERIVING A LESSON."

OO. [AND THAT WAS THE SITUATION THAT PREVAILED] UNTIL R. AQIBA CAME ALONG AND TAUGHT CONCERNING THE VERSE THAT PLACES THE ACCUSATIVE PARTICLE BEFORE THE WORD "LORD," NAMELY, "THE LORD YOUR GOD YOU SHALL FEAR" (DT. 10:20), "THE ACCUSATIVE PARTICLE SERVES TO ENCOMPASS WITHIN THE COMMANDMENT THE DISCIPLES OF SAGES THEMSELVES."

PP. *But what about produce of a tree in the first three years after planting, for though the All-Merciful has said,* "Three years shall it be forbidden unto you, it shall not be eaten" (Lev. 19:23), *yet it has been taught on Tannaite authority:* "Uncircumcised: it shall not be eaten of" (Lev. 19:23) — I know only the prohibition concerning eating it. How do I know that one may derive no benefit from it or use it for dye or light a candle with it? Scripture says, "You shall count the fruit thereof as uncircumcised; uncircumcised it shall not be eaten of" — encompassing all these other usages."

QQ. *So the operative consideration is that Scripture has said,* "You shall count the fruit thereof as uncircumcised; uncircumcised it shall not be eaten of." *Then if Scripture had not said so, I would have supposed that the prohi-*

bition covers eating but not deriving benefit!

The present composite is appropriately cited by Theodor-Albeck, because the topic, the accusative article, is the same, and so is the principal player, Aqiba. But now the point is completely different. This is not a "parallel" at all.

Yerushalmi Sotah 5:5 I:5

[I:5 A] R. *Aqiba was on trial before Tonosteropos the Wicked. The time for reciting the Shema came. He began to recite it and smiled.*

[B] *[The wicked one] said to him, "Old man, old man! You are either a wizard or you have contempt for pain [that you smile]."*

[C] *He said to him, "May the soul of that man perish. I am no wizard, nor do I have contempt for pain. But for my whole life I have been reciting this verse: 'And you shall love the Lord your God with all your heart, with all your soul, and with all your might' (Dt. 5:6). I loved God with all my heart, and I loved him with all my might. But 'with all my soul' until now was not demanded of me. And now that the time has come for me to love him with all my soul, as the time for reciting the Shema has arrived, I smile that the occasion has come to carry out the verse at that very moment at which I recite the Scripture."*

[H] NEHEMIAH IMSONI, WHO SERVED R. AQIBA FOR TWENTY-TWO YEARS, WOULD SAY, "[WHEN WE SEE IN SCRIPTURE THE WORDS] 'ET [THE OBJECT MARKER] AND GAM ['ALSO'], [THEY SERVE AS EXEGETICAL TOOLS FOR] ENCOMPASSING AN UNSTATED SUBJECT. [WHEN WE SEE THE WORDS] AKH AND RAK ['ONLY'], [THEY SERVE TO] LIMIT [AND EXCLUDE].

[I] HE SAID TO HIM, "WHAT IS THE MEANING OF THAT WHICH IS WRITTEN, 'YOU SHALL FEAR [+ 'ET] THE LORD YOUR GOD'" (DT. 6:13).

[J] HE SAID TO HIM, "HIM AND HIS TORAH [SHALL YOU FEAR]."

Once more, we have the form but not the substance: Aqiba, the accusative particle, Aqiba's solution. But the point has shifted. We turn to the final unit of Genesis Rabbah, another that is tacked on outside of the main structure of the Parashah.

Genesis Rabbah Parashah One Continued
I:XV.

L. A. ["...THE HEAVEN AND THE EARTH" (GEN. 1:1):] THE HOUSE OF SHAMMAI SAY, "THE HEAVEN WAS CREATED FIRST."

B. THE HOUSE OF HILLEL SAY, "THE EARTH WAS CREATED FIRST."

C. IN THE VIEW OF THE HOUSE OF SHAMMAI THE MATTER MAY BE COMPARED TO THE CASE OF A KING WHO FIRST MADE A THRONE FOR HIMSELF AND AFTERWARD THE FOOTSTOOL FOR THE THRONE, AS IT IS SAID, "THE HEAVEN IS MY THRONE, AND THE EARTH THE DUST OF MY FEET" (IS. 66:1).

D. IN THE VIEW OF THE HOUSE OF HILLEL THE MATTER IS TO BE COMPARED TO THE CASE OF A KING WHO BUILT A FIRST PALACE FOR HIMSELF. ONLY AFTER HE HAD BUILT THE BOTTOM FLOOR DID HE BUILD THE UPPER FLOOR, FOR SO IT IS WRITTEN, "ON THE DAY ON WHICH THE LORD GOD MADE EARTH AND [ONLY THEN] HEAVEN" (GEN. 2:4).

E. SAID R. JUDAH BAR ILAI, "THE FOLLOWING VERSE OF SCRIPTURE SUPPORTS THE VIEW OF THE HOUSE OF HILLEL: 'OF OLD YOU LAID OUT THE FOUNDATIONS OF THE EARTH..., ' AND AFTERWARD, '...AND THE HEAVENS ARE

THE WORK OF YOUR HANDS' (PS. 102:25).

F. SAID R. HANIN, "ON THE BASIS OF THE VERSE OF SCRIPTURE THAT SUPPORTS THE POSITION OF THE HOUSE OF SHAMMAI THE HOUSE OF HILLEL FIND EVIDENCE TO REJECT THAT SAME VIEW: 'THE EARTH WAS...' (GEN. 1:2), MEANING THAT IT HAD ALREADY COME INTO BEING."

G. R. YOHANAN [SAID] IN THE NAME OF SAGES, "AS TO THE ACT OF CREATION, HEAVEN CAME FIRST. AS TO THE PROCESS OF FINISHING OFF CREATION, THE EARTH CAME FIRST."

H. Said. R. Tanhuma, "I shall supply a verse of Scripture to support that statement. As to creation, the heaven came first: 'In the beginning God created [the heaven, then the earth]' (Gen. 1:1). But as to the process of finishing off creation, the earth came first: 'On the day on which the Lord God made heaven and earth' (Gen. 2:4)."

I. SAID R. SIMEON, "I SHOULD BE SURPRISED IF THE FATHERS OF THE WORLD DISPUTED CONCERNING THIS MATTER. FOR BOTH OF THEM WERE CREATED ONLY AS ARE THE POT AND ITS LID [WHICH IS TO SAY, IN A SINGLE ACT]. IN THIS REGARD I RECITE THE FOLLOWING VERSE OF SCRIPTURE: '[MY HAND ESTABLISHED THE EARTH, AND MY RIGHT HAND SPREAD OUT THE HEAVEN.] WHEN I CALL THEM, THEY STAND UP TOGETHER' (IS. 48:13)."

J. SAID R. ELEAZAR B. R. SIMEON, "ACCORDING TO THIS OPINION OF MY FATHER, WHY IS IT THAT SOMETIMES HEAVEN COMES BEFORE EARTH, SOMETIMES EARTH COMES BEFORE HEAVEN. BUT WHAT IT TEACHES IS THAT THE TWO

OF THEM ARE EQUAL [HAVING BEEN CREATED AT THE SAME INSTANT]."

2. A. [T. KER. 4:14: R. SIMEON SAYS,] "IN EVERY PLACE SCRIPTURE GIVES PRECEDENCE TO ABRAHAM OVER ISAAC, AND TO ISAAC OVER JACOB. BUT IN ONE PASSAGE SCRIPTURE SAYS, 'AND I REMEMBERED MY COVENANT WITH JACOB [...ISAAC AND ABRAHAM...]' (LEV. 26:42).

B. "THIS TEACHES THAT THE THREE OF THEM ARE EQUIVALENT TO ONE ANOTHER.

C. "IN EVERY PASSAGE SCRIPTURE ACCORDS PRECEDENCE TO MOSES OVER AARON, BUT IN ONE PLACE SCRIPTURE STATES, 'THAT IS AARON AND MOSES' (EX. 6:26).

D. "THIS TEACHES THAT THE TWO OF THEM ARE EQUIVALENT TO ONE ANOTHER.

E. "IN EVERY PASSAGE SCRIPTURE GIVES PRECEDENCE TO JOSHUA OVER CALEB, BUT IN ONE PASSAGE IT SAYS, 'EXCEPT FOR CALEB, THE SON OF JEPHUNNEH THE KENIZZITE, AND JOSHUA, THE SON OF NUN' (NUM. 32:12).

F. "THIS TEACHES THAT THE TWO OF THEM ARE EQUIVALENT TO ONE ANOTHER.

G. "AND IN EVERY PASSAGE SCRIPTURE GIVES PRECEDENCE TO THE HONOR OWING TO THE FATHER OVER THE HONOR OWING TO THE MOTHER, WHILE IN ONE PLACE IT SAYS, 'A MAN MUST FEAR HIS MOTHER AND HIS FATHER' (LEV. 19:3), TEACHING THAT THE TWO OF THEM ARE EQUAL TO ONE ANOTHER."

What we find is, the entire composite, which is free-standing in Genesis Rabbah, also turns out to be extra-documentary, within the definitions given throughout this study. Apart from minor variations in wording or attribution, the passage is replicated in Yerushalmi, as follows:

Yerushalmi Hagigah 2:1 III:15

[III:15 A] THE HOUSE OF SHAMMAI SAY, "HEAVEN WAS CREATED FIRST, THE EARTH AFTERWARD."

[B] THE HOUSE OF HILLEL SAY, "THE EARTH WAS CREATED FIRST, AND HEAVEN AFTERWARD."

[C] THEY BOTH ADDUCE SUPPORTING REASONS FOR THEIR OPINIONS.

[D] *WHAT IS THE REASONING OF THE HOUSE OF SHAMMAI?*

[E] "IN THE BEGINNING GOD CREATED THE HEAVEN AND THE EARTH." [THIS IS TO BE COMPARED] TO A KING WHO MADE A THRONE; AFTER HE HAD MADE IT, HE MADE ITS FOOTSTOOL: "HEAVEN IS MY THRONE AND EARTH MY FOOTSTOOL" (IS. 66:1).

[F] *WHAT IS THE REASONING OF THE HOUSE OF HILLEL?*

[G] "IN THE DAY WHEN GOD MADE THE EARTH AND THE HEAVEN" (GEN. 2:4). [THIS IS TO BE COMPARED] TO A KING WHO BUILT A PALACE. AFTER HE HAD BUILT THE LOWER STORIES HE BUILT THE UPPER STORIES.

[H] "MY HAND ESTABLISHED THE EARTH AND [77D] MY RIGHT HAND SPREAD OUT THE HEAVEN" (IS. 48:13].

[I] *R. JUDAH BAR PAZZI SAYS, "THIS SUPPORTS THE HOUSE OF HILLEL, 'OF OLD YOU LAID THE FOUNDATION OF THE EARTH, AND THE HEAVEN IS THE WORK OF YOUR HANDS'"*

(PS. 102:26).

[J] R. HANINA SAID, "FROM THE [VERY] PLACE FROM WHICH THE HOUSE OF SHAMMAI ADDUCE SUPPORT FOR THEIR OPINION, THE HOUSE OF HILLEL REFUTE [LIT., REMOVE] THEM. WHAT IS THE SUPPORT FOR THE HOUSE OF SHAMMAI? 'IN THE BEGINNING GOD CREATED THE HEAVEN AND THE EARTH.' FROM THERE THE HOUSE OF HILLEL REFUTE THEM: 'AND THE EARTH WAS' (GEN. 1:2) — ALREADY *WAS* [I.E., GEN. 1:2 REFERS TO THE STATE OF THE EARTH BEFORE CREATION]."

[K] R. YOHANAN [SAID] IN THE NAME OF THE SAGES, "AS REGARDS CREATION, HEAVEN WAS FIRST; AS REGARDS COMPLETION, EARTH WAS FIRST. AS REGARDS CREATION, HEAVEN WAS FIRST: 'IN THE BEGINNING GOD CREATED.' AS REGARDS COMPLETION, EARTH WAS FIRST: 'IN THE DAY WHEN GOD MADE THE EARTH AND THE HEAVEN.'"

[L] According to the House of Shammai he made heaven on the first [day]. There was an interval of three days, then it produced offspring — first, second, third. On the fourth, "Let there be lights."

[M] According to the House of Shammai he made the sea on the second [day]. There was an interval of three days, then it produced offspring — second, third, fourth; on the fifth, "Let the seas swarm."

[N] According to the House of Shammai he made the earth on the third [day]. There was an interval of three days, then it produced offspring — third, fourth, fifth; on the sixth, "Let the earth bring forth" (Gen. 1:24).

[O] According to the House of Hillel he made the earth on the first [day]. There was an interval of two days, then it produced offspring — first, second; on the third, "Let the earth put forth vegetation" (Gen. 1:11).

[P] According to the House of Hillel he made

heaven on the second [day]. There was an interval of two days, then it produced offspring — second, third; on the fourth, "Let there be lights."

[Q] According to the House of Hillel he made the sea on the third [day]. There was an interval of two days, then it produced offspring — third, fourth; on the fifth, "Let the seas swarm."

[R] R. SIMEON BEN YOHAI SAID, "I AM AMAZED THAT THE FATHERS OF THE WORLD WERE SPLIT ON THE QUESTION OF THE CREATION OF THE WORLD, FOR I SAY, HEAVEN AND EARTH WERE CREATED ONLY LIKE THIS POT AND ITS LID [VIZ., IN ONE ACT]."

[S] What is the support [for this view]? "My hand established the earth and my right hand spread out the heavens" (Is. 48:13).

[T] R. ELEAZAR B. R. SIMEON SAID, "ACCORDING TO THIS OPINION OF MY FATHER, SOMETIMES HEAVEN PRECEDES EARTH, SOMETIMES EARTH PRECEDES HEAVEN. BUT [THE VERSES] TEACH [US] THAT THEY ARE BOTH EQUAL."

YERUSHALMI AND GENESIS RABBAH INTERSECT EXCEPT AT THE AMPLIFIED MATERIALS, L-Q. THESE CLEARLY ARE INTERPOLATED INTO THE ESSENTIAL STATEMENT, GIVEN IN LOWER CASE CAPS AND IN YERUSHALMI UNDERLINED. NOW TO THE BAVLI'S COUNTERPART.

BAVLI HAGIGAH 12A/2;1 III:9

9. A. *OUR RABBIS HAVE TAUGHT ON TANNAITE AUTHORITY:*

B. THE HOUSE OF SHAMMAI SAY, "HEAVEN WAS CREATED FIRST, THEN THE EARTH WAS CREATED: 'IN THE BEGINNING GOD CREATED HEAVEN AND EARTH' (GEN. 1:1).

C. AND THE HOUSE OF HILLEL SAY, "THE

EARTH WAS CREATED FIRST, THEN HEAVEN: 'IN THE DAY THAT THE LORD GOD MADE EARTH AND HEAVEN' (GEN. 2:4)."

D. SAID THE HOUSE OF HILLEL TO THE HOUSE OF SHAMMAI, "IN ACCORD WITH YOUR VIEW, SOMEONE FIRST BUILDS THE UPPER STORY, AND THEN THE BASIC HOUSE ITSELF: 'IT IS HE WHO BUILDS HIS UPPER CHAMBERS IN THE HEAVEN AND HAS FOUNDED HIS VAULT UPON THE EARTH' (AMOS 9:6)."

E. Said the House of Shammai to the House of Hillel, "In your view a person makes the footstool first, then the throne: 'Thus says the Lord, the heaven is my throne and the earth is my footstool' (Is. 66:1)."

F. But sages say, "Both were created at the same instant: 'Yes, my hand has laid the foundation of the earth, and my right hand has spread out the heavens; when I call to them they stand up together' (Is. 48:13)."

10. A. *And how do the other parties deal with the word* "together"?

B. *It means, they cannot be separated from one another.*

11. A. *One way or the other, the verses contradict one another!*

B. Said R. Simeon b. Laqish, "When they were created, he created heaven, then he created earth, but when he spread them out, he spread out the earth, then he spread out the heaven."

THE BAVLI'S VERSION IS THE LESS ARTICULATED, BUT IT COVERS THE SAME POINTS. WE SHALL NOW SEE THAT THE WHOLE IS TACKED IN AS A TOPICAL COMPOSITE IN LEVITICUS RABBAH.

LEVITICUS RABBAH PARASHAH THIRTY-SIX
XXXVI:I

1. A. "Of old you laid out the foundation of the earth, and the heavens are the work of your hands" (Ps. 102:25).

TOPICAL COMPOSITE ON PRECEDENCE

B. THE HOUSE OF SHAMMAI AND THE HOUSE OF HILLEL:

C. THE HOUSE OF SHAMMAI SAY, "THE HEAVEN WAS CREATED FIRST, AND THEN THE EARTH."

D. THE HOUSE OF HILLEL SAY, "THE EARTH WAS CREATED FIRST, THEN THE HEAVEN."

E. THIS PARTY BRINGS A PROOF TEXT FOR ITS OPINION, AND THAT PARTY BRINGS A PROOF TEXT FOR ITS VIEW.

F. IN THE VIEW OF THE HOUSE OF SHAMMAI, WHO MAINTAIN THAT THE HEAVEN WAS CREATED FIRST AND THEN THE EARTH, WE MAY MAKE A COMPARISON. TO WHAT IS THE MATTER COMPARABLE?

G. TO THE CASE OF A KING WHO MADE A THRONE. ONLY AFTER HE MADE THE THRONE DID HE MAKE ITS FOOTSTOOL. THUS: "SO SAYS THE LORD, 'THE HEAVEN IS MY THRONE, AND THE EARTH THE DUST AT MY FEET'" (IS. 66:1).

H. IN THE VIEW OF THE HOUSE OF HILLEL, WHO MAINTAIN THAT THE EARTH WAS CREATED FIRST AND THEN THE HEAVEN, WE MAY MAKE A COMPARISON. [TO WHAT IS THE MATTER COMPARABLE?]

I. TO THE CASE OF A KING WHO BUILT HIMSELF A PALACE. ONLY AFTER HE BUILDS THE LOWER FLOORS DOES HE BUILD THE UPPER FLOORS.

J. SO IT IS WRITTEN, "MY HAND LAID THE FOUNDATION OF THE EARTH, AND MY RIGHT HAND [THEN] SPREAD OUT THE HEAVEN" (IS. 48:13).

K. SAID R. HANINAH, "ALSO THE FOLLOWING VERSE OF SCRIPTURE SUPPORTS THE POSITION OF THE HOUSE OF HILLEL: 'OF OLD YOU LAID OUT THE FOUNDATIONS OF THE EARTH,' AND AFTERWARD: 'AND THE HEAVENS ARE THE WORK OF YOUR HANDS'" (PS. 102:25).

L. SAID R. JUDAH, "FROM THE VERY PASSAGE

OF SCRIPTURE WHICH IS ADDUCED IN SUPPORT OF THE POSITION OF THE HOUSE OF SHAMMAI, THE HOUSE OF HILLEL FIND PROOF TO DISMISS THAT SAME POSITION.

M. "IN THE VIEW OF THE HOUSE OF SHAMMAI, WHO MAINTAIN THAT THE HEAVEN WAS CREATED FIRST AND THEN THE EARTH, [THE FOLLOWING PROOF TEXT CONFIRMS THEIR POSITION:] 'IN THE BEGINNING GOD CREATED THE HEAVEN AND THE EARTH' [GEN. 1:1].

N. "IN THE VIEW OF THE HOUSE OF HILLEL, WHO SAY THAT THE EARTH WAS CREATED FIRST, THEN THE HEAVEN: 'AND THE EARTH WAS UNFORMED AND VOID' [GEN. 1:2], INDICATING THAT THE EARTH ALREADY WAS IN BEING."

2. A. R. YOHANAN SAID IN THE NAME OF SAGES, "AS TO THE ACT OF CREATION, HEAVEN CAME FIRST. AS TO THE PROCESS OF FINISHING OFF CREATION, THE EARTH CAME FIRST.

B. "AS TO THE ACT OF CREATION, THE HEAVEN CAME FIRST: 'IN THE BEGINNING GOD CREATED [THE HEAVEN AND THE EARTH]' [GEN. 1:1].

C. "AS TO THE PROCESS OF FINISHING OFF CREATION, THE EARTH CAME FIRST: 'ON THE DAY ON WHICH THE LORD GOD MADE HEAVEN AND EARTH'" (GEN. 2:4).

3. A. SAID R. SIMEON B. YOHAI, "I AM AMAZED THAT THE FATHERS OF THE WORLD [THE HOUSES OF SHAMMAI AND HILLEL] WERE SPLIT ON THE QUESTION OF THE CREATION OF THE WORLD, FOR I SAY, HEAVEN AND EARTH WERE CREATED ONLY LIKE A POT AND ITS LID [THAT IS, IN A SINGLE ACT].

B. "THAT IS IN LINE WITH THE FOLLOWING VERSE OF SCRIPTURE: 'MY HAND ESTABLISHED THE EARTH, AND MY RIGHT HAND SPREAD OUT THE HEAVEN. WHEN I CALL THEM, THEY STAND UP TOGETHER'" (IS. 48:13).

C. SAID R. ELEAZAR B. R. SIMEON, "ACCORD-

ING TO THIS OPINION OF MY FATHER, SOMETIMES HEAVEN PRECEDES EARTH, SOMETIMES EARTH PRECEDES HEAVEN. BUT HE [REALLY] TEACHES THAT THEY ARE BOTH EQUAL [HAVING BEEN CREATED AT THE SAME INSTANT]."

4. A. (T. KER. 4:14: R. SIMEON SAYS,) "IN EVERY PLACE [SCRIPTURE] HAS GIVEN PRECEDENCE TO THE CREATION OF HEAVEN OVER THE CREATION OF EARTH. IN ONE PLACE, HOWEVER, IT SAYS, 'ON THE DAY OF THE LORD GOD'S CREATING OF EARTH AND HEAVEN' [GEN. 2:4], TEACHING THAT THE TWO ARE DEEMED EQUIVALENT.

B. "IN EVERY PLACE SCRIPTURE HAS GIVEN PRECEDENCE TO MOSES OVER AARON. BUT IN ONE PLACE IT SAYS, 'IT IS AARON AND MOSES' [EX. 6:26]. THIS TEACHES THAT THE TWO ARE DEEMED EQUIVALENT.

C. "IN EVERY PLACE SCRIPTURE HAS GIVEN PRECEDENCE TO JOSHUA OVER CALEB. BUT IN ONE PLACE IT SAYS, 'EXCEPT FOR CALEB, THE SON OF JEPHUNNEH THE KENIZZITE, AND JOSHUA, THE SON OF NUN' [NUM. 32:12]. THIS TEACHES THAT THE TWO ARE DEEMED EQUIVALENT.

D. "[M. KER. 6:9I-L:] IN EVERY PLACE SCRIPTURE HAS GIVEN PRECEDENCE TO THE HONOR OF THE FATHER OVER THAT OF THE MOTHER. IN ONE PLACE, HOWEVER, IT SAYS, 'YOU SHALL FEAR EVERYONE HIS MOTHER AND HIS FATHER' [LEV. 19:3]. THIS TEACHES THAT THE TWO ARE DEEMED EQUIVALENT.

E. "IN EVERY PLACE SCRIPTURE HAS GIVEN PRECEDENCE TO DOVES BEFORE YOUNG PIGEONS. BUT IN ONE PLACE IT SAYS, 'A YOUNG PIGEON OR A DOVE FOR A SIN OFFERING' [LEV. 12:6]. THIS TEACHES THAT THE TWO OF THEM ARE DEEMED EQUIVALENT.

F. "IN EVERY PLACE SCRIPTURE HAS GIVEN PRECEDENCE TO ABRAHAM OVER THE OTHER PATRIARCHS. BUT IN ONE PLACE IT SAYS, 'AND

I REMEMBERED MY COVENANT WITH JACOB, [
... ISAAC ... AND ABRAHAM ...]' [LEV. 26:42].
THIS TEACHES THAT THE THREE ARE
DEEMED EQUIVALENT TO ONE ANOTHER."

Leviticus Rabbah goes over the same ground as Genesis Rabbah, in much the same way. The upshot is now self-evident. Extra-documentary writing distinguishes itself in every document in which it occurs; it is not primary to any one of them.

The documentary hypothesis thus encompasses a theory of the writing of Rabbinic traditions that accommodates both documentary and non- and extra-documentary writing as well. As I said at the outset, the basic theory maintains that two kinds of writing took place. Some writing was undertaken with a plan and program for a cogent document in mind. Some writing was carried on without any intent in creating a cogent composition as part of an encompassing, purposeful composite. The difference is, writing that adheres to documentary conventions as a matter of hypothesis was undertaken with those conventions in full view; that writing will rarely serve in any other document but the one for which it was prepared. Writing that is non-documentary was carried on without any interest in the ultimate disposition of the completed composition or even sizable composite. That is the kind of writing that presents candidates for inclusion without regard to the documentary context in which it is set. That non-documentary writing constitutes the principal source for extra-documentary writing.

Now let us return to our sample of Genesis Rabbah and ask our questions of proportion and position: how large a part of the Parashah derives from extra-documentary writing, and how significant a role in the exposition of the Parashah is assigned to that writing?

III. The Considerable Proportion of Free-standing Stories

Genesis Rabbah Parashah One in my translation contains approximately 5400 words. Of these, by my estimate, in that same translation approximately 1600 are shared with other documents, somewhat under 30%. That proportion is not negligible. If we examine the proportions of autonomous and shared materials as indicated in the outline, set forth in part iv, we find 2900 words, of which 750 words are shared, thus approximately 26%. The results correspond: somewhere between a fourth and a third of the compositions of Parashah One of Genesis Rabbah occur in other documents as well. That result contrasts with our findings in the Mishnah, which contains a negligible proportion of free-standing compositions, and Tosefta, with approximately 11% in our sample, let alone Sifra, with under 6%. We therefore cannot characterize the proportion of free-standing stories as negligible at all. It is considerable.

But these shared, free-standing compositions bear in common two traits that account for the higher proportion of extra-documentary writing.

The first is formal and documentary. The autonomous compositions in Genesis Rabbah are not asked to bear the principal message of our Parashah. Nearly all the materials of Genesis Rabbah that have parallels in other documents take up, in Genesis Rabbah, subordinated positions in the composite in which they occur. And, we have seen in a most elaborate way, the same is so in the comparable documents, those that contain the same stories and exegetical compositions. Materials that are shared among documents rarely undertake a role primary to one of the documents and secondary in the others. Those paralleled materials tend to stand autonomous of the documentary programs of all of the documents in which they occur. What we see is that some composites and compositions circulated independently of documents. Then, when taken up for use in documents, they enrich, but they do not materially affect, the character of the documents that use them.

The second trait that accounts for the higher proportion of extra-documentary writing is particular to Genesis Rabbah. All of the document's free-standing compositions link to verses of Scripture. They serve as conventional readings of those verses. When a given verse is cited, the composition that accompanies it makes its appearance. If we wish to make the point sustained by, e.g., Ps. 31:19, that it is arrogant to delve into hidden matters, then we cite that verse and its attached proposition. Were we to compile a florilegium of verses and their fixed propositions for Genesis Rabbah, our sample suggests, we should also find in hand a compilation of the bulk of the extra-documentary compositions of our sample — the bulk, if not the entirety thereof.

The upshot is, in our sample, and I think, in our document, free-standing compositions bear a distinctive type of writing, namely, a verse and its exegesis, which may then serve in a variety of contexts. The extra-documentary writing is always introduced by the documentary compilers for their purposes, and, more to the point, it is everywhere subordinate to those purposes. This very distinctive assignment of the free-standing compositions — amplify the established meaning of a given verse of Scripture — underscores the documentary control that governs the selection and inclusion of non- and extra-documentary writing.

And that fact underscores the main point. Even where non- and extra-documentary writing constitutes a meaningful proportion of a large documentary composite such as our sample-Parashah, the free-standing compositions play a peripheral role in the document. To that matter we now turn.

IV. THE PERIPHERAL ROLE OF FREE-STANDING STORIES

What we find here in Genesis Rabbah Parashah One takes the form of a commentary, but the commentary turns out, as in the later Midrash-compilations, to mask the real program, which is propositional. So when I judge that free-standing or extra-documentary writing undertakes a peripheral role in our sample, I mean, that writing does not convey the document's main point or proposition. The propositions that predominate at each unit thereof are expressed in compositions that are particular to Genesis Rabbah.

With that hypothesis in hand, we turn to the outline of the Parashah. My task is to show precisely how Genesis Rabbah holds together and carries out its purposes. Since the entire document is organized following the sequence of the verses of the book of Genesis, that defines the framework of the outline, which is worked out through visual signals, indentations and variations in type-faces. To show the non-documentary components of the whole, I use indentation in particular. That is, specifically, where I find reason to remove a composition or composite from the mainstream of the document's flow, I indent the entry; that signals the judgment that an entry is secondary. It may be intruded, or it may develop a prior, primary point. Or in some other way it impedes the systematic and orderly progress of the whole. These are the principal media by which I identify the components of the document and so identify the aberrational or extra-documentary compositions and composites. At the end I specify what I think the outline yields.

Genesis Rabbah utilizes the intersecting-verse/base-verse construction as a way of realizing its documentary program and laying out its principal propositions. These then form the main beams of the construction and require particular attention. They constitute the documentary definition of Genesis Rabbah in the union of form and topical proposition. To differentiate the intersecting-verse/base-verse construction from the routine exegetical construction, I underline the former as it occurs. In that way we see the extent to which the former construction plays a role here, as it rarely does in any temporally-prior compilation (e.g., Sifra, the two Sifrés, and the like). My sense is that, once the intellectual possibilities of the new construction were recognized, with the promise of imposing a single, encompassing proposition on diverse exegetical compositions and so formulating a quite powerful hermeneutical medium, the exegetical form that had earlier predominated tended to lose all appeal. The outcome of Genesis Rabbah, some time thereafter, is the triumph of Leviticus Rabbah, with its complete shift away from the step-by-step exegetical exposition. And that led to the still more imaginative achievement of Pesiqta deRab Kahana, with its theologization of the liturgical calendar — not to mention the magnificent abstractions of symbolic discourse achieved in Song of Songs Rabbah.

I indent the topical appendices and miscellanies as well. In this way the three major components of the document — the intersecting-verse/base-verse constructions, the systematic exegetical compositions, and the topical appendices (so important to the present study) are clearly identified and the proportions of the whole contributed by each are precisely marked.

What about our particular interest in the extra-documentary components of our sample? To signal passages that occur both in Genesis Rabbah and in other compilations,

I resort to **BOLD FACE LOWER CASE CAPITALS.** In that way I underscore what turns out to be the peripherality of the extra-documentary components of the whole.

PART ONE: PARASHAT BERESHIT

I:I. 1. "In the beginning God created" (Gen. 1:1): R. Oshaia commenced [discourse by citing the following verse:] "'Then I was beside him like a little child, and I was daily his delight [rejoicing before him always, rejoicing in his inhabited world, and delighting in the sons of men]' (Prov. 8:30-31). "The word for 'child' uses consonants that may also stand for 'teacher,' 'covered over,' and 'hidden away.' "Some hold that the word also means 'great.' "The word means 'teacher,' in line with the following: 'As a teacher carries the suckling child' (Num. 11:12). "The word means 'covered over,' as in the following: 'Those who were covered over in scarlet' (Lam. 4:5). "The word means 'hidden,' as in the verse, 'And he hid Hadassah ' (Est. 2:7). "The word means 'great,' in line with the verse, 'Are you better than No-Ammon?' (Nah. 3:8). This we translate, 'Are you better than Alexandria the Great, which is located between rivers.'"

2. Another matter: The word means "workman." [In the cited verse] the Torah speaks, "I was the workplan of the Holy One, blessed be he." In the accepted practice of the world, when a mortal king builds a palace, he does not build it out of his own head, but he follows a work-plan. And [the one who supplies] the work-plan does not build out of his own head, but he has designs and diagrams, so as to know how to situate the rooms and the doorways. Thus the Holy One, blessed be he, consulted the Torah when he created the world. So the Torah stated, "By means of 'the beginning' [that is to say, the Torah] did God create..." (Gen. 1:1). And the word for "beginning" refers only to the Torah, as Scripture says, "The Lord made me as the beginning of his way" (Prov. 8:22).

The next entry marks the one point at which a fundamental building block of our document is extra-documentary.

> I:V.1. R. Huna in the name of Bar Qappara commenced [discourse by citing the following verse]: "'Let the lying lips be made dumb [which arrogantly speak matters kept secret against the righteous]' (Ps. 31:19). "[Translating the Hebrew word for dumb into Aramaic one may use words meaning] 'bound,' 'made dumb,' or ' silenced.' "Let [the lying lips] be bound,' as in the following verse: 'For behold, we were binding sheaves' (Gen. 37:7). "'Let the lying lips be made dumb,' as in the usage in this verse: 'Or who made a man dumb ' (Ex. 4:11). "'Let them be silenced' bears the obvious meaning of the word." "Which arrogantly speak matters kept secret against the righteous" (Ps. 31:19): "...which speak against the Righteous," the Life of the Ages, matters that he kept secret from his creatures [the mysteries of creation]. "With pride" (Ps. 31:19): That is so as to take pride, saying, "I shall expound the work of creation." "And contempt" (Ps. 31:19): Such a one treats with contempt the honor owing to me. And what is written after the cited verse [Ps. 31:19]? How abundant is your goodness, which you have stored away for those who revere you" (Ps. 31:20).

As we see, only the attribution shifts. Otherwise we have a conventional florilegium of verses deemed by convention to register, and prove, the specified propositions. This is the only example of a composition that is primary to Genesis Rabbah and also shared with other documents.

> **I.VI.1.** R. Judah bar Simon commenced discourse [by citing the following verse:] "'And he reveals deep and secret things' (Dan.2:22). "The word for deep things refers to Gehenna, as it is written, 'But he does not know that the shades are there, that in the depths of

the nether world are her guests' (Prov. 9:18). "And the word for 'secret things' speaks of the Garden of Eden, as it is written, 'And for a refuge and for a hiding place' (Is. 4:6). [This hiding place, using the same word, is taken to mean the Garden of Eden]."

2. Another matter: "And he reveals deep and secret things" (Dan. 2:22): This refers to deeds performed by the wicked [which God brings out into the open], as it is said, "Woe to the ones who try to hide their plans from the Lord" (Is. 29:15). "He knows what is in the darkness" (Dan. 2:22): This refers to deeds performed by the wicked, as it is written, "And their works are in the darkness" (Is. 4:6). "But the light dwells with him" (Dan. 2:22): This refers to deeds performed by the righteous, as it is said, "Light is sown for the righteous" (Ps. 97:11).

3. Said R. Abba of Sarangayya, "'Light dwells with him' (Dan. 2:22) refers to the messiah-king."

4. Said R. Judah bar Simon, "To begin with, when the world was being created, 'He reveals deep and secret things,' for it is written, 'In the beginning God created the heaven (Gen. 1:1).' But the matter was not spelled out. Where then was it spelled out? Elsewhere: 'Who stretches out the heaven as a curtain' (Is. 40:22). '....and the earth' (Gen. 1:1). But this matter, too, was not then spelled out. Where then was it spelled out?

The same trait — established reading of specified verses to make a given point — registers once again.

I.VII.1. R. Isaac commenced [discourse by citing the following verse]: "'The beginning of your word is truth [and all your righteous ordinance endures forever]' (Ps. 119:16)." Said R. Isaac [about the cited verse], "From the beginning of the creation of the world, 'The beginning of your word was truth.' "'In the beginning God created' (Gen. 1:1). ""And the Lord God is truth '(Jer. 10:9). "Therefore: 'And all your righteous ordinance endures forever' (Ps. 119:16). "For as to every single decree which you lay down for your creatures, they accept that degree as righteous and receive it in good faith, so that no creature may differ, saying ' , 'Two powers gave the Torah, two powers created the world.' "[Why not?]' Because here it is not written, 'And gods spoke,' but rather, 'And God spoke' (Ex. 20:1). "'In the beginning [gods] created is not written, but rather, 'in the beginning [God] created' [in the singular]."

I.II.1. R. Joshua of Sikhnin in the name of R. Levi commenced [discourse by citing the following verse]: "'He has declared to his people the power of his works, in giving them the heritage of the nations' (Ps. 111:6). "What is the reason that the Holy One, blessed be he, revealed to Israel what was created on the first day and what on the second? "It was on account of the nations of the world. It was so that they should not ridicule the Israelites, saying to them, 'Are you not a nation of robbers [having stolen the land from the Canaanites]?' "It allows the Israelites to answer them, 'And as to you, is there no spoil in your hands? For surely: "The Caphtorim, who came forth out of Caphtor, destroyed them and dwelled in their place" (Dt. 2:23)! "'The world and everything in it belongs to the Holy One, blessed be he. When he wanted, he gave it to you, and when he wanted, he took it from you and gave it to us.' "That is in line with what is written, '….in giving them the heritage of the nations, he has declared to his people the power of his works' (Ps. 111:6).. [So as to give them the land, he established his right to do so by informing them that he had created it.] "He told them about the beginning: 'In the beginning God created…" (Gen. 1:1)."

I.III.1. R. Tanhum commenced discourse, "For you are great and do wonderful things, you alone are God "(Ps. 86:10). Said R. Tanhum b. R. Hiyya, "As to a skin, if it has a hole as small as the eye of a needle, all of the air will escape for from it. "But as to a human being, a person is made with many apertures and holes, but the spirit does not go forth through them. "Who has done it in such a way? 'You alone are God' (Ps. 86:10)."

2. When were the angels created? R. Yohanan said, "On the second day of creation [Monday] were they created. R. Hanina said, "They were created on the fifth day of creation [Thursday]. For it is written, 'Let fowl fly above the earth' (Gen. 1:20), and it is written, 'And with two did the angel fly' (Is. 6:21)."

3. Said R. Tanhuma, "'For you are great and do wonderful things' (Ps. 86:10). Why so? Because: 'You alone are God' (Ps. 86:10). You by yourself created the world. In the beginning God created' (Gen. 1:1)."

Topical Composite
WHAT WAS IN BEING BEFORE CREATION

I:IV.1 ["In the beginning God created" (Gen. 1:1):] Six things came before the creation of the world, some created, some at least considered as candidates for creation. **THE TORAH AND THE THRONE OF GLORY WERE CREATED [BEFORE THE CREATION OF THE WOR-----LD].** The patriarchs were considered as candidates for creation, as it is written, "I saw your fathers as the first-ripe in the fig tree at her first season" (Hos. 9:10). Israel was considered [as a candidate for creation], as it is written, "Remember your congregation, which you got aforetime" (Ps. 74:2). The Temple was considered as a candidate for creation], as it is written, "You, throne of glory, on high from the beginning, the place of our sanctuary" (Jer. 17:12). The name of the Messiah was kept in mind, as it is written, "His name exists before the sun" (Ps. 72:17).

Two items on the list occur elsewhere, with the same proof-texts to be sure. This is not an important example of the utilization of a composition in more than a single document. We note, in any event, that the extra-documentary writing is peripheral to the program of our Parashah.

> **2.** R. Huna, R. Jeremiah in the name of R. Samuel b. R. Isaac: "Intention concerning the creation of Israel came before all else.
>
> **3. SAID. R. BENAIAH, "THE WORLD AND EVERYTHING IN IT WERE CREATED ONLY ON ACCOUNT OF THE MERIT OF THE TORAH. "'THE LORD FOR THE SAKE OF WISDOM [TORAH] FOUNDED THE EARTH' (PROV. 3:19)." R. BEREKHIAH SAID, "IT WAS FOR THE MERIT OF MOSES. "'AND HE SAW THE BEGINNING FOR HIMSELF, FOR THERE A PORTION OF A RULER [MOSES] WAS RESERVED' (DT. 33:21)."**

What was said about extra-documentary writing in the fore-going entry applies here without variation. We have a fixed repertoire of verses, Prov. 3:19 and Dt. 33:21, which sustain a set of conventional propositions: facts based on evidence of a probative character. This once more is not what people mean when they invoke extra-documentary writing.

> **4.** R. Huna in the name of Rab repeated [the following]: "For the merit of three things was the world created, for the merit of dough-offerings, tithes, and first fruits. "For it is said, 'On account of [the merit of] what is first, God created...' (Gen. 1:1). "And the word 'first' refers only to dough-offering, for it is written, 'Of the first of your dough' (Num. 15:20). "The same word refers to tithes, as it is written, 'The first fruits of your grain' (Dt. 18:4). "And the word 'first ' refers to first fruits, for it is written, 'The choicest of your land's first fruit' (Ex. 23:19)."
>
> **I:VIII.1** R. Menahem and R. Joshua b. Levi in the name of R. Levi: "One who builds requires six things: water, dust, wood, stones, canes, and iron. And should you say that [since God] is rich, he will not need canes [which are used only in hovels], lo, he requires a

cane for measuring, for it is written, 'And a measuring reed in his hand' (Ez. 40:3). The Torah came before those six things [as indicated by Prov. 8:22]."

I:IX.1 A philosopher asked Rabban Gamaliel, saying to him, "Your God was indeed a great artist, but he had good materials to help him." He said to him, "What are they?" He said to him, "Unformed [space], void, darkness, water, wind, and the deep."

I:X.1 ["In the beginning God created" (Gen. 1:1):] R. Jonah in the name of R. Levi: "Why was the world created with [a word beginning with the letter] B? Just as [in Hebrew] the letter B is closed [at the back and sides but] open in front, so you have no right to expound concerning what is above or below, before or afterward."

BAR QAPPARA SAID, "'FOR ASK NOW OF THE DAYS PAST WHICH WERE BEFORE YOU, SINCE THE DAY THAT GOD CREATED MAN UPON THE EARTH' (DT. 4:32). CONCERNING THE DAY *AFTER* WHICH DAYS WERE CREATED, YOU MAY EXPOUND, BUT YOU MAY NOT MAKE AN EXPOSITION CONCERNING WHAT LIES BEFORE THEN.' 'AND FROM ONE END OF THE HEAVEN TO THE OTHER' (DT. 4:32). [CONCERNING THAT SPACE] YOU MAY CONDUCT AN INVESTIGATION, BUT YOU MAY NOT CONDUCT AN INVESTIGATION CONCERNING WHAT LIES BEYOND THOSE POINTS."

Bar Qappara's reading of Dt. 4:32 is tacked on, because it makes the point that one is not supposed to investigate what came before Creation, which is the proposition of the exegetical composition particular to Genesis Rabbah, I:X.1.

2. Why with a B? To tell you that there are two ages [this age and the age to come, for the letter B bears the numerical value of two].

3. Another matter: Why was the world created [with a word beginning with the letter] B? Because that is the letter that begins the word for blessing. And why not with an A? Because that is the first letter of the Hebrew word for curse.

4. Another matter: Why not with an A? So as not to give an opening to the *minim* to claim, "How can the world endure, when it has been created with a word meaning curse!"

5. Another matter: Why with a B? Because the letter B has two points, one pointing upward, the other backward, so that [if] people say to it, "Who created you?" it will point upward.

6. R. Eleazar bar Abinah in the name of R. Aha: "For twenty-six generations the letter A made complaint before the Holy One, blessed be he, saying to him, 'Lord of the world! I am the first among all the letters of the alphabet, yet you did not create your world by starting with me!' Said the Holy One, blessed be he, to the A, 'The world and everything in it has been created only through the merit of the Torah. Tomorrow I am going to come and give my Torah at Sinai, and I shall begin only with you: "I [beginning with the A] am the Lord your God" (Ex. 20:1).'"

7. Bar Hutah said, "Why is it called '*alef*'? Because that is the word for a thousand: 'The word which he commanded for a thousand [*elef*] generations' (Ps. 105:8)."

I:XI.1 R. Simon in the name of R. Joshua b. Levi: "[The fact that the letters] M, N, S, P, and K [when appearing at the end of the word have a form different from that used when they appear at the beginning or the middle of a word] is a law revealed to Moses at Sinai."

2. ONCE ON AN OVERCAST DAY, ON WHICH SAGES DID NOT COME INTO THE ASSEMBLY HOUSE, THERE WERE CHILDREN THERE. THEY SAID, "LET'S TAKE UP [THE TOPIC OF THE FINAL FORM OF THE LETTERS AS THESE HAVE BEEN ORDAINED BY] THE SEERS." THEY SAID, "WHAT IS THE REASON THAT THERE ARE TWO FORMS FOR THE WRIT-

ING OF THE LETTERS M, N, S, P, AND K?

The story about Eliezer and Joshua circulates from one document to another, a fine instance of extra-documentary writing, which is afforded a tangential place in some, but not all, comparable contexts.

> I:XII.1 ["In the beginning God created..." (Gen. 1:1):] R. Yudan in the name of Aqilas: "*This* one it is appropriate to call God. [Why so?] Under ordinary circumstances a mortal king is praised in province even before he has built public baths for the population or given them private ones. [God by contrast created the world before he had received the praise of humanity, so it was not for the sake of human adulation that he created the world.]"
>
> 2. Simeon b. Azzai says, "'And your modesty has made me great' (2 Sam. 22:36). A mortal person mentions his name and afterward his title, for example, 'Mr. So-and-so, the prefect,' 'Mr. Such-and-such, and whatever title he gets.' But the Holy One, blessed be he, is not that way.
>
> I:XIII.1 R. Simeon b. Yohai taught, "How [on the basis of Scripture] do we know that one should not say, 'For the Lord, a burnt offering,' 'For the Lord, a meal-offering,' 'For the Lord, a peace-offering.' Rather one should say, 'A burnt-offering for the Lord,' 'A meal-offering for the Lord,' 'A peace-offering for the Lord'?

Simeon's saying, an exegesis of the specified verse, circulates in a number of documents, always intact. It is a good example of the extra-documentary formation of exegetical compositions. Interestingly, as we noted earlier, it invariably stands by itself, not participating in an unfolding exposition, let alone argument, of a continuous character.

2. ["...the heaven and the earth" (Gen. 1:1):] Rabbis said, "When a mortal builds a building, if the building goes as planned, he may continue to broaden the structure as it rises, but if not, he has to make it broad at the bottom but narrow at the top. But that is not how things are for the Holy One, blessed be he. But: '...*the* heaven' meaning that very form of heaven as it had come to mind, first, and then: '...and *the* earth...,' as it had originally been planned."

3 R. Huna in the name of R. Eliezer, son of R. Yosé the Galilean: "Even those concerning which Scripture states, 'For behold, I create a new heaven' (Is. 65:17) were in fact created from the six days of creation."

A Miscellany

I:XIV.1. ["...THE HEAVEN AND THE EARTH" (GEN. 1:1):] R. ISHMAEL ASKED R. AQIBA, SAYING TO HIM, "BECAUSE YOU SERVED NAHUM OF GIMZO AS DISCIPLE FOR TWENTY-TWO YEARS, [LEARNING FROM HIM THE EXEGETICAL PRINCIPLES THAT] THE WORDS 'EXCEPT' AND 'ONLY' ARE TO BE INTERPRETED AS EXCLUSIONARY, AND THE ACCUSATIVE PARTICLE '*ETH*' AND 'ALSO' SERVE AS INCLUSIONARY WORDS [INDICATING THAT MORE IS COVERED BY THE STATEMENT AT HAND THAN THAT WHICH IS EXPLICITLY MENTIONED IN IT], AS TO THE ACCUSATIVE PARTICLE IN THE VERSE BEFORE US [GEN. 1:1], WHAT IS THE EXEGESIS THAT THAT USAGE APPLIES?"

I:XV.L. ["...THE HEAVEN AND THE EARTH" (GEN. 1:1):] THE HOUSE OF SHAMMAI SAY, "THE HEAVEN WAS CREATED FIRST." THE HOUSE OF HILLEL SAY, "THE EARTH WAS CREATED FIRST."

2. [T. Ker. 4:14: R. Simeon says,] "In every

> place Scripture gives precedence to Abraham over Isaac, and to Isaac over Jacob. But in one passage Scripture says, 'And I remembered my covenant with Jacob [...Isaac and Abraham...]' (Lev. 26:42). This teaches that the three of them are equivalent to one another. In every passage Scripture accords precedence to Moses over Aaron, but in one place Scripture states, 'That is Aaron and Moses' (Ex. 6:26). This teaches that the two of them are equivalent to one another.

The concluding appendix of our Parashah is comprised by materials that are common to a number of compilations — a complete composite of extra-documentary writing. In no document do these compositions play a critical role in constructing the main lines of exposition and argument. In all documents in which they occur, the compositions amplify or illustrate or simply enrich the discourse.

V. DOCUMENTARY, NON-DOCUMENTARY, AND EXTRA-DOCUMENTARY WRITING: THE CASE OF GENESIS RABBAH

Having examined a sample of the document, we may now draw some conclusions of a theoretical character, forming a hypothesis for testing in other documents. Here we systematically recapitulate observations already made in detail.

1. DOCUMENTARY WRITING

Documentary writing in Genesis Rabbah accomplishes the goals of the compilers of that document, conforms to the pattern that predominates throughout, and delivers the messages, makes the statements, that the compilers have created the document to set forth. As we have seen in the outline above, in Genesis Rabbah documentary writing takes the basic forms of the intersecting-verse/base-verse construction and the exegetical composition. More to the point, those passages that register the main propositions of the document viewed whole, propositions specified in a moment, fall into the category of documentary writing. The outline has shown what that means.

2. NON-DOCUMENTARY WRITING

Free-standing compositions and composites ignore the definitive traits of rhetoric and topic (and even logic of coherent discourse) that characterize a particular document, whether Genesis Rabbah or any other. They fall into two principal classifications, narratives[18] and exegetical sets (verse of Scripture, some words of amplification or generalization of the proposition yielded by said verse).

Our sample yields compositions that do not conform to the formal or topical program governing the whole. In theory these compositions can have found a position elsewhere than in Genesis Rabbah, and that can have been for a purpose other than that which defines the composition and compilation of Genesis Rabbah. But these find no parallels in other documents, and hence require classification as non-documentary, even though they are unique to this compilation.

3. EXTRA-DOCUMENTARY WRITING

---

[18] But not all narratives are non- or extra-documentary. The ma'aseh in the Mishnah and the Tosefta exhibits distinctive and definitive traits, which distinguish it from all other narrative writing. I offer a typology of Rabbinic stories in my *Judaism and Story: The Evidence of The Fathers According to Rabbi Nathan*. Chicago, 1992: University of Chicago Press.

As is clear, some compositions occur in other documents in addition to Genesis Rabbah. They are, by definition, extra-documentary. They violate all documentary lines and definitions. They represent a kind of writing not generated by the program of making a coherent statement through cogent propositions set forth in a fixed repertoire of forms. These have been amply instantiated. They are of two sorts: comments on verses and stories. The former are ordinarily brief and stereotypical. The latter are striking for their fixed wording.[19]

VI. THE DOCUMENTARY COMPLEX

To assess the role — central or peripheral — of the free-standing stories and sayings we have examined, an account of the focus and purpose of the document is required. Let me, then, present my reading of the document as a whole, and with that picture in hand, we may rapidly determine whether the free-standing compositions have been assigned a critical task in the documentary program. To spell out our main result with appropriate emphasis:

Genesis Rabbah is a composite document. It is comprised by writing undertaken in accord with the distinctive conventions of the document itself. But it contains, in addition, compositions that can have served, and did serve, in

---

[19] A study of the forms and other conventional traits of the extra-documentary stories will prove fruitful. But such a study must be compendious and comprehensive. Studies of the story in Rabbinic literature to date have proved superficial, because they generalize on the basis of trivial samples of we know not what. My own study of stories limited itself to a single document and classified its stories in documentary context. It is *Judaism and Story: The Evidence of The Fathers According to Rabbi Nathan.* Chicago, 1992: University of Chicago Press.

Proportion and Position: Evidence in a Sample of Genesis Rabbah

other compilations as well. As with the Talmud that it accompanies, the Yerushalmi, so in Genesis Rabbah, some of the material in the compilation can be shown to have been composed before that material was used for the purposes of the compilers of this particular document. Many times a comment entirely apposite to a verse of Genesis has been joined to a set of comments in no way pertinent to the verse at hand. Proof for a given syllogism, furthermore, will derive from a verse of Genesis as well as from numerous verses of other books of the Bible. Such a syllogistic argument therefore has not been written for exegetical purposes particular to the verse at hand. On the contrary, the particular verse subject to attention serves that other, propositional plan; it is not the focus of discourse; it has not generated the comment but merely provided a proof for a syllogism. That is what it means to say that a proposition yields an exegesis.

Why all this? What relationship do I discern between the forms of a document and its program? The answer for Genesis Rabbah is clear. The document's framers have chosen a particular, appropriate book of Scripture to make their statement, and they could have accomplished their goals only in the setting of that book and no other. So the topical program, the exegesis of the book of Genesis, is critical to the documentary definition. Then it is time, at the end, to ask, what, specifically, is that fundamental proposition, displayed throughout Genesis Rabbah, that yields the specific exegeses of many of the verses of the book of Genesis and even whole stories? It is that the beginnings point toward the endings, and the meaning of Israel's past points toward the message that lies in Israel's future. The things that happened to the fathers and mothers of the family, Israel, provide a sign for the things that will happen to the children later on.

What is at stake is the discovery, among the facts provided by the written Torah, of the social rules that govern Israel's history. At stake is the search for the order yielded by the chaos of uninterpreted data. It follows that, as with the Mishnah, the governing mode of thought in Genesis Rabbah (as in Leviticus Rabbah) is that of natural philosophy. It involves the classification of data by shared traits, yielding descriptive rules, the testing of propositions against the facts of data, the whole aimed at the discovery of underlying rules out of a multiplicity of details, in all, the proposing and testing, against the facts provided by Scripture, of the theses of Israel's salvation that demanded attention just then. But the issues were not so much philosophical as religious, in the sense that while philosophy addressed questions of nature and rules of enduring existence, religion asked about issues of history and God's intervention in time. Within that rough and ready distinction between nature, supernature, and sanctification, typified by the Mishnah and the Tosefta and the legal enterprise in general, on the one side, and society, history, and salvation, typified by Genesis Rabbah, as well as by Leviticus Rabbah and Pesiqta deRab Kahana, and the theological inquiry into teleology, on the other, we may distinguish our documents.

Specifically, we may classify the document before us and its successors and companions as works of profound theological inquiry into God's rules for history and society in the here and now and for salvation at the end of historical time. That fundamental proposition concerning the search, in the account of the beginnings, of the ending and meaning of Israel's society and history — hence the rules that govern and permit knowledge of what is to come — constitutes the generative proposition that yielded the specific exegesis of the book of Genesis in Genesis Rabbah.

Formally and programmatically, Genesis Rabbah in its documentary definition (if not in its final form as we know it![20]) emerges at ca. 400-450, from that momentous age of the fourth and fifth centuries in which the Rome Empire passed from pagan to Christian rule, and, in which, in the aftermath of the Julian's abortive reversion to paganism, in 360, which endangered the Christian character of the Roman empire, Christianity adopted that politics of repression of paganism that rapidly engulfed Judaism as well. The issue confronting Israel in the Land of Israel therefore proved immediate: the meaning of the new and ominous turn of history, the implications of Christ's worldly triumph for the other-worldly and supernatural people, Israel, whom God chooses and loves. The message of the exegete-compositors addressed the circumstance of historical crisis and generated remarkable renewal, a rebirth of intellect in the encounter with Scripture, now in quest of the rules not of sanctification — these had already been found — but of salvation. So the book of Genesis, which portrays how all things had begun, would testify to the message and the method of the end: the coming salvation of patient, hopeful, enduring Israel.

That is why in the categories of philosophy, including science and society, and religion, including a prophetic interpretation of history and teleology, Genesis Rabbah presents a deeply *religious* view of Israel's historical and salvific life, in much the same way that the Mishnah provides a profoundly *philosophical* view of Israel's everyday and sanctified existence. Just as the main themes of the Mishnah evoke the consideration of issues of being and becoming, the potential and the actual, mixtures and blends and other problems of physics, all in the interest of philosophical analysis, so Genesis Rabbah presents its cogent and coherent agendum as well. That program of inquiry concerns the way in which, in the book of

---

[20] In that formulation I complete my response to the ideas, such as they are, of the Goldberg-Schaefer-Becker school. That suffices.

Genesis, God set forth to Moses the entire scope and meaning of Israel's history among the nations and salvation at the end of days. The mode of thought by which the framers of Genesis Rabbah work out their propositions dictates the character of their exegesis, as to rhetoric, logical principle of cogent and intelligible discourse, and, as is clear, even as to topic.

In the view of the framers of the compilation, the entire narrative of Genesis is so formed as to point toward the sacred history of Israel, the Jewish people: its slavery and redemption; its coming Temple in Jerusalem; its exile and salvation at the end of time. In the reading of the authors at hand, therefore, the powerful message of Genesis proclaims that the world's creation commenced a single, straight line of events, leading in the end to the salvation of Israel and through Israel of all humanity. That message — that history heads toward Israel's salvation — the sages derived from the book of Genesis and contributed to their own day. Therefore in their reading of Scripture a given story will bear a deeper truth about what it means to be Israel, on the one side, and what in the end of days will happen to Israel, on the other. True, their reading makes no explicit reference to what, if anything, had changed in the age of Constantine. But we do find repeated references to the four kingdoms, Babylonia, Media, Greece, Rome — and beyond the fourth will come Israel, fifth and last. So sages' message, in their theology of history, was that the present anguish prefigured the coming vindication, of God's people.

It follows that sages read Genesis as the history of the world with emphasis on Israel. So the lives portrayed, the domestic quarrels and petty conflicts with the neighbors, all serve to yield insight into what was to be. Why so? Because the deeds of the patriarchs taught lessons on how the children were to act, and, it further followed, the lives of the patriarchs signaled the history of Israel. Israel constituted one extended family, and the metaphor of the family, serving the nation as it did, imparted to the stories of Genesis the character of a family record. History become genealogy conveyed the message of salvation. These propositions really laid down the same judgment, one for the individual and the family, the other for the community and the nation, since there was no differentiating one from the other. Every detail of the narrative therefore served to prefigure what was to be, and Israel found itself, time and again, in the revealed facts of the history of the creation of the world, the decline of humanity down to the time of Noah, and, finally, its ascent to Abraham, Isaac, and Israel.

Now to return to our question in the exposition of the documentary reading of the canonical compilations of Rabbinic Judaism: what of variations in the wording of extra-documentary writings? Do these not call into question the very notion of formed, purposive documents? To deal with that question, in Volume Three I present my systematic account of what happens when stories and sayings make the journey from one compilation to another.

Conclusion

I. Summary

To summarize the argument of this book, only a few words are required.

The question is, If documentary programs define the canonical writing of Rabbinic Judaism as I claim, how do I make provision for the free-standing, broadly-circulating sayings and stories that the documents encompass? My answer is in two parts.

In the first, in part one, Chapter One, I addressed the large-scale, unformalized composites of the Bavli, a huge corpus of free-standing writings. These call into question the documentary definition of the single most important writing of Rabbinic Judaism and have to be dealt with. My response is to show the task that the free-standing composites carry out for the Bavli. Here we learn about the interplay between, on the one side, writing compositions and composites outside of all documentary framework and, on the other side, the ultimate formation of documents.

Second, in part two, Chapters Two, Three, and Four, for the Mishnah and the Tosefta, Sifra, and Genesis Rabbah, I turned to sample the generality of the canonical writings, asking about the compositions and composites that, in general, lack documentary traits. I show two facts. First, free-standing compositions — stories and constructions of verses and their exegesis — add up to very little in proportion to the volume of the documents in which they occur. Second, they ordinarily contribute little or nothing to the achievement of the documentary purpose, being tacked on or tangential. They do more than fill space, but less than constitute building blocks where they occur. Above all, they simply do not fill gaps in the documentary argument. Rather, they function as do protracted footnotes and appendices.

II. POINTLESS PARALLELS, PALTRY PARALLELS

Let me at the end place into a single theoretical context this exercise and its paired companion within this trilogy, *The Pointless Parallel: The Myth of the Autonomous Tradition in Rabbinic Documents*. At issue in both monographs is the character of the Rabbinic canonical documents of late antiquity. These are the Mishnah, tractate Abot, the Tosefta, Sifra, Sifré to Numbers, Sifré to Deuteronomy, Mekhilta Attributed to R. Ishmael, the Talmud of the Land of Israel, the Talmud of Babylonia, the four Rabbah-Midrash-compilations of late antiquity, Genesis, Leviticus, Lamentations, Song of Songs, Abot deR. Natan, as well as some minor compilations. These represent the bulk of the canon of formative Judaism down to the end of late antiquity with the advent of Islam. Under debate are the following alternative propositions:

Are these writings, respectively, subject to characterization as a whole, or do they lack traits of coherence, whether formal or substantive?

Do they in the aggregate exhibit purpose and plan, or are they mere random collections of free-standing ("autonomous") compositions and composites?

In a long sequence of monographs, devoted to each of the compilations of the Rabbinic canon of the formative age,[21] I have invoked the indicative criteria of rhetoric (form), topic (propositional program), and logic of coherent dis-

---

[21] Listed in the bibliography of my writings, given at the end of the book.

course. On the strength of those criteria I have argued that we may define each of the named documents in comparison and contrast with all the others. The documents are shown to relate in three ways: autonomy, connection, and continuity. Each is distinct from all the others in its particular traits of rhetoric, topic, and logic. None may be characterized as a mere scrapbook, collected we know not how or why. All exhibit traits that show them to be purposive and pointed. The Rabbinic documents, severally and jointly, constitute components of a coherent canon of ideas, not merely random collections of writings about this and that. I have defined in detail the indicative traits of each of the principal documents, with the result just now summarized.

The documentary hypothesis requires the reading of the writings start to finish and the systematic categorization, by reference to rhetoric, topic, and logic of coherent discourse, of each of the components of each of the writings. That work has been done and has produced sustained results. The rejectionists call attention to the indeterminacy of the manuscript evidence, rich as it is in variant readings, as an argument that the entire documentary enterprise is hopeless to begin with: there are no documents susceptible of characterization, only diverse manuscript testimonies to we know not what. They further point to compositions and composites, as well as singleton-sayings, that are shared among two or more documents. These by definition testify against the documentary hypothesis of the Rabbinic canon.

The principal task, then, for those who hold the parallels to be pointless and the autonomous tradition to be subordinate to its documentary setting(s) is in two parts, affirmative and negative. The former requires exercises in documentary characterization, encompassing both form-analysis and propositional characterization (rhetoric, topic). The latter demands the testing of a null-hypothesis. That is carried out in

The Pointless Parallel. This companion maintains that the parallels form a negligible proportion of the whole and never bear the main burden of a document but are tangential and tacked-on.

III. IMAGINING THE RABBINIC CANON: TOWARD A GENERAL THEORY

How in light of these findings should we imagine the canonical writings and their life-situation as data of the Rabbinic culture? The upshot is, the Rabbinic canon is comprised by a community of texts, related in three dimensions: autonomy, connection, and continuity. Documents stand on their own. They intersect at specific points with other documents. And they form a continuity with all other documents, constituting a canon.

To clarify this perspective, let us consider the analogy of a library. Books brought together form a library. Each title addresses its own program and makes its own points. But books produced by a cogent community constitute not merely a library but a canon: a set of compositions each of which contributes to a statement that transcends its own pages. The books exhibit intrinsic traits that make of them all *a community of texts*. We should know on the basis of those characteristics that the texts form a community even if we knew nothing more than the texts themselves. In the Judaic writings, moreover, the documents at hand are held by Judaism to form a canon.

Seeing the whole as continuous, which is quite natural, later theology maintains that all of the documents of Rabbinic literature find a place in the Torah. But that is an imputed, and theological, not an inductive and intrinsic fact. It is something we know only on the basis of information — theological convictions about the one whole Torah God gave to Moses in two media — deriving from sources other than the texts at hand, which, on their own, do not link each to all and all to every line of each. Extrinsic traits, that is imputed ones, make of the discrete writings a single and continuous, uniform statement: one whole Torah in the mythic language of Judaism. The community of Judaism imputes those traits, sees commonalities, uniformities, deep harmonies: one Torah of one God. In secular language, that community expresses its system — its world view, its way of life, its sense of itself as a society — by these choices, and finds its definition in them. Hence, in the nature of things, the community of Judaism forms a *textual community*. That cogent community that forms a canon out of a selection of books therefore participates in the process of authorship, just as the books exist in at least two dimensions.

    Let us turn to the problem of the community of texts, utilizing the dimensions just now defined in our description of the canon. We take the measure of two of the three dimensions now introduced, *autonomy*, on the one side, and *connection*, on the second. Continuity among all documents introduces theological, not literary problems for analysis. That is to say, a book enjoys its own autonomous standing, but it also situates itself in relationship to other books of the same classification. Each book bears its own statement and purpose, and each relates to others of the same classification. The community of texts therefore encompasses individuals who (singly or collectively) comprise (for the authorships: compose) books. But there is a set of facts that indicates how a book does not stand in isolation. These facts fall into several categories. Books may go over the same ground or make use in some measure of the same materials. The linkages between and among them therefore connect them. Traits of rhetoric, logic, and topic may place into a single classification a number of diverse writings. Then there is the larger consensus of members who see relationships between one book and another and so join them together on a list of authoritative writings. So, as is clear, a book exists in the dimensions formed of its own contents and covers, but it also takes its place in the second and third dimensions of relationship to other books.

Then the relationships in which a given document stands may be expressed in the prepositions *between* and *among*. That is to say, in its intellectual traits a document bears relationship, to begin with, to some other, hence we describe relationships between two documents. These constitute formal and intrinsic matters: traits of grammar, arrangements of words and resonances as to their local meaning, structures of syntax of expression and thought. But in its social setting a document finds bonds among three or more documents, with all of which it is joined in the imagination and mind of a community. These range widely and freely, bound by limits not of form and language, but of public policy in behavior and belief. Documents because of their traits of rhetoric, logic, and topic form a community of texts. Documents because of their audience and authority express the intellect of a textual community.

The principal issue worked out in establishing a community of texts is hermeneutical, the chief outcome of defining a textual community, exegetical, social and cultural. The former teaches us how to read the texts on their own. The latter tells us how to interpret texts in context. When we define and classify the relationships between texts, we learn how to read the components — words, cogent thoughts formed of phrases, sentences, paragraphs — of those texts in the broader context defined by shared conventions of intellect: rhetoric, logic, topic. More concretely, hermeneutical principles tell how, in light of like documents we have seen many times, to approach a document we have never before seen. Hermeneutics teaches the grammar and syntax of thought. Memorizing a passage of a complex text will teach the rhythms of expression and thought that make of the sounds of some other document an intelligible music. Not only so, but documents joined into a common classification may share specific contents, not only definitive traits of expression — meaning and not solely method. That, in the context of the debate on intertextuality, represents the results of my inquiry into the status of the Rabbinic canonical writings, a status captured in the single word, "document," with its explicit definition now set forth.

IV. THE TWO THEORIES OF THE RABBINIC CANON: DOCUMENTS *VERSUS* SCRAPBOOKS — AND WHY THEY MATTER

The choices are clear. I have spelled them out in the Preface and recapitulate for this conclusion. One theory is that a document serves solely as a convenient repository of ready-made sayings and stories, available materials that will have served equally well (or poorly) wherever they took up their final location. In accord with that theory it is quite proper in ignorance of all questions of circumstance and documentary or canonical context to compare the exegesis of a verse of Scripture in one document with the exegesis of that verse of Scripture found in some other document. Documentary boundaries demarcate nothing. Their lines of structure and order are null.

The other theory is that a composition exhibits a viewpoint, a purpose of authorship distinctive to its framers or collectors and arrangers. Such a characteristic, literary purpose — by this other theory — is so powerfully particular to one authorship that nearly everything at hand can be shown to have been (re)shaped for the ultimate purpose of the authorship at hand, that is, collectors and arrangers who demand the title of authors. In accord with this other theory context and circumstance form the prior condition of inquiry, the result, in exegetical terms, the contingent one.

To resort to a less than felicitous neologism, I thus ask what signifies or defines the "document-ness" of a document and what makes a book a book. I therefore wonder whether there are specific texts in the canonical context of Judaism or whether all texts are merely contextual. In framing the question as I have, I of course lay forth the mode of answering it. . We have to confront a single Rabbinic composition, and ask about its definitive traits and viewpoint. When we investigate the textuality of a document, we therefore raise these questions: is it a composition or a scrap book, a cogent proposition made up of coherent parts, or a collage?

The answers help us to determine the appropriate foundations for comparison, the correct classifications for comparative study. Once we know what is unique to a document, we can investigate the traits that characterize all the document's unique and so definitive materials. We ask about whether the materials unique to a document also cohere, or whether they prove merely miscellaneous. If they do cohere, we may conclude that the framers of the document have followed a single plan and a program. That would in my view justify the claim that the framers carried out a labor not only of conglomeration, arrangement and selection, but also of genuine authorship or composition in the narrow and strict sense of the word. If so, the document emerges from authors, not merely arrangers and compositors. For the same purpose, therefore, we also take up and analyze the items shared between that document and some other or among several documents. We ask about the traits of those items, one by one and all in the aggregate. In these stages we may solve for the case at hand the problem of the Rabbinic document: do we deal with a scrapbook or a collage or a cogent composition? A text or merely a literary expression, random and essentially promiscuous, of a larger theological context? That is the choice at hand and defines what is at stake in these companion-research papers.

What is at stake in these recondite problems of literary description and analysis? The ultimate issue is, can we speak of "Judaism" as a coherent religious construction, a system and structure of cogency? Or is there only a mass — a mess, really — of discrete, chaotic facts, insusceptible of rational composition? The testimony of history favors the documentary construction of the Rabbinic canon and challenges the nihilism of the Goldberg-Schaefer-Becker effort to bring about the literary deconstruction and then the historical demolition of that ancient, enduring religious tradition: Judaism, the coherent religious structure and system that are set forth in the dual Torah at Sinai.

BIBLIOGRAPHY

These are the titles of mine that contribute to the arguments and data of the present book.

The Talmud of the Land of Israel. A Preliminary Translation and Explanation. Chicago: The University of Chicago Press: 1983. XXXV. Introduction. Taxonomy.

The Integrity of Leviticus Rabbah. The Problem of the Autonomy of a Rabbinic Document. Chico, 1985: Scholars Press for Brown Judaic Studies.

Comparative Midrash: The Plan and Program of Genesis Rabbah and Leviticus Rabbah. Atlanta, 1986: Scholars Press for Brown Judaic Studies.

From Tradition to Imitation. The Plan and Program of Pesiqta deRab Kahana and Pesiqta Rabbati. Atlanta, 1987: Scholars Press for Brown Judaic Studies. [With a fresh translation of Pesiqta Rabbati *Pisqaot* 1-5, 15.]

Canon and Connection: Intertextuality in Judaism. Lanham, 1986: University Press of America. *Studies in Judaism* Series.

Midrash as Literature: The Primacy of Documentary Discourse. Lanham, 1987: University Press of America *Studies in Judaism* series.

The Bavli and its Sources: The Question of Tradition in the Case of Tractate Sukkah. Atlanta, 1987: Scholars Press for Brown Judaic Studies.

Sifré to Deuteronomy. An Introduction to the Rhetorical, Logical, and Topical Program. Atlanta, 1987: Scholars Press for Brown Judaic Studies.

Uniting the Dual Torah: Sifra and the Problem of the Mishnah. Cambridge and New York, 1989: Cambridge University Press.

Sifra in Perspective: The Documentary Comparison of the Midrashim of Ancient Judaism Atlanta, 1988: Scholars Press for Brown Judaic Studies.

Mekhilta Attributed to R. Ishmael. An Introduction to Judaism's First Scriptural Encyclopaedia. Atlanta, 1988: Scholars Press for Brown Judaic

Studies.

The Midrash Compilations of the Sixth and Seventh Centuries. An Introduction to the Rhetorical Logical, and Topical Program. I. Lamentations Rabbah. Atlanta, 1990: Scholars Press for Brown Judaic Studies

The Midrash Compilations of the Sixth and Seventh Centuries: An Introduction to the Rhetorical Logical, and Topical Program. II. Esther Rabbah I. Atlanta, 1990: Scholars Press for Brown Judaic Studies

The Midrash Compilations of the Sixth and Seventh Centuries: An Introduction to the Rhetorical Logical, and Topical Program. III. Ruth Rabbah. Atlanta, 1990: Scholars Press for Brown Judaic Studies

The Midrash Compilations of the Sixth and Seventh Centuries: An Introduction to the Rhetorical Logical, and Topical Program. IV. Song of Songs Rabbah. Atlanta, 1990: Scholars Press for Brown Judaic Studies

Making the Classics in Judaism: The Three Stages of Literary Formation. Atlanta, 1990: Scholars Press for Brown Judaic Studies.

The Canonical History of Ideas. The Place of the So-called Tannaite Midrashim, Mekhilta Attributed to R. Ishmael, Sifra, Sifré to Numbers, and Sifré to Deuteronomy. Atlanta, 1990: Scholars Press for South Florida Studies in the History of Judaism.

Tradition as Selectivity: Scripture, Mishnah, Tosefta, and Midrash in the Talmud of Babylonia. The Case of Tractate Arakhin. Atlanta, 1990: Scholars Press for South Florida Studies in the History of Judaism.

Language as Taxonomy. The Rules for Using Hebrew and Aramaic in the Babylonian Talmud. Atlanta, 1990: Scholars Press for South Florida Studies in the History of Judaism.

The Bavli That Might Have Been: The Tosefta's Theory of Mishnah-Commentary Compared with That of the Babylonian Talmud. Atlanta, 1990: Scholars Press for South Florida Studies in the History of Judaism.

The Rules of Composition of the Talmud of Babylonia. The Cogency of the Bavli's Composite. Atlanta, 1991: Scholars Press for South Florida Studies in the History of Judaism.

The Bavli's One Voice: Types and Forms of Analytical Discourse and their Fixed Order of Appearance. Atlanta, 1991: Scholars Press for South Florida Studies in the History of Judaism.

The Bavli's One Statement. The Metapropositional Program of Babylonian Talmud Tractate Zebahim Chapters One and Five. Atlanta, 1991: Scholars Press for South Florida Studies in the History of Judaism.

How the Bavli Shaped Rabbinic Discourse. Atlanta, 1991: Scholars Press for South Florida Studies in the History of Judaism.

The Bavli's Massive Miscellanies. The Problem of Agglutinative Discourse in the Talmud of Babylonia. Atlanta, 1992: Scholars Press for South Florida Studies in the History of Judaism.

Sources and Traditions. Types of Composition in the Talmud of Babylonia. Atlanta, 1992: Scholars Press for South Florida Studies in the History of Judaism.

The Law Behind the Laws. The Bavli's Essential Discourse. Atlanta, 1992: Scholars Press for South Florida Studies in the History of Judaism.

The Bavli's Primary Discourse. Mishnah Commentary, its Rhetorical Paradigms and their Theological Implications in the Talmud of Babylonia Tractate Moed Qatan. Atlanta, 1992: Scholars Press for South Florida Studies in the History of Judaism.

The Discourse of the Bavli: Language, Literature, and Symbolism. Five Recent Findings. Atlanta, 1991: Scholars Press for South Florida Studies in the History of Judaism.

How to Study the Bavli: The Languages, Literatures, and Lessons of the Talmud of Babylonia. Atlanta, 1992: Scholars Press for South Florida Studies in the History of Judaism.

Form-Analytical Comparison in Rabbinic Judaism. Structure and Form in The Fathers *and* The Fathers According to Rabbi Nathan. Atlanta, 1992: Scholars Press for South Florida Studies in the History of Judaism.

The Bavli's Intellectual Character. The Generative Problematic in Bavli Baba Qamma Chapter One and Bavli Shabbat Chapter One. Atlanta, 1992: Scholars Press for South Florida Studies in the History of Judaism.

Decoding the Talmud's Exegetical Program: From Detail to Principle in the Bavli's Quest for Generalization. Tractate Shabbat. Atlanta, 1992: Scholars Press for South Florida Studies in the History of Judaism.

The Principal Parts of the Bavli's Discourse: A Final Taxonomy. Mishnah-Commentary, Sources, Traditions, and Agglutinative Miscellanies. Atlanta, 1992: Scholars Press for South Florida Studies in the History of Judaism.

The Bavli's Unique Voice. A Systematic Comparison of the Talmud of Babylonia and the Talmud of the Land of Israel. Volume One. *Bavli and Yerushalmi Qiddushin Chapter One Compared and Contrasted.* Atlanta, 1993: Scholars Press for South Florida Studies in the History of Judaism.

The Bavli's Unique Voice. A Systematic Comparison of the Talmud of Babylonia and the Talmud of the Land of Israel. Volume Two. *Yerushalmi's, Bavli's, and Other Canonical Documents' Treatment of the Program of Mishnah-Tractate Sukkah Chapters One, Two, and Four Compared and Contrasted. A Reprise and Revision of* The Bavli and its Sources. Atlanta, 1993: Scholars Press for South Florida Studies in the History of Judaism.

The Bavli's Unique Voice. A Systematic Comparison of the Talmud of Babylonia and the Talmud of the Land of Israel. Volume Three. *Bavli and Yerushalmi to Selected Mishnah-Chapters in the Division of Moed. Erubin Chapter One, and Moed Qatan Chapter Three.* Atlanta, 1993: Scholars Press for South Florida Studies in the History of Judaism.

The Bavli's Unique Voice. A Systematic Comparison of the Talmud of Babylonia and the Talmud of the Land of Israel. Volume Four. *Bavli and Yerushalmi to Selected Mishnah-Chapters in the Division of Nashim. Gittin Chapter Five and Nedarim Chapter One. And Niddah Chapter One.* Atlanta, 1993: Scholars Press for South Florida Studies in the History of Judaism.

The Bavli's Unique Voice. A Systematic Comparison of the Talmud of Babylonia and the Talmud of the Land of Israel. Volume Five. *Bavli and Yerushalmi to Selected Mishnah-Chapters in the Division of Neziqin. Baba Mesia Chapter One and Makkot Chapters One and Two.* Atlanta, 1993: Scholars Press for South Florida Studies in the History of Judaism.

The Bavli's Unique Voice. A Systematic Comparison of the Talmud of Babylonia and the Talmud of the Land of Israel. Volume Six. *Bavli and Yerushalmi to a Miscellany of Mishnah-Chapters. Gittin Chapter One, Qiddushin Chapter Two, and Hagigah Chapter Three.* Atlanta, 1993: Scholars Press for South Florida Studies in the History of Judaism.

The Bavli's Unique Voice. Volume Seven. *What Is Unique about the Bavli in Context? An Answer Based on Inductive Description, Analysis, and Comparison.* Atlanta, 1993: Scholars Press for South Florida Studies in the History of Judaism.

Introduction to Rabbinic Literature. N.Y., 1994: Doubleday. The Doubleday Anchor Reference Library. Religious Book Club Selection, 1994. Paperback edition: 1999.

Talmudic Dialectics: Types and Forms. Atlanta, 1995: Scholars Press for South Florida Studies in the History of Judaism. I. *Introduction. Tractate Berakhot and the Divisions of Appointed Times and Women.*

Talmudic Dialectics: Types and Forms. Atlanta, 1995: Scholars Press for South Florida Studies in the History of Judaism. II. *The Divisions of Damages and Holy Things and Tractate Niddah.*

Rationality and Structure: The Bavli's Anomalous Juxtapositions. Atlanta, 1997: Scholars Press for South Florida Studies in the History of Judaism.

Judaism. The Evidence of the Mishnah. Chicago, 1981: University of Chicago Press. *Choice,* "Outstanding academic book list" 1982-3. Paperback edition: 1984. Second printing, 1985. Third printing, 1986. Second edition, augmented: Atlanta, 1987: Scholars Press for Brown Judaic Studies.

Hayyahadut le'edut hammishnah. Hebrew translation of *Judaism. The Evidence of the Mishnah*. Tel Aviv, 1987: Sifriat Poalim.

Il Giudaismo nella testimonianza della Mishnah. Italian translation by Giogio Volpe. Bologna, 1995: Centro editoriale Dehoniane.

Judaism in Society: The Evidence of the Yerushalmi. Toward the Natural History of a Religion. Chicago, 1983: The University of Chicago Press. *Choice*, "Outstanding Academic Book List, 1984-1985." Second printing, with a new preface: Atlanta, 1991: Scholars Press for South Florida Studies in the History of Judaism.

Judaism and Scripture: The Evidence of Leviticus Rabbah. Chicago, 1986: The University of Chicago Press. [Fresh translation of Margulies' text and systematic analysis of problems of composition and redaction.] Jewish Book Club Selection, 1986.

Judaism: The Classical Statement. The Evidence of the Bavli. Chicago, 1986: University of Chicago Press. *Choice*, "Outstanding Academic Book List, 1987."

Judaism and Story: The Evidence of The Fathers According to Rabbi Nathan. Chicago, 1992: University of Chicago Press.

The Making of the Mind of Judaism. Atlanta, 1987: Scholars Press for Brown Judaic Studies.

The Formation of the Jewish Intellect. Making Connections and Drawing Conclusions in the Traditional System of Judaism. Atlanta, 1988: Scholars Press for Brown Judaic Studies.

The Four Stages of Rabbinic Judaism. London, 2000: Routledge.

What, Exactly, Did the Rabbinic Sages Mean by "the Oral Torah"? An Inductive Answer to the Question of Rabbinic Judaism. Atlanta, 1999: Scholars Press for South Florida Studies in the History of Judaism.

A Theological Commentary to the Midrash. I. *Pesiqta deRab Kahana*. Lanham, 2001: University Press of America. STUDIES IN ANCIENT JUDAISM SERIES.

A Theological Commentary to the Midrash: II. *Genesis Rabbah*. Lanham, 2001: University Press of America. STUDIES IN ANCIENT JUDAISM SERIES.

A Theological Commentary to the Midrash: III. *Song of Songs Rabbah*. Lanham, 2001: University Press of America. STUDIES IN ANCIENT JUDAISM SERIES.

A Theological Commentary to the Midrash. IV. *Leviticus Rabbah*

A Theological Commentary to the Midrash: V. *Lamentations Rabbati*

A Theological Commentary to the Midrash VI. *Esther Rabbah I and Ruth Rabbah*

A Theological Commentary to the Midrash VII. *Sifra*

A Theological Commentary to the Midrash VIII. *Sifré to Numbers*

A Theological Commentary to the Midrash IX. *Sifré to Deuteronomy*

A Theological Commentary to the Midrash X. *The Theological Foundations of Rabbinic Midrash*

The Talmud of Babylonia. A Complete Outline. Atlanta, 1995-6: Scholars Press for *USF Academic Commentary Series*.

I.A	Tractate Berakhot and the Division of Appointed Times. Berakhot, Shabbat, and Erubin.
I.B	Tractate Berakhot and the Division of Appointed Times. Pesahim through Hagigah.
II.A.	The Division of Women. Yebamot through Ketubot
II.B.	The Division of Women. Nedarim through Qiddushin
III.A	The Division of Damages. Baba Qamma through Baba Batra
III.B	The Division of Damages. Sanhedrin through Horayot
IV.A	The Division of Holy Things and Tractate Niddah. Zebahim through Hullin

IV.B The Division of Holy Things and Tractate Niddah. Bekhorot through Niddah

The Talmud of The Land of Israel. An Outline of the Second, Third, and Fourth Divisions. Atlanta, 1995-6: Scholars Press for USF Academic Commentary Series.

I.A Tractate Berakhot and the Division of Appointed Times. Berakhot and Shabbat
I.B Tractate Berakhot and the Division of Appointed Times. Erubin, Yoma, and Besah
I.C Tractate Berakhot and the Division of Appointed Times. Pesahim and Sukkah
I.D Tractate Berakhot and the Division of Appointed Times. Taanit, Megillah, Rosh Hashanah, Hagigah, and Moed Qatan
II.A. The Division of Women. Yebamot to Nedarim
II.B. The Division of Women. Nazir to Sotah
III.A The Division of Damages and Tractate Niddah. Baba Qamma, Baba Mesia, Baba Batra, Horayot, and Niddah
III.B The Division of Damages and Tractate Niddah. Sanhedrin, Makkot, Shebuot, and Abodah Zarah

The Two Talmuds Compared. Atlanta, 1995-6: Scholars Press for USF Academic Commentary Series.

I.A Tractate Berakhot and the Division of Appointed Times in the Talmud of the Land of Israel and the Talmud of Babylonia. Yerushalmi Tractate Berakhot
I.B Tractate Berakhot and the Division of Appointed Times in the Talmud of the Land of Israel and the Talmud of Babylonia. Tractate Shabbat.
I.C Tractate Berakhot and the Division of Appointed Times in the Talmud of the Land of Israel and the Talmud of Babylonia. Tractate Erubin
I.D Tractate Berakhot and the Division of Appointed Times in the Talmud of the Land of Israel and the Talmud of Babylonia. Tractates Yoma and Sukkah
I.E Tractate Berakhot and the Division of Appointed Times in the Talmud of the Land of Israel and the Talmud of Babylonia. Tractate Pesahim

I.F   Tractate Berakhot and the Division of Appointed Times in the Talmud of the Land of Israel and the Talmud of Babylonia. Tractates Besah, Taanit, and Megillah
I.G   Tractate Berakhot and the Division of Appointed Times in the Talmud of the Land of Israel and the Talmud of Babylonia. Tractates Rosh Hashanah, Hagigah, and Moed Qatan
II.A   The Division of Women in the Talmud of the Land of Israel and the Talmud of Babylonia. Tractates Yebamot and Ketubot.
II.B   The Division of Women in the Talmud of the Land of Israel and the Talmud of Babylonia. Tractates Nedarim, Nazir, and Sotah.
II.C   The Division of Women in the Talmud of the Land of Israel and the Talmud of Babylonia. Tractates Qiddushin and Gittin.
III.A   The Division of Damages and Tractate Niddah in the Talmud of the Land of Israel and the Talmud of Babylonia. Tractates Baba Qamma and Baba Mesia
III.B   The Division of Damages and Tractate Niddah in the Talmud of the Land of Israel and the Talmud of Babylonia. Baba Batra and Niddah.
III.C   The Division of Damages and Tractate Niddah. Sanhedrin and Makkot.
III.D   The Division of Damages and Tractate Niddah. Shebuot, Abodah Zarah, and Horayot.

The Components of the Rabbinic Documents: From the Whole to the Parts. Volume I. *Sifra.* Atlanta, 1997: Scholars Press for USF Academic Commentary Series.

Part i.   Introduction. And Parts One through Three, Chapters One through Ninety-Eight
Part ii.   Parts Four through Nine. Chapters Ninety-Nine through One Hundred Ninety-Four
Part iii. Parts Ten through Thirteen. Chapters One Hundred Ninety-Five through Two Hundred Seventy-Seven
Part iv.   A Topical and Methodical Outline of Sifra

The Components of the Rabbinic Documents: From the Whole to the Parts. Volume II. *Esther Rabbah I.* Atlanta, 1997: Scholars Press for USF Academic Commentary Series.

The Components of the Rabbinic Documents: From the Whole to the Parts. Volume

III. *Ruth Rabbah.* Atlanta, 1997: Scholars Press for USF Academic Commentary Series.

The Components of the Rabbinic Documents: From the Whole to the Parts. Volume IV. *Lamentations Rabbati.* Atlanta, 1997: Scholars Press for USF Academic Commentary Series.

The Components of the Rabbinic Documents: From the Whole to the Parts. Volume V. *Song of Songs Rabbah.* Atlanta, 1997: Scholars Press for USF Academic Commentary Series.

Part i. *Introduction. And Parashiyyot One through Four*
Part ii. *Parashiyyot Five through Eight. And a Topical and Methodical Outline of Song of Songs Rabbah*

The Components of the Rabbinic Documents: From the Whole to the Parts. VI. *The Fathers Attributed to Rabbi Nathan.* Atlanta, 1997: Scholars Press for USF Academic Commentary Series.

The Components of the Rabbinic Documents: From the Whole to the Parts. VII. *Sifré to Deuteronomy.* Atlanta, 1997: Scholars Press for USF Academic Commentary Series.

Part i. *Introduction. And Parts One through Four*
Part ii. *Parts Five through Ten*
Part iii. *A Topical and Methodical Outline of Sifré to Deuteronomy*

The Components of the Rabbinic Documents: From the Whole to the Parts. VIII. *Mekhilta Attributed to R. Ishmael.* Atlanta, 1997: Scholars Press for USF Academic Commentary Series.

Part i. *Introduction. Pisha, Beshallah and Shirata*
Part ii *Vayassa, Amalek, Bahodesh, Neziqin, Kaspa and Shabbata*
Part iii. *A Topical and Methodical Outline of Mekhilta Attributed to R. Ishmael.*

The Components of the Rabbinic Documents: From the Whole to the Parts. IX. *Genesis Rabbah.* Atlanta, 1998: Scholars Press for USF Academic Commentary Series.

Part i.   Introduction. *Genesis Rabbah Chapters One through Twenty-One*
Part ii. *Genesis Rabbah Chapters Twenty-Two through Forty-Eight*
Part iii. *Genesis Rabbah Chapters Forty-Nine through Seventy-Three*
Part iv. *Genesis Rabbah Chapters Seventy-Four through One Hundred*
Part v.   *A Topical and Methodical Outline of Genesis Rabbah. Bereshit through Vaere, Chapters One through Fifty-Seven*
Part vi. *A Topical and Methodical Outline of Genesis Rabbah. Hayye Sarah through Miqqes. Chapters Fifty-Eight through One Hundred*

The Components of the Rabbinic Documents: From the Whole to the Parts. X. *Leviticus Rabbah*. Atlanta, 1998: Scholars Press for USF Academic Commentary Series.

Part i.   Introduction. *Leviticus Rabbah Parashiyyot One through Seventeen*
Part ii. *Leviticus Rabbah Parashiyyot Eighteen through Thirty-Seven*
Part iii. *Leviticus Rabbah. A Topical and Methodical Outline*

The Components of the Rabbinic Documents: From the Whole to the Parts. XI. *Pesiqta deRab Kahana*. Atlanta, 1998: Scholars Press for USF Academic Commentary Series.

Part i.   Introduction. *Pesiqta deRab Kahana Pisqaot One through Eleven*
Part ii. *Pesiqta deRab Kahana Pisqaot Twelve through Twenty-Eight*
Part iii. *Pesiqta deRab Kahana. A Topical and Methodical Outline*

The Components of the Rabbinic Documents: From the Whole to the Parts. XII. *Sifré to Numbers*. Atlanta, 1998: Scholars Press for USF Academic Commentary Series.

Part i.   Introduction. *Pisqaot One through Eighty-Four*
Part ii   *Pisqaot Eighty-Five through One Hundred Twenty-Two*
Part iii *Pisqaot One Hundred Twenty-Three through One Hundred Sixty-One*
Part iv   *Sifré to Numbers. A Topical and Methodical Outline*

The Documentary Form-History of Rabbinic Literature. I. *The Documentary Forms of the Mishnah*. Atlanta, 1998: Scholars Press for USF Academic

Commentary Series.

The Documentary Form-History of Rabbinic Literature II. *The Aggadic Sector: Tractate Abot, Abot deRabbi Natan, Sifra, Sifré to Numbers, and Sifré to Deuteronomy.* Atlanta, 1998: Scholars Press for USF Academic Commentary Series.

The Documentary Form-History of Rabbinic Literature III. *The Aggadic Sector: Mekhilta Attributed to R. Ishmael and Genesis Rabbah.* Atlanta, 1998: Scholars Press for USF Academic Commentary Series.

The Documentary Form-History of Rabbinic Literature IV. *The Aggadic Sector: Leviticus Rabbah, and Pesiqta deRab Kahana.* Atlanta, 1998: Scholars Press for USF Academic Commentary Series.

The Documentary Form-History of Rabbinic Literature V. *The Aggadic Sector: Song of Songs Rabbah, Ruth Rabbah, Lamentations Rabbati, and Esther Rabbah I.* Atlanta, 1998: Scholars Press for USF Academic Commentary Series.

The Documentary Form-History of Rabbinic Literature. VI. *The Halakhic Sector. The Talmud of the Land of Israel.* A. *Berakhot and Shabbat through Taanit.* Atlanta, 1998: Scholars Press for USF Academic Commentary Series.

The Documentary Form-History of Rabbinic Literature. VI. *The Halakhic Sector. The Talmud of the Land of Israel.* B. *Megillah through Qiddushin.* Atlanta, 1998: Scholars Press for USF Academic Commentary Series.

The Documentary Form-History of Rabbinic Literature. VI. *The Halakhic Sector. The Talmud of the Land of Israel.* C. *Sotah through Horayot and Niddah.* Atlanta, 1998: Scholars Press for USF Academic Commentary Series.

The Documentary Form-History of Rabbinic Literature. VII. *The Halakhic Sector. The Talmud of Babylonia.* A. *Tractates Berakhot and Shabbat through Pesahim.* Atlanta, 1998: Scholars Press for USF Academic Commentary Series.

The Documentary Form-History of Rabbinic Literature. VII. *The Halakhic Sector.*

The Talmud of Babylonia. B. *Tractates Yoma through Ketubot*. Atlanta, 1998: Scholars Press for USF Academic Commentary Series.

The Documentary Form-History of Rabbinic Literature. VII. *The Halakhic Sector. The Talmud of Babylonia*. C. *Tractates Nedarim through Baba Mesia*. Atlanta, 1998: Scholars Press for USF Academic Commentary Series.

The Documentary Form-History of Rabbinic Literature. VII. *The Halakhic Sector. The Talmud of Babylonia*. D. *Tractates Baba Batra through Horayot*. Atlanta, 1998: Scholars Press for USF Academic Commentary Series.

The Documentary Form-History of Rabbinic Literature. VII. *The Halakhic Sector. The Talmud of Babylonia*. E. *Tractates Zebahim through Bekhorot*. Atlanta, 1998: Scholars Press for USF Academic Commentary Series.

The Documentary Form-History of Rabbinic Literature. VII. *The Halakhic Sector. The Talmud of Babylonia*. F. *Tractates Arakhin through Niddah. And Conclusions*. Atlanta, 1998: Scholars Press for USF Academic Commentary Series.

How Adin Steinsaltz Misrepresents the Talmud. Four False Propositions from his "Reference Guide." Atlanta, 1998: Scholars Press for South Florida Studies in the History of Judaism.

WITHDRAWN